Spirituality, Inc.

Spirituality, Inc.

Religion in the American Workplace

Lake Lambert III

NEW YORK UNIVERSITY PRESS
New York and London

NEW YORK UNIVERSITY PRESS
New York and London
www.nyupress.org

Library of Congress Cataloging-in-Publication Data

Lambert, Lake.
Spirituality, Inc. : religion in the American workplace / Lake Lambert III.
p. cm.
Includes bibliographical references (p.   ) and index.
ISBN-13: 978-0-8147-5246-3 (cl : alk. paper)
ISBN-10: 0-8147-5246-2 (cl : alk. paper)
1. United States—Religious life and customs. 2. Religion in the
workplace—United States. 3. Businesspeople—Religious life—United
States. I. Title.
BL2500.L36   2009
261.8'5—dc22   2009021702

New York University Press books are printed on acid-free paper,
and their binding materials are chosen for strength and durability.
We strive to use environmentally responsible suppliers and materials
to the greatest extent possible in publishing our books.

Manufactured in the United States of America

10 9 8 7 6 5 4 3 2 1

Contents

Acknowledgments

Every book has a history, and this one is no different. More than fifteen years ago, an acquaintance told me that she was reading *Jesus, CEO* with her book club and asked if I had heard of it. I had not, but I was curious from her description and the resonance it found among the members of the club. For several years after, I collected anecdotes like this, book titles, newspaper articles, and other resources all around the theme of "workplace spirituality." I had long been interested in "vocation" as a theological theme, and while related, this seemed different. After awhile, it became clear that I was tracking not a collection of disparate events but a religious trend worthy of additional attention. Soon, an explosion of books, articles, and conferences confirmed my suspicions.

The first support for *Spirituality, Inc.* came from a summer stipend by the Louisville Institute, and I remain grateful to the Institute's executive director, Jim Lewis, for recognizing this as a significant project. While she may not remember it, Dorothy Bass was especially encouraging of the project when the summer stipend recipients met as a group, and she made several helpful suggestions that shaped the project. A few years later, Wartburg College, the institution where I teach, received a major grant from the Lilly Endowment's Program for the Theological Exploration of Vocation (PTEV), and I was tapped to serve as the project director. Because the endowment was supportive of research and writing related to vocation in addition to the grant's programmatic emphasis, I have been able to devote additional time and attention to the subject of workplace spirituality, and I have been influenced by the flurry of programmatic and research activity on vocation that has been fostered at the eighty-eight colleges and universities with PTEV grants. Special thanks go to Kim Maphis-Early and Chris Coble at the Lilly Endowment for their support of Wartburg's program, my leadership role, and my related scholarship. A sabbatical granted by Wartburg College was also instrumental in bringing the book to completion.

Initial research for *Spirituality, Inc.* has been presented in several venues, and I am grateful for the feedback I have received. Regional and national meetings of the American Academy of Religion have been especially important, but the Wartburg Philosophical and Literary Society—a weekly gathering of faculty, staff, and students—has also proven valuable, especially because of its interdisciplinary composition. In 2006 Charles Lippy invited me to submit a greatly condensed version of my research as a chapter for *Faith in America: Changes, Challenges, New Directions*, the three-volume series he edited, and I am appreciative of his support. Other colleagues and friends have also read and provided feedback on various drafts, including Jim Legler, professor of business and director of the Center for Ethical Leadership at Concordia College, Max L. Stackhouse, professor emeritus at Princeton Theological Seminary, and Kathryn Kleinhans, professor of religion and chair of the Religion and Philosophy Department at Wartburg College. Two outstanding undergraduate students at Wartburg, David Rewarts and Shannon Geisinger, served as research assistants, and many other students either read chapter drafts in their classes or offered clerical assistance.

While it may not pass muster as scholarly evidence, I continue to recognize the influence of family and friends who have modeled, often in very different ways, the expression of faith and spirituality at work. My parents were small business owners whose faith led them to pay their employees first even though there was sometimes not enough money left for themselves and our family. My wife, Kelly, has a quiet integrity that makes her a good accountant and trusted colleague, and I know that our children, Bailey and Zack, continue to learn much from her. Many friends and acquaintances have shared with me the challenges that they have faced trying to remain faithful or spiritually whole in the workplace, and I have learned much from their experiences and struggles. One of my hopes is that this work of scholarship, at least in some small way, honors all of them and their efforts.

Finally, a word of thanks is due to Jennifer Hammer at New York University Press. She recognized this project as something worthwhile, identified several areas needing attention, offered valuable editorial guidance, and shepherded it (and me) to its completion.

1

Finding Meaning in Business

When Patricia Aburdene issued her latest book in the *Mega-trends* franchise, she and her sometime partner, John Naisbitt, had been offering their prophecies on American business culture for almost twenty years. The newest edition was unique, however, because it blurred the line between religion and commerce in a way unexpected for a business best seller. *Megatrends 2010* promised to reveal "the rise of conscious capitalism" as the new revolution in corporate operations, consumer behavior, investing, business leadership, and work itself. Filled with interviews, anecdotes, and predictions in bold face, *Megatrends 2010* concluded that capitalism was being transformed from an egoistic survival of the fittest built around greed to a new vision of commerce grounded in compassion and enlightened self-interest that is, at its heart, a spiritual phenomenon. No longer would God and mammon be separate, and the path to enlightenment would no more require the renunciation of worldly possessions. Instead, they were coming together in new and creative ways. The "power of spirituality," Aburdene asserted, was making an impact and demanded notice as the next big trend in American business.

What Aburdene predicted is today not hard to see. At the food giant Tyson Foods, workplace chaplains roam the corporate halls and processing floors. Corporations like Ford and Xerox sponsor spiritual retreats to spark creativity, and small businesses include Bible verses and Christian symbols on their advertising. In the fast-food industry, Chick-fil-A honors the Sabbath by closing on Sunday, and amid rapid growth they dedicate each new store to God's glory. Prominent business theorists like *The One-Minute Manager*'s Kenneth Blanchard write books about Jesus as a leader, and even Wal-Mart sells the publications. At the same time, major American universities including Virginia Tech, Notre Dame, and Columbia University offer courses touting the value of spirituality to future business managers, and in Washington, DC, public policy makers wonder how to respond to a rising tide of religious discrimination complaints.

Not to be left out, churches and many new religious organizations support workplace spirituality. Domino's Pizza founder Tom Monaghan established Legatus as an organization exclusively for Roman Catholic CEOs and other high-level business executives. Evangelical Christians have a similar organization in Fellowship of Companies for Christ, and now Muslim CEOs can connect through the Minaret Business Association. For major league and minor league baseball players, including Cy Young Award–winner Jake Peavy, Baseball Chapel connects sports and faith through team Bible studies and worship. For PBS correspondent Judith Valente, the Coalition for Ministry in Daily Life is a faith-at-work-resource.

For many Americans throughout our recent history, spirituality and business have seemed like exact opposites. The former is concerned with questions of meaning and ultimate significance while the latter is supposedly devoted to making money and to affairs of this world. Aburdene reported there had traditionally been a "firewall" between spirituality and business, but it was a barrier that was breaking down as both individuals and organizations undergo a spiritual awakening. Individuals are seeking to bring their whole selves to the workplace, including their spirituality, and businesses today are dependent upon the creativity that only "consciousness" and spirituality can provide. Thus, capitalism is being transformed from the inside and the outside, changing the way Americans do business.[1]

Six years earlier, a *BusinessWeek* cover and feature story had already heralded spirituality in business as a hot trend, and the magazine offered evidence to prove it. The article reported that Americans desired meaning and fulfillment in their work more than additional pay or time off.[2] Although surprising on a certain level, this finding revealed not only how many people were beginning to realize that there was potentially more to work than getting a paycheck, but also that the inability to find workplace meaning had the potential to create personal anxiety and even crisis. The search for meaning in work, the connection between work and faith or the divine, and the relationship between work and other areas of life like family and health were being raised more frequently and acted on in new, creative ways individually and organizationally. These same developments were prompting profound moral, philosophical, and religious questions not normally asked or answered in American business.

Beginning in the 1990s, different forms of spirituality in work seemed to pop up all the time. An explosion of books on the subject could be found in both religious bookstores and mainstream retailers with titles such as *The Business Bible, Your Soul at Work, The Soul of a Business, Angels in the Workplace, Soul at Work, Jesus, CEO,* and *Leading with Soul.* Individuals sought out like-minded co-workers for lunchtime discussion groups and Bible studies, and a variety of organizations began to emerge that hosted meetings and conferences to connect work and spirituality. Employers, especially when faced with labor shortages for highly skilled workers, adopted programs and accommodations that created holistic and family-friendly work environments, all of which were more open and accommodating to the spiritual and emotional needs of employees.[3] Corporations and the individuals who work in them recognized that child care concerns, depression, or even poor fitness could impede optimal work performance, and so programs and services to meet those needs were created and used. Why not spirituality too? Professional training also adopted this concern for holism and forms of spirituality, and employees appreciated the accommodation and vision of these workplaces while the companies themselves hoped that short-term costs would eventually result in greater economic success. In 1990 John Naisbitt and Patricia Aburdene had noted in *Megatrends 2000* that companies were spending $4 billion for spiritual consultants and "consciousness raising," and they were correct when they predicted that this trend would only continue to grow.[4]

Something was indeed happening. Many of the developments in workplace spirituality related easily to the traditional theological identities of Christians or the practices of diverse religious traditions, but others expressed forms of spirituality outside the boundaries of established faiths. Some of the changes could easily be understood as new forms of professional development or programs to increase morale and productivity; other activities, programs, and services appeared unrelated to the affairs of commerce. Still others seemed to tap into Americans' incredible love for "self-help" methodologies and, perhaps most of all, their love of success. Whatever it was, the apparent novelty made spirituality big news and a worthy subject for trend-watchers like Aburdene. But while there are always new things, very few developments, if any, come into existence ex nihilo. This was the case for workplace spirituality as well. In fact, the efforts to find meaning in work extend at least as far back as the founding of America and were a recurring theme in much of the modern Western tradition, and within that tradition, the Christian notion of calling was central.

The Idea of Vocation

When the Puritan divine Richard Steele wrote his treatise *The Religious Tradesman* in 1684, he too was claiming a connection between business and spirituality. Steele praised business as worthy work for a Christian, and he hoped that parents would "be persuaded to educate their children for a life of business and usefulness."[5] Offering careful advice for discerning whether business was one's appropriate vocation, Steele suggested self-examination as to vocational fit, consultation with experienced businessmen, and prayer to God for direction and assistance. For the remainder of his book Steele described in detail the virtues that were necessary for a Christian in business, including prudence, justice, truth, and contentment. Steele did not worry about business as a potential challenge to faith as much as he feared sloth—a sin that an industrious businessman was sure to avoid. The great English hymnist and fellow minister Isaac Watts found the volume so inspirational that he wrote an introduction to a new printing in 1747.[6] For Steele and his admirers, the justification for Christians in commerce was biblically derived from fusing the economic division of labor with the gifted diversity of the Body of Christ, thus making some Christians literally called to business.[7]

It was from his study of Puritans specifically and Calvinists more generally that the great sociologist Max Weber developed his famous "Protestant ethic" thesis on the origins of capitalism and modern business practices. In looking at the development of business life and capitalist systems at the end of the nineteenth century, Weber was struck by how overwhelmingly Protestant everything was. Why, he asked, were business owners and capitalists more often Protestant, and why were Calvinists even more prevalent? In particular he was struck by the Puritans and their rigorous piety in all areas of life, coupled with the successful commerce they developed in New England. He concluded that these religious traditions and the forms of economic organization known as capitalism had an affinity for one another.

In *The Protestant Ethic*, Weber also offered a definition of capitalism that still deserves attention. He argued that capitalism is not about the maximization of wealth or even its pursuit. Long before the rise of capitalism, humans sought money and riches, but greed has "nothing to do with capitalism." Rather, Weber argued, capitalism is an economic system with inherent values, including self-discipline and rationality, that result not in profit but "forever renewed profit."[8] Unfortunately, popular opinion has not changed a great deal from Weber's time until now. From Gordon Gecko in the film *Wall Street* touting that "greed is good" to the perception that business is all about making a lot of money, business is associated with many values, but few are seen as good ones.

Despite his being misinterpreted frequently, Weber asserted that the relationship between economics and religion was directly connected to the values and behaviors that each fostered and demanded, and perhaps most important, the connection was never one way. Whereas Adam Smith saw economics as shaped by religion and morality, and Karl Marx asserted that economics determined religion, Weber argued for a more complex relationship with each influencing the development of the other. Religion, he said, has the power to shape economic life, and economic realties can make certain religious groups and certain religious ideas more or less available.[9] For his "Protestant ethic" thesis, Weber asserted that on the economic side, capitalism demanded hard work and asceticism; on the faith side, Calvinism's teaching on predestination produced anxiety and a need to prove eternal salvation in this world while, at the same time, proclaiming that everyone was assigned a vocation—places and roles to which one was called to serve God. This form of faith and this pattern of economics were then attracted by their "elective affinity."

The idea of vocation had deep roots in the Hebraic and Christian traditions, from the biblical text to the Protestant reformers, roots of which both Steele and Weber were well aware. The Hebrew and Christian scriptures frequently speak of human work, its meaning, and its difficulty. In the Genesis stories of creation, humanity is called into being as workers. God gives to humans "dominion" over the newly created earth, and in Eden, the man is placed in the garden "to till it and to keep it."[10] Yet another part of Genesis speaks of the difficulty found in work. The sin of Adam and Eve in the Garden of Eden is mythically connected to the demeaning of work in that human labor is cursed as a consequence of disobedience. God's words to Adam foretell the trouble ahead, "Cursed is the ground because of you; in toil you shall eat of it all the days of your life; thorns and thistles it shall bring forth for you; and you shall eat the plants of the field. By the sweat of your face you shall eat bread until you return to the ground."[11] Adam and Eve are expelled from the rich productivity of the garden and forced to work in alienation from God's presence.

The New Testament has similar tensions in consideration of work. Jesus often calls individuals away from their daily work to a life of discipleship free from mammon and affairs of the world, but at the same time he repeatedly tells stories about daily work and what work will be like in the Kingdom of God. Jesus teaches about faithful managers, dishonest and lazy workers, and ungrateful laborers. He states that as his Father in heaven is working, so he as the Son of God must also be working, and certainly humans can be no different. The call of Jesus to discipleship is a call to be part of a community that will work to make disciples of all nations.[12] This need not involve grand schemes or so-called important work. Even the most minor task is claimed by Jesus and made part of God's work: Jesus teaches that even fetching a cup of cold water can have spiritual meaning.[13]

However, it was in the writings of St. Paul that the Protestant reformers found their greatest inspiration. It was Paul and his *Epistle to the Galatians* that in 1517 prompted the German Protestant reformer Martin Luther to question the monastic life to which he had sworn himself. He began to ask whether the spiritual works of monasticism were better than the good works of the common layman, and he wondered whether good works mattered at all in one's relationship with God. His conclusion was that all Christians are "called" and not just a spiritual elite group of bishops, priests, monks, and nuns. In fact, Luther said that the supposed good works of monks and nuns were far surpassed by the simple work of a common maid. For Luther, you know you are serving God when you serve others, and any work that does not serve is demonic and to be avoided. A "calling" or a vocation was for all Christians, and so the Christian life should be seen as living out one's calling in the everyday world of work, family, community, and church.

Working in Geneva several years later, John Calvin adopted Luther's larger project on vocation with a few alterations. A vocation, for Calvin, was a "station" or "sentry post," which God gives to Christians to prevent them from wandering. Monasticism is unsuitable as a Christian vocation because it is not a defined area of responsibility where spirituality daily engages materiality, nor does it provide service.[14] The vow taken by monks is false, said Calvin, because it is likely in conflict with one's true calling to marriage, family, occupation, and social participation.[15] In his great work, *The Institutes*, Calvin considered a main problem of the Christian life to be human mobility and restlessness that would lead Christians to abandon God-given work because of the hardships associated with it. His fear was not that Christians would hold too fast to the status quo, but rather they would be too likely to roam, looking for a nonexistent occupation without hardship.[16] In his commentary on 1 Corinthians 7:20,

Calvin allowed for occupational change only if a sufficient reason is available, and he interprets Paul in this passage as condemning the eagerness by which many switch jobs for little or no reason. Change is possible but must be made with prayerful consideration of motive, merit, and the will of God.[17] This reinforced the conviction that the meaning of work was not to be found in personal satisfaction but rather in service to others.

The Puritans in Britain and the American colonies received this rich tradition and added to it as well. Less than fifty years after Calvin's death, William Perkins put forth a theology of vocation that distinguished the "general call" from the "particular call." The general call referred to faithfulness in Jesus Christ and as such was the same for all Christians, but the particular call directed individual Christian to their specific roles, occupations, and stations in life. Because all Christians have a particular calling, Perkins wanted to ensure that all understood the divine rules that governed them. Faith and work were to be joined; a person was to be confident and steady in a calling; and since all are called to work, begging should be outlawed.[18] Another Puritan pastor and theologian, Cotton Mather, later added that the two types of call were like the oars on a rowboat, and each must be pulled equally.[19]

The theological clarifications of Mather and the Puritans of the early 1700s defined subtle but important changes to the idea of vocation established by Luther and Calvin. Mather's rowboat metaphor included in it that the boat was the Christian's transportation to heaven, meaning that faith and holiness were to be combined with diligent work in one's particular calling to merit salvation. Whereas Luther asserted that one could serve God only by serving one's neighbor, the later Puritans claimed that a vocation served God, society, and oneself. The individual was aided because one's vocation was a path to salvation. Richard Baxter, the Puritan writer most influential on Weber and his study of the Protestant ethic, claimed that in one's calling the worker could obtain proof of salvation.[20] With its focus on eternal rewards, this change in vocation made the particular call a place where great spiritual meaning might be found. It tied the materiality of work to the divine. And soon, Puritans would claim that the connection also went the other way. Richard Steele declared in *The Tradesman's Calling* that God would bless hard work and diligence in one's vocation with prosperity, making work a path to both salvation and riches.[21] These developments grounded Weber's thesis that faith was aided by capitalism as a way to "prove" one's salvation, and capitalism was aided by faith as a motivation toward hard work and asceticism.

As it emerged in late Puritan theology, the theology of vocation did not closely resemble the teachings of the Protestant reformers and was considerably more complex. But it was also more American. A vocation was not about service to neighbor alone; it served the eternal, spiritual ends of the one who was called, and it offered something in this life as well. This threefold character of vocation is what continued and continues today, albeit with somewhat different language. Contemporary discussions of workplace spirituality all claim that one can serve others, be truly and deeply spiritual, and derive wealth all at the same time. If it has one, this is the thesis of Aburdene's *Megatrends 2010*. Working in business can be a path to spiritual growth, a means to creating a better world, and a path to prosperity. In fact, she contends, harnessing these truths in today's new economic paradigm will result in greater prosperity yet.

Not a Puritan New England Economy

Just as theologies developed and transformed, so did economies, and the institutional structures of commerce have evolved substantially since the days of colonial America. While early forms of corporate organization were present in Puritan New England and as far back as the Middle Ages, the modern business corporation emerged full steam in the nineteenth century. Legal changes made it possible, but the Industrial Revolution was the key factor in this development, making corporations more prominent in their numbers and especially in their size. In the United States, a national economy—as opposed to several regional ones—and large corporations of truly national scope challenged the face-to-face, human interaction that had so often governed economic life and replaced it with rational, bureaucratic structures of management. Work was organized differently, and efficiency as a value gained the highest prominence in commerce, substituting for the relational and religious values that had guided the Puritans and others who practiced business in the early years of the American republic. As the era of "big business" emerged, sometimes tempered by governmental regulations, the American economy came to dominate the globe. By the mid-twentieth century, business and national interest were conflated, leading the president of General Motors to make the famous assertion that "what's good for the country is good for General Motors, and vice versa." Amid the boom, there was great work stability in large organizations, and sociologists and social critics commented on these developments in such books as William Whyte's *The Organization Man* (1956).

But by the 1980s it was clear that the great industrial economy of the United States was waning. A new economic transformation was underway, yet few if any knew what it was changing into. As with the Industrial Revolution a century earlier, technology was an important factor since it allowed some tasks to be automated and others eliminated as unnecessary. In the 1980s and early 1990s massive layoffs occurred, and "downsizing" became a way of life for corporate employees. This created severe anxiety among workers, including those who remained in the downsized organizations. Experts warned that there was no such thing as lifetime employment. These days, workers now expect to move from job to job; temporary work is common; and there is little sense of company loyalty because companies have proven they have no loyalty to their employees. This "new employee contract" led many workers to feel unappreciated, anxious, and frankly scared about their future.[22] Frequently, those who remained in downsized companies actually felt worse because they were asked to absorb the work of departing co-workers at the same rate of pay, making them feel even more abused.[23] A new crisis of workplace meaning emerged in the midst of job loss and economic change.

At the same time companies were pushing employees to the maximum level, they were also realizing that the postindustrial economy, with new products like software and new "lean and mean" models of corporate organization, relied on the knowledge, creativity, and initiative of employees more than ever. In addition to new products, technology made less hierarchical organizations possible. In this environment, trend-watcher Aburdene concluded that there must be more self-management. Everyone had to be a leader because power had shifted from the organizational system to the individual. Even large corporate cultures were seeking to encourage creative entrepreneurship in order to produce innovative products and to manage more efficiently.[24] Ideally, a new type of worker was highly educated and innovative. This was significant to the rising interest in workplace spirituality because creativity was increasingly understood to be an inherently spiritual process involving the whole person and not just the intellect, manual skill, or brute strength.

Along with Aburdene, a whole host of academics, journalists, and trend-watchers attempted to explain the new economic developments. They were also developing clever names for the new class or classes of workers that emerged to meet the economy's new demands. In 1991 Robert Reich coined the term "symbolic analyst" to describe the new worker who creates economic value by manipulating symbols and using tools such as "mathematical algorithms, legal arguments, financial gimmicks, scientific principles, psychological insights about how to persuade or amuse, systems of induction or deduction, or any other set of techniques for doing conceptual puzzles."[25] The symbolic analyst is usually highly educated, often works in teams, and is not dependent upon any one location to do his or her work. Reich, who went on to serve as secretary of labor in the Clinton administration, was careful to emphasize that symbolic analysts as a category of workers did not easily overlap with existing categories like "professional" and "managerial." For example, he said that all lawyers may be professionals but not all are symbolic analysts because their work may be entirely routine, and "special deftness in solving, identifying, or brokering new problems" is more important than supervision.[26]

In 1995 *Newsweek* coined the term "overclass" to describe the new breed of Americans who, it stated, were hard to define "because it is a state of mind and also a slice on the income curve." While the group was diverse, the one thing *Newsweek* could say with assurance was that high levels of education were the foundation of the overclass, and their list of "The Overclass 100" included individuals in business, finance, law, government, education, arts, and the media.[27] The journalist David Brooks offered his take and definitely the most creative of all descriptors in his book *Bobos in Paradise* (2000). Brooks's thesis was that this new class combined both bourgeois and bohemian values for the first time in history, and with a short abbreviation of those two words (*bo*-urgeoise and *bo*-hemian), the term "Bobo" was born. Because of their high levels of education, Brooks claimed that Bobos have been very successful in the new economy, but they have "anxiety about abundance." They worry that their economic success is incompatible with their bohemian values.[28] The results, said Brooks, is that Bobos are "countercultural capitalists" who seek new ways to do business, which honors their bohemian values, and he offered examples such as Ben Cohen and Jerry Greenfield of Ben & Jerry's Ice Cream to make his point. Bobos are more focused on creativity than money, so they view business as an art, and like the Puritans, they also want to understand their work as a vocation or calling. Brooks noted how "the weird thing is that when employees start thinking like artists and activists, they actually work harder for the company."[29] By this fusion, a new form of work ethic was supposedly born.

In another attempt to make sense of the new economy and its workers, in 2002 Richard Florida at Carnegie Mellon University invented the
term "creative class" to describe a new group of workers. Florida argued
that the creative class included as many as 30 percent of all Americans for
whom "every aspect and every manifestation of creativity—technological,
cultural, economic—is interlinked and inseparable."[30] Like Brooks's Bobos, the creative class Florida described also has a longing for personal
fulfillment and self-expression. They desire "a creative life full of intense,
high-quality, multidimensional experiences."[31] To create economic value
requires active and authentic experiences of creativity in multiple are-
nas. Rather than interpreting time at a funky music joint as recreation,
the creative class counts it as complimentary. These diverse experiences
feed the creative process, and they want to be in those environments that
support creativity. Channeling a prototypical member of the class, Florida
wrote that it is a "way of both disconnecting and recharging, it is part of
what we need to do as creative people."[32] What appears to be hedonistic
to others outside that class is, in fact, a necessity for the class to exist. The
creative class treats experiences as consumables and desires pleasure and
happiness in all areas of life, including work. This is not counter to economic productivity, but in a strange reversal of the Protestant work ethic's
emphasis on asceticism, is required for the work of the creative class to be
most productive.[33]

In describing the new type of worker, however, the most common term
in use has been the "knowledge class." Drawing upon high levels of education and training, and working in fields as diverse as medicine, marketing, and manufacturing, knowledge workers simply "think for a living." Of
course, most types of work require some level of expertise, but for knowledge workers, thinking is their primary if not exclusive contribution to
economic productivity. While some people have done knowledge work for
centuries (e.g., monks and professors), their numbers have grown astro-
nomically, and they are more essential in today's complex global economy
than ever before. Scholars estimate that a quarter to a half of all workers in advanced industrial economies like the United States are knowledge
workers. This new type of worker also likes certain features to accompany
their work, including autonomy, and their effectiveness requires a higher
level of commitment than other types of work: Unlike manual labor or
many services, you cannot think about other things while you work if you
are paid only to think.[34] Likewise, you cannot turn off your brain when
you leave the office, and maybe there is no need to do so. The desire for

autonomy coupled with technology often allows those in the knowledge class to work at home or at their own hours, designing their own work processes rather than being dependent upon what has been established for them.[35] Knowledge work has no assembly lines—a process that is metaphorically and literally linear in its design. Knowledge work is more like a spider's web with multiple points of connection and interface, all in support of a common goal.

The new knowledge class also devotes more of their time to work. Increased demands require it, and the meaning found in creativity, exciting corporate cultures, and new areas of enterprise facilitates it. As *Fortune* stated in 2000, "Overwork in part seems to be a class thing. While hours for unskilled workers have actually been falling slightly (even taking multiple-job holders into account), they've been headed skyward for highly educated professionals, suggesting a semantic flip-flop: The working class now has more leisure, and the leisure class has more work."[36] In many cases, the workplace becomes the only form of community that workers know, and bonds between co-workers become those of a pseudo-family.[37] One's closest relationship may be drawn from the workplace, and for single people, it may be the main source one has for meeting a mate. The importance of the workplace as a community also makes the workplace a hospitable environment for spirituality in the same way that it is hospitable to friendship and even love. Sociologist Arlie Hoschild has even argued that work is so comfortable that people often prefer the office to the demands of home.[38]

Regardless of the particular title adopted, whether symbolic analyst or creative class, the centrality of work in people's lives made attention to the meaning of work all the more important, and an increasing focus on creativity, collaboration, and personal relationships at the office provided openings for spiritual dialogue. These things also channeled the managerial concern for increasing the productivity of knowledge workers. Forty years ago, the great management theorist Peter Drucker predicted that productivity gains for knowledge workers would be the next great managerial challenge. The old, highly rational and hierarchical forms of command and control over work processes would not be effective with the knowledge class. To impose old-fashioned industrial structures would destroy the environment of autonomy, community, and creativity that make knowledge work possible. What was promising instead was an enhancement of what already worked. Creativity, community, autonomy, and holistic concern became new employee benefits that supported the productivity of the new knowledge class, and a particular type of spirituality found a partner in knowledge work.

Religious Developments

More traditional theological forms of vocation remained after the Puritans, but they tended to be hidden from view except for a few Protestant exemplars and periodic efforts by Lutherans, Presbyterians, Episcopalians, and other mainline Protestants to foster a vocational revival. Perhaps the most important of those renewal efforts appeared soon after World War II when the newly formed World Council of Churches (WCC) devoted special attention at its first two assemblies to the significance of the laity in the life of the church. In its early statements and studies, the WCC asserted that all Christians had the power to transform the world through their daily work, and the church must be in concord with the laity so that "the laity in their turn (will) become genuine representatives of the church in areas of modern life to which the church has no access."[39] This claim seemed strange since it followed one of the world's greatest encounters with systemic evil, the Nazi state, but reflecting on that challenge, the Protestant leaders of the WCC attended not to systemic reform, such as new models of Christian government or a Christianized economic order, but to individual empowerment, faithful living, and vocation. In Europe, these same commitments gave rise to the Evangelical Academies that offered retreats and other resources for Protestants to consider their life and work as ministry.

Noteworthy developments occurred among Romans Catholics as well. Beginning in the late nineteenth century, Catholic leaders began to take seriously the religious meaning of work in their response to industrialization and as the result of a series of papal encyclicals. Pope Leo XIII's *Rerum Novarum: The Condition of Labor* (1891) began the process, and it continued to Pope John Paul II's *Laborem Exercens: On Human Work* (1981) and *Centesimus Annus: On the Hundredth Anniversary of Rerum Novarum* (1991). In his statements, John Paul II affirmed that work is necessary because it both expresses humanity's creation in the image of God and can serve the common good; he also wrote specifically about a "spirituality of work."[40] John Paul II's writings on work, coupled with his efforts to reign in Marxist influences on the church's theology, led some Roman Catholics to conclude that John Paul II was a capitalist. Michael Novak, a conservative Roman Catholic scholar at the American Enterprise Institute, wrote *Business as a Calling* (1996) to make these very claims and to affirm that there was a "Catholic ethic" with an affinity to capitalism as much as there was a Protestant one.

But by the 1960s, the WCC and its member churches were changing their social witness away from the idea of vocation and toward the critique of economic, political, and social structures. Business was not to be engaged through vocation but opposed through advocacy and movements of transformation. Some efforts to revive vocation among mainline Protestants continued, but with limited effort and little effect. Lutheran layman William Diehl, an executive at Bethlehem Steel, expressed his discontent over the loss of vocation in a series of books, as did others, but to no avail.[41] Likewise, centuries of a clergy-only meaning for vocation were hard to reverse among Roman Catholics in particular, and "having a vocation" was still widely understood by the faithful as having a call to be a priest, monk, or nun. In 1997 a survey by the sociologist Robert Wuthnow revealed that few mainline Protestant or Catholics saw the link between faith and work in their lives, and many were skeptical about churches seeking to address workplace issues.[42] The effect, Wuthnow reported, was that "those who attend religious services every week are almost as likely as those who attend less often to say that they are dissatisfied with their work and to complain of burnout . . . (and) the two groups are virtually indistinguishable in terms of motives for working hard and doing their work well."[43] A Protestant ethic—or even a Catholic one—was effectively absent, and despite the rich theological resources, the link between the historic European denominations and modern American commerce was, at best, unclear.

Evangelical Christians, because of their Protestant roots, were also heirs to the tradition of vocation, but as in so many things in American religious life and history, they offered a marked contrast to Catholics and their fellow Protestants. In their formative history, American evangelicals had readily embraced business and market culture as an economic system, means of evangelism, and form of ecclesiastical organization. Fervent anticommunism in the early twentieth century was one important reason. Yet even earlier, the nineteenth-century revivals of Charles Finney had made use of emerging forms of advertising and business organization, and marketplace methods became allied with the evangelical's personal decision for faith as well as a commitment to individual choice in finding a congregation (sometimes described as "church shopping"). The best contemporary example of these practices has been the megachurch flagship Willow Creek in suburban Chicago, which was founded based on a marketing study. It continues to use worship styles that speak to their "target demographic."

Numerous commentators have noted how, for at least the last thirty years, evangelical Christianity has been rising in numbers of adherents and cultural influence. Most recently, the evangelicals' style of vocation has made a cultural impact, not through the traditional language of the Reformation but via concern for meaning-making and purpose. In early 2005, the Reverend Rick Warren's *The Purpose Driven Life* (2002) made front-page news—a recovering methamphetamine addict in Georgia read from the book to the man who held her hostage and who had just shot a judge, court reporter, and deputy sheriff. According to media reports, she attempted to show her captor, through passages from the book, that he too had a purpose in life.[44] Warren's book offered a contemporary compilation of vocational ideas but seldom used the term "calling," relying instead on a host of potential synonyms such as identity, plan, design, mission, and purpose. Yet it did maintain the more traditional Puritan division of the general and particular call, speaking repeatedly of service to God and neighbor, while also reminding readers that this life is about "preparing for eternity."[45]

Warren's *The Purpose Driven Life* has been a huge market success. *Publishers Weekly* reported that it was the best-selling book in 2003 and 2004 with 20.5 million copies sold in those two years. It has also been translated into twenty-eight different languages.[46] The book did what American evangelicals have done well for over two centuries: blend the values of popular culture with biblical Christianity. And like their Puritan forebears, many evangelicals do not stop where Warren leaves them, going farther to connect having a purpose with being prosperous. In a similar integration of American values and religion, the "gospel of health and wealth" has become a significant force among evangelical Christians with work serving as a primary point of reception for God's abundant blessing. As a result, if the potential affinities with other forms of Christianity are in decline, connections between evangelicals and commerce proliferate.

Of course, mainline Protestants, Catholics, and evangelicals are not a religious monopoly, and religion in the United States is not—nor has it ever been—exclusively Christian. However, the other main tradition of American religion is a faith that some would regard as no faith at all. In *A Republic of Mind and Spirit* (2007), Catherine Albanese referred to it as the "metaphysical tradition," encompassing theories of mind power, mysticism, energy, therapy, and healing, plus forms of occultism that existed alongside orthodox Christianity even in Puritan New England.[47] In popular language today, the descriptor has been "spiritual but not religious." Spirituality is supposedly free, universal, and open, while religion is dogmatic, particular, and proselytizing. It is thus possible, in the minds of many, to be religious without being spiritual, and most important, it is possible to be spiritual without being religious.[48] And it is within this perceived dichotomy that new sets of affinities with business have begun to emerge.

Increasingly, spirituality is understood as a private realm of thoughts and experiences whereas "religion" is a public realm of institutions, creeds, and rituals.[49] The Baby Boomers led the way in this change as they have done in other areas of American culture. Beginning in the 1960s, large numbers of Boomers left the religious traditions of their youth never to return or to return with considerable skepticism toward institutional religion.[50] Yet they were not the first Americans to engage in metaphysical religion. While it greatly frustrated Puritan religious leaders, even American colonials practiced a religious eclecticism alongside their traditional Christian beliefs. In his book *Spiritual but Not Religious* (2001), Robert Fuller concludes that even for the Puritan faithful, "an aloof, judgmental God failed to mesh with colonists' desire to fashion a vital spirituality."[51] They too wanted something that worked, and they were willing to go outside institutional boundaries to find it.

What they found was abundant and ever present in American life. Over the last decade, as spirituality has seemed to trump religion in the popular imagination, scholars of American religious life have sought to demonstrate how spirituality *apart* from Christianity is nothing new. Leigh Schmidt, author of *Restless Souls* (2005), named the same tradition "religious liberalism" and included within it the desire for mystical experience, valuing meditation and silence, a fascination with Eastern religious traditions, the idea that all religions have common ideals, and "an emphasis on creative self-expression and adventure-some seeking."[52] Together, Albanese's "metaphysical tradition," Schmidt's "religious liberalism," and what Fuller called "unchurched traditions" form a triumvirate, all identifying the important role of spirituality throughout American history and all trying to contextualize the current explosion in spiritual expressions and practices today.

The Baby-Boom generation still matters to an understanding of American religious life, and so do the 1960s as the decade most important in shaping the Boomers' identity. In his monumental work on the Boomers' faith, Wade Clark Roof noted that the Boomer generation is a "lead cohort" or national trend setter, simply because of their numbers.[53] The key to understanding their impact, however, is the degree to which Boomers, born between 1946 and 1964, engaged the 1960s counterculture of drugs, music, and political activism. Using an index based on surveys, Roof concluded that all Boomers were more prone to drop out of religious institutions than previous generations, but those Boomers with higher levels of exposure to the counterculture dropped out at a rate of 84 percent.[54] In addition, the higher the level of exposure, the more likely Boomers were to identify themselves as "spiritual" and the less likely they were to understand themselves as "religious." The rates for "spirituality" topped 80 percent while those with low exposure only identified themselves as spiritual at a rate of 33 percent.[55]

Beginning in the 1990s, advocates for workplace spirituality, usually Boomers themselves, began to claim that Boomers were an obvious source for the new interest in spiritual work. In age, they were reaching a period of life when self-reflection and introspection are common. Often they had raised children and reached high points in their career, and after achieving success they wondered what it all meant in the big scheme of things. They were also asking questions about ultimate meaning and significance generally, and when such basic questions were asked, it was only logical that similar questions would be addressed to and in the workplace since this was the location where a majority of their time was spent.[56]

The impact of the 1960s also extended beyond the counterculture. In 1965 a groundbreaking immigration reform law began a religious transformation in the United States so that it was no longer a nation with only different denominations of Christianity as its primary basis of religious diversity. Large numbers of adherents to Islam, Hinduism, Buddhism, and many other smaller sects joined the Christian majority and the long-present Jewish minority. Jews, Muslims, Hindus, and Buddhists have all addressed questions about the meaning of work in some way. Hinduism's dharma or duty and a caste system connected to occupation, along with Islam's affirmation of work as an assignment from God, share with Christian theologies of vocation the idea that work has meaning. In Buddhism, which sees human labor as the result of greed, work has a meaning (albeit negative) in the tradition's cosmology. In understanding contemporary workplace spirituality, the religious traditions of new immigrants are significant, but so too is the religious eclecticism that it intensifies. Religious traditions now mix and mingle, creating an opportunity for individuals to pick and choose, and for different, religiously defined meanings of work to absorb, morph, and transform.

New Elective Affinities

This book examines contemporary practices of workplace spirituality and demonstrates that they constitute an important religious movement, shaping and being shaped by American business culture. These trends have historical, sociological, and theological contexts that reveal how workplace spirituality frequently serves diverse and sometimes competing functions. Personal fulfillment, increased economic productivity, and moral guidance occur simultaneously amid new economic realities and new forms of economic institutions. But perhaps more important, expressions of workplace spirituality are best interpreted as creative collaborations between the practices and values of contemporary commerce and the diverse meanings of religious and spiritual life. Returning to the language of Max Weber, new forms of both economic life and religion create new opportunities for "elective affinities," and workplace spirituality as a term captures and consolidates a variety of new affinities into a single yet diverse social movement.

The next chapter traces the roots of spirituality in the business corporation, stretching from the industrial transformation of the nineteenth century to the new knowledge economy of the current day. Looking closely at the history of business in America, it notes the affinity between spirituality and the larger economic movement known as "welfare capitalism" in which corporations rather than the state provide social services. The development of the "human relations" school of management also provided a crucial foundation for workplace spirituality with its concern for personal development and emerging interest in corporate culture. A spiritual workplace is often seen as a more profitable workplace, transforming again the structure of work and creating either a possible win-win situation or a religiously manipulative environment.

Chapter 3 turns to the significance of "Christian companies" as an evangelical expression of spirituality in business. Although most Christian companies are small, this chapter profiles several larger organizations such as Chick-fil-A, ServiceMaster, and Hobby Lobby that have created a different model of workplace spirituality with great attention to personal morality and religious devotion. Small Christian businesses are also making their mark by joining networks and alerting evangelicals to a distinctive Christian subculture in the American economy. As something of an alternative case, the chapter examines Jewish diamond merchants in New York as another business model with a faith-based network. Both large and small faith-based businesses are important sources for workplace spirituality practices, but they may have a more limited impact in an economically complex and religiously diverse nation.

Outside the office, many resources for workplace spirituality are on sale at the local bookstore. The fourth chapter profiles and places into context the plethora of books that appeal to both evangelicals and secular wisdom seekers, in an attempt to make Jesus into a source of leadership and management guidance. Current books like *Jesus, CEO* have important predecessors, but they are best understood in relationship to other contemporary "business guru" books and the increased interest in character following Stephen Covey's highly successful and influential *The 7 Habits of Highly Effective People.* Within the American religious and economic marketplace, books offer a "do-it-yourself" approach to workplace spirituality and are a significant feature of the overall movement.

As workplace spirituality has gained prominence in corporate offices and American life, business faculties at colleges and universities have taken notice. Chapter 5 describes and analyzes the various ways spirituality has become a part of the business curricula at both public and church-related colleges and universities. Several education institutions are highlighted, including Maharishi University of Management, where Vedic philosophy and transcendental meditation are embedded in all courses, and David Lipscomb University, where students must participate in "Business Administration Students Imitating Christ (BASIC) Training Camp." The chapter also considers the impact of the Lilly Endowment's Program for the Theological Exploration of Vocation on the business curricula of the eighty-eight participating college and universities as well as the role of the Academy of Management's "Management, Spirituality, and Religion" Interest Group in making workplace spirituality a more mainstream academic area.

Outside academia, those seeking a personal guide to workplace meaning may employ a life coach. Chapter 6 describes the field of "life coaching" and its role as a new form of vocational counseling. Mainline Protestants, Roman Catholics, and other faith-based organizations are responding to the workplace spirituality movement by trying to provide their own form of life coaching, reasserting the significance of Christian theologies of vocation and trying to connect again to business life and practice. This chapter also examines more secular responses to the different forms of the workplace spirituality movement, including the dramatic rise in civil rights complaints related to religion in the workplace and the comic strip *Dilbert's* satiric look at spirituality as another business fad. The presence of affinities may best be known by the reactions against them.

While some would argue that religion and spirituality in America have been de-centered from traditional religious institutions, they are not totally free floating and have found other institutional homes. The corporate office, the local bookstore, the family business, and the university's business department provide the setting for the new religious movement of workplace spirituality. The concluding chapter situates the workplace spirituality movement within the context of American religious life and assesses its future impact on business, higher education, and traditional religious communities.

While much has been written about workplace spirituality in the last fifteen years, little of it has been scholarly, and among scholars of religion it has received even less attention. For these reasons alone, *Spirituality, Inc.* fills a troublesome scholarly void. But there will always be skeptics. When I presented my early research on workplace spirituality books at an academic meeting, a professional colleague and friend asked, "Why would you want to study that?" My answer then and my answer now is that workplace spirituality is an important frontier in American religion, and it is a means to understand the complex relationship between business and religious faith that has existed for centuries. The "elective affinities" between business and religion will undoubtedly continue. *Spirituality, Inc.* engages several of those that exist today, offering insights into the future of American business culture, American religious life, and their ongoing relationship.

2

The Genealogy of
Corporate Spirituality

One way of viewing the phenomenon of corporate spirituality is to see the corporation as the new οικος of our time. In the ancient world, the Greek word for household—οικος—captured as part of its meaning all areas of human life. Used throughout the New Testament, οικος meant much more than "household" does today; in that time the household was truly the center of economic production, faith, and family life. On the land and in the household all the necessities of life were produced, and at the hearth symbols of faith and devotion would remind the family of the gods and their ancestors. The centrality of the household in so many areas can be seen in the diversity of English words that have been derived from οικος, including economy, ecology, and ecumenical.

Whereas the home had once been the center for all of human life, it has increasingly become a base camp for a lifestyle that involves constant movement between different institutions, activities, and places. Much of modern Western history can be understood as the effort to divide the household into distinctive spheres with their own institutions, leaders, and logics. The new corporate spirituality seeks to reverse this trend by creating a "holistic workplace" that centers life at work rather that at home. Historically, the Christian tradition sought to affirm the spiritual character of work through the theological doctrine of calling and vocation, but this chapter looks at the spirituality of work from the economic institutions in which most work is based today—the business corporation. To understand how corporations and the people in them are seeking to unite spirituality and work, we first need to consider how the meaning of work was lost through changes in the structure and organization of human labor, and how it is being revived in response to new economic realities and the same quest for higher productivity that drove the previous shifts. With multiple expressions and examples, corporate spirituality is beginning to change the very identity of the business corporation.

Changing Character of Human Work

In the late nineteenth century, George Pullman was an elite industrialist who reshaped the nature of modern enterprise through his use of holistic business practices. Pullman's Palace Car Company had brought about a revolution in transportation, for the first time making it enjoyable to travel long distances by train. Through a combination of decorative and technical features, the passenger cars that Pullman's company designed and built rode smoothly and provided the conveniences of meals, comfortable chairs, sleeping quarters, and lavatories. To ensure total quality, the Pullman Company staffed and maintained full ownership of their cars even while they were being used by various railroad companies of the day. Passengers paid a premium over regular ticket prices to ride in a Pullman car, and the name "Pullman" was a sign of excellence that was considered worth the additional charge. As a result, the fortunes of George Pullman and his company expanded dramatically.[1]

Pullman's success exemplified the changing character of work from the Middle Ages into the industrial era. Three distinctive features defined this change, and Pullman along with his industrialist peers utilized them all with great results. The first was the large-scale factory that combined many men and multiple trades in one central location, creating convenience as well as economy. The second was the use of more sophisticated technology and machinery in that production, including reliance on outside sources of power. A new form of bureaucratic management was the third feature, which provided a sophisticated means to control acquisition, production, distribution, and capital formation in newly emerging business corporations. For Pullman, these factors meant that he could mass produce elegant train cars, staff them, and track their use across the nation and with multiple railroad companies.

In the economic history of the West, the earliest developments were increased specialization and concentration on limited areas of economic production. In the Middle Ages, a division of labor had increasingly produced a multitude of craftsmen in a variety of fields, even as most people labored at home and on small farms. As far back as the ancient world, specialists were present, with early texts mentioning the work of the blacksmith, potter, shipbuilder, and armorer. The Bible included employment descriptions as well, noting for example that Jesus was a carpenter (Mark 6:3), Andrew and Peter were fisherman (Matt. 4:18), and Lydia was a dealer in purple cloth (Acts 16:14). Craftsmen would sometimes congregate in a city for the ease of suppliers and customers, and this led to the development of a guild system that regulated the quality of workmanship among members and stipulated the requirements for training and admission into a particular craft. The guilds also included a religious-ethical dimension, with the organization providing support for needy members, widows, and orphans. Rules stipulating the quality of goods and the limits of competition were also developed. In ancient times and into the medieval era, guild members worshiped together in communal services, and specific fields of work became identified with devotion to particular saints.[2] While specialization may have more sharply distinguished work and home, much of life remained unified, including work and spirituality.

In the earliest phases of industrialization, a variety of methods were used to increase production but without changing the fundamental character of the work. Some master producers would include several apprentices and journeyman workers in their shops, producing a greater volume of goods but still under the supervision of a master. In the manufacturing of cloth, an elaborate means of work organization developed known as the "putting-out" system: a single merchant would take raw wool or other fibers to one house for spinning and weaving and to another house for cleaning and dying before finally selling the finished product.[3]

The factories of the later Industrial Revolution placed an even greater variety of workers under one roof with more mechanized means of production and the power (steam, water, electricity) to run the machines. The use of machines gradually decreased the need for some skilled laborers since the worker no longer needed to understand the full scope of production. This increased division of labor was noted by Adam Smith in the *Wealth of Nations* with his classic example of the pin factory:

> One man draws out the wire, another straightens it, a third cuts it, a fourth points it, a fifth grinds it at the top for receiving the head; to make the head requires two or three distinct operations; to pin it on is a peculiar business, to whiten the pins is another; it is even a trade by itself to put them into the paper; and the important business of making a pin is, in this manner, divided into about eighteen distinct operations.[4]

Smith noted that this division of labor provided substantial gains in productivity that benefited both workers and society overall. But more importantly, Smith emphasized that the worker who does one task need not be able to do another related task or even understand how the various tasks fit together in the final product.

In the new industrial organization, there was an increased effort to break skilled work into several unskilled parts so that anyone could do the work with only limited training and that the overall work processes could be streamlined. The problem with such efforts was that any creativity exercised by workers in accomplishing a task was taken away. Industrial work became increasingly monotonous, with no use for the intellectual (and some would say, spiritual) contribution of the worker.

The large scale of factory work was facilitated by the rise of the corporation as a form of economic organization and the emergence of "management" as a distinctive field and type of work. During the Middle Ages, European kings chartered schools and guilds as corporations to confer legitimacy and to regulate the quality and price of products. Later, in the age of exploration, governments incorporated trading companies to finance colonialism and foreign trade.[5] Since incorporation was granted only on authority of the regime, the early business corporation was distinct but not entirely independent from the state itself. In America, colonial legislatures issued individual charters for both business and benevolent corporations, including churches. Those issued for businesses were most often for large-scale projects with explicit public purposes such as turnpikes and canals. Private gain was not disallowed in corporations by such ventures, but private ends were always subsumed to social ones.[6]

Ironically, a growing distrust of corporations themselves fueled the drive for reform and more lax rules for incorporation. Since incorporation required a special action by (most often) state legislatures, political and economic power remained intertwined. Incorporation was the preferred business option of the elite, who could muster the political influence to pass a special act for private purposes. Opening incorporation to all under general laws was seen as a democratic reform.[7] By the late nineteenth and early twentieth centuries, corporations were the primary unit of nonagricultural production, and many grew to what was considered then enormous size. In 1900 most workers were still self-employed, but by the time the United States entered World War II, a transformation had occurred. Large corporations became the norm.[8]

The corporate form of organization offered a rational means to consolidate financial capital and control the operation of large-scale organizations. At the turn of the twentieth century, however, large corporations were in most cases connected to the work and wealth of an individual or small groups. Although organized as corporations, most if not all the assets of these and other large corporations were controlled by individuals or families. But even here the corporation was distinguished from the home because managers from outside the ranks of family and owners were required for administration. The need for and importance of managers was further exacerbated by the creation of gigantic firms through mergers and vertical integration of various industries.[9] In the United States, the emergence of the transcontinental railroad created the first megacorporations, but the Industrial Revolution in general created other large corporations, which could no longer be owned or run solely by individual entrepreneurs and their extended families.[10] While on the one hand bringing diverse people together for a single economic purpose, the large-scale corporation also threatened the social aspect of work by isolating co-workers and replacing face-to-face interactions and trust with bureaucratic rules and regulations.

The joint effect of rational corporate organization and a specialized division of labor combined at the dawn of the twentieth century to further change the character of human work. The most well-known advocate for this new style of industrialization was Frederick W. Taylor, a mechanical engineer who was determined to bring even greater efficiency to industrial organizations. Taylor's basic contribution was to systematically study different tasks performed by workers. He would time the activities and measure the productivity of different techniques. By observing individual shovelers at the Bethlehem Iron Works in Pennsylvania, Taylor was able to determine the optimal shovel size and design as well as the best method for removing coal from rail cars and then loading it into furnaces. Taylor's study then led the iron works' management to mandate the most productive methods, requiring the workers to give up their own tools and techniques as well as the variety of shoveling methods they might use throughout the day. In return for their lost control, the workers received a 63 percent raise.[11]

Taylor proposed a new relationship between labor and management that would give more authority to management over the organization of work. As Taylor described it,

All of the planning which under the old system was done by the work-man, as a result of his personal experience, must of necessity under the new system be done by the management in accordance with the laws of science; because even if the workman were well suited to the development and use of scientific data, it would be impossible for him to work at his machine and at a desk at the same time.[12]

An expanded role for management was needed to bring about the increased productivity necessary to benefit both workers and owners. In fact, Taylor later claimed that his methods were essential for reducing tension between labor and capital since they would provide the increased productivity necessary for substantive wage increases.[13]

Learning from Taylor and his predecessors, Henry Ford created a system in 1914 for mass producing identical cars that not only used multiple, low-skilled tasks but also automated the process. Previously, automobiles had been almost exclusively custom made, but in the factory Ford opened in Dearborn, Michigan, the workers stood still and the work flowed to them along a conveyor belt, producing the famous identical black cars that were the Ford trademark. This increased productivity even more than simple Taylorism. Ford thus invented the "assembly line" as we know it today, but he also offered workers an eight-hour workday and the premium pay of $5 per day. Ford hoped to establish a class of industrial workers who would have the time and the money to consume mass produced items—like his cars.[14]

Both Taylorism and Fordism were significant in the history of work because they had no room for spirituality in the secular rationality of workplace activity. Industrialization in general and the de-skilling of work by Taylorism treated the human body as a machine to be controlled. Creativity and intellectual engagement were lost for the average worker, and with these the "spirit" or inherent meaning of the work was lost too.[15] In the new systems of industrial organization with their radical divisions of labor, workers may not have known how their small piece of work fit into the larger process of the factory and product(s) made there. Henry Ford then focused the workers attention not on the work being done but exclusively on the wages earned and what those wages could buy. Wages were the "fuel," and it was assumed that wages alone were the motivation for employee effort. In other words, the Faustian trade for less meaning at work was for leisure and a lifestyle of consumption—a process we continue to see to this day. Many people may find their work wholly meaningless, but it is necessary to support a certain consumer lifestyle that they are unwilling to abandon.

Ironically, the dehumanization of work by Taylorism and the assembly line has been made into a source of great humor. Charlie Chaplin's 1936 *Modern Times* is the classic with Chaplin exploiting the mechanization of human work for comic effect. Scratching and shooing a fly upsets the assembly line and forces Chaplin's Tramp to make emergency adjustments. At an especially ludicrous moment, the factory owner decides to use a mechanical feeding machine on Chaplin in order to save the time and expense of providing a lunch break. The character Lucy Ricardo in *I Love Lucy* exploits similar comic themes in the episode where Lucy works in an automated candy factory. Instead of Lucy being fed by the machine, however, she frantically stuffs her mouth with candy to avoiding getting behind the pace of the candy-making machine. These works of entertainment have become a form of satire that highlight the dehumanization that can result from certain forms of automated work.

Of course, work does not have to be automated to be antithetical to spiritual longing. In fact, most of the contemporary interest in workplace spirituality comes from white-collar workers. These workers, however, still suffer similar indignities to their industrial counterparts when bureaucracy and the logic of the market strip work of creativity, relationship, service, and ethical guidance. White-collar workers are also faced with increased work hours, fear of layoffs, and an increasing work pace. An executive in a center-city office building may not face an assembly line, but she might well describe her work as being on a quickening treadmill. A factory worker may not be able to fully understand how his task relates to the whole, but he can often point to the final product, while white-collar work is often less tangible. White-collar workers more than others also are immersed in complex bureaucracies, settings that sociologist Max Weber would liken to an "iron cage" of restraint.

Spirituality and Welfare Capitalism

Anxious to consolidate his growing manufacturing operations, George Pullman began work in 1881 on a new factory located southeast of Chicago near Lake Calumet. That site would include more than a factory. Pullman hired both an architect and a landscape architect to design an entire city that would surround the production facilities. The city of Pullman would eventually include a hotel, shops, parks, and a combination of single-family homes and apartments that would result in a population of 8,600 in 1885.[16] Having lived most of his adult life in Chicago, Pullman had observed the social disorder of industry-fostered urbanization, and this new city became his counter to it. He made a direct connection between the aesthetics of a neighborhood or home and the morality of its residents.[17] By building a model town where his workers would reside, Pullman hoped to foster an improved moral ethos. Pullman was also able to maintain absolute control over the continued use and upkeep of the property by retaining full ownership and allowing only renters.[18]

Included in plans for Pullman's new city was a single church located near the town's center. Pullman was raised in a Universalist church, and he had two brothers who became Universalist ministers. The religious life of his home was focused more on values and ethics than doctrine, which characterized his spirituality as an adult.[19] With little concern for doctrinal differences, Pullman saw no need to provide more than one church for the multiple religious traditions that might be present among workers. Moreover, a large church was deemed more aesthetically pleasing and a better fit for the town overall. Traditionally Protestant in design, the church sported stained-glass windows and a Gothic exterior of serpentine stone. It seated six hundred and was eponymously named the Greenstone Church.[20]

Over seven hundred miles away in Gaston County, North Carolina, company towns and villages were being built around growing cotton mills. Attracted by low wages and abundant supplies of water power, North Carolina's Piedmont was becoming a center for the textile industry. The large migration of workers to the county as well as the often rural location of the mills led managers and owners to construct housing and provide a variety of services. In these company towns, mill employees and their families might have access to medical care as well as opportunities for recreation organized and financially supported by the mill owner.[21]

As with Pullman, southern mill owners also provided large amounts of support for the construction of churches in mill villages. Since the mill usually owned all the land in the village, one of the major gifts was property for churches, but the mill corporations and mill owners as individuals often made large cash contributions to the construction of church buildings. Even more, many mills provided direct support to ministers serving churches in the mill villages. In some cases this included the minister receiving a regular or annual check from the company's account just like the employees of the mill itself, and some ministers were provided with a parsonage at the mill's expense.[22] Mill owners, managers, and foremen were also expected to be prominent leaders within the congregations of the villages, and it was common for the owners to supervise work during the week and then teach their employees in Sunday schools on the weekend.[23] Support of churches gave mill owners significant control over the types of religious expression allowed in mill villages, and owners of nearby mills would often coordinate the location and denominational type of churches to avoid duplication.[24]

Except for a few occupations (like pastors), the idea of living in housing owned by your employer sounds odd today, but by 1916 approximately 3 percent of the U.S. population lived in company-owned housing and "company towns."[25] Companies also built and supported churches in many of these locales with pastors as part of the regular corporate payroll. Together with recreation opportunities, schools, company-employed social workers, and various provisions for medical care, American businesses during this period showed a growing attention to the overall well-being of employees by meeting a wide scope of human needs as part of the business enterprise. While Henry Ford certainly wanted his own employees to buy Ford cars, he also exercised a paternalistic interest in their other consumer and lifestyle choices; this included, in 1916, sending social workers to the homes of employees to "teach" immigrant workers how to live an appropriate middle class lifestyle.[26]

The package of holistic concerns and responses by corporate America during the industrialization of the nineteenth and early twentieth centuries would later become known as "welfare capitalism." It was an industrial form of enlightened self-interest that drew upon communitarian ideals and themes from the Social Gospel to emphasize the importance of sharing wealth and respecting workers as more than mere cogs in the industrial machine. Welfare capitalism was not, however, a move toward a socialist ideal of industrial community. Rather, as a system of benefits and controls, it sought to protect American capital and capitalists from the perceived dangers of unionism and from the welfare policies being adopted in Europe states. The enlightened solution was a distinctively American system of welfare benefits that were provided by employers and not the state.[27]

The workplace spirituality of early industrial America, like all expressions of welfare capitalism, mixed the diverse desires and values of owners, workers, and society at large. Company towns, with their many community services, were a far cry from the urban slums and tenements where most industrial workers were forced to live and toil, and corporate concerns for workers as holistic, spiritual beings warranted praise over the dehumanizing forms of Taylorism. While both Pullman's ideal community and Gastonia's mill towns would be forever changed by strikes, they were honorable efforts to reconcile the values of capitalism and the Social Gospel. As American life became more urban and industrial, "the city" became a great concern for the Protestant advocates of the Social Gospel's more socially conscious Christianity, and its influence spread and found partners in business and progressive political movements of the same period. Industrialists even found models for welfare capitalism in the many utopian communities and philosophies that flourished in the nineteenth century.[28]

Specific programs of welfare capitalism sought to improve morale, foster a healthy home life, and acculturate new, often rural, workers to the rigors (and perils) of industrialization and urbanism.[29] Welfare capitalism sought to "shield workers from the strains of industrialism," but it did so not by altering the structure or type of work; it focused instead almost exclusively on employees' time away from the factory. Taylorism as a system of industrial organization remained in effect on the factory floor, but even the Society for the Promotion of Scientific Management (later the Taylor Society) began to take seriously those critics who questioned the personal and social costs of Taylorism.[30] Welfare capitalism thus sought to build community and a new model of the οἶκος that was company controlled. Company-sponsored unions and welfare benefits provided a type of community but without affecting work itself. Included in this focus was a concern for the morality and religious practices of employees since this would lead to more stable, loyal, dependable, and productive workers in the long term. One of the most common practices of the time was for companies to organize YMCA-led Bible studies among employees; in 1904 the YMCA reported that the organization was working in 175 factories in 115 cities with an average attendance of 25,000.[31]

However, as welfare capitalism developed further, it was not spirituality that assumed predominance. Rather, the behavioral sciences, foreshadowed in the use of social workers by Henry Ford, became the primary resources. During and soon after World War I, large American companies began to establish personnel departments that drew upon the emerging discipline of "industrial psychology" to appease, avoid, and (if necessary) negotiate with workers and unions.[32] While new personnel departments often assumed responsibility for the welfare activities of companies, the tie to psychology can also be viewed as an extension of scientific management. Whereas foremen had traditionally hired and fired workers, this was now the role of the personnel department; new rules and regulations further systematized the employee-employer relationship—often in the interest of fairness and good relationships.[33]

But personnel managers also began to rebel from the rigid orthodoxy of Taylorism. They sought to develop new methods and systems of motivation and work organization that would be persuasive rather than domineering like that of Taylorism. The historian Stanford Jacoby notes that "behavioral scientists defended their approach by arguing that consensus forms of persuasion were preferable to the drive system and to the *spiritless* [emphasis mine] ideas—such as Taylorism—that underpinned it."[34] Personnel managers and professional industrial psychologists used interviews to gauge employee attitudes and morale, and foremen were trained to be more sensitive, appealing to an employee's feelings rather than resorting to harsh disciplinary measures. Some, like John Dewey, thought that these initiatives were a more democratic management style since they at least considered employee ideas, wants, and needs, but others, such as Walter Lippman, accused industrial psychology of social engineering.[35]

Most importantly, business leaders and theorists in the 1920s began to rethink their assumptions that workers were motivated exclusively by increased wages and economic benefits. "Economic man" was replaced by "social man," and, according to Bruce Kaufman, that shift:

> provided an intellectual justification for the abandonment of drive methods of motivation that relied on fear and intimidation and the adoption of positive employment methods (e.g. supervisor training, employment security, profit sharing) that not only encouraged hard work by linking personal gain with corporate gain but also fostered an atmosphere of fair treatment and personal growth.[36]

Relationships were now valued not only outside the workplace on softball teams and in company-town churches but also inside the plant and as part of the work process itself.

The empirical confirmation for this new theory of employee-employer relations came in a surprising way. In 1924 at the Western Electric plant in Hawthorne, Illinois, what began as a scientific management study in the end undermined the basic assumptions of Taylorism. George Pennock, the assistant plant manager, began an experiment to determine what level of lighting in the plant would lead to the most productivity, using a test group of workers who were placed in a separate room with their own supervisors. The study was later expanded to include a fluctuating variety of workplace changes, including incentive pay systems, different break schedules, and revised work hours. The surprising result for both the lighting study and the later study with multiple variables was that none of the variables seemed to matter. Regardless of the change made, the test group's productivity continued to rise. In their confusion, officials from the plant sought the assistance of Elton Mayo, a professor at Harvard University.[37]

Mayo and his assistants interviewed thousands of workers at the Hawthorne plant, and they continued to monitor worker productivity in both the main production area and in the test area. Mayo's conclusion was that the increases in productivity by the test workers had nothing to do with the test variables (a conclusion that even the plant officials had reached), but instead the tests themselves had brought about the increased productivity. Strangely, the employees in the test area were affected by variables that had not been measured as part of the original study. Workers perceived the test room as being more relaxed, and they also sensed that they had greater freedom to offer suggestions and organize their work.[38] Each test was discussed in advance with workers, creating a dialogue and a relationship that before had not been present between labor and management. Mayo concluded that it was this sense of participation and cooperation as well as the improved relationship between supervisor and employee that brought about the productivity gains.[39]

Mayo's conclusions had been influenced by the sociology of Emile Durkheim, even though it is unclear whether he actually read Durkheim as a primary source. For Durkheim, a social organization always has a religious reality that is present, and his own study of work in *The Division of Labor in Society* (originally published in 1893) affirmed the division of labor as the basis for the new industrial society and thus of that society's moral and religious reality.[40] Like Durkheim, Mayo worried about the feelings of isolation and the lack of an organic social system that had been brought about by industrialization, and both men affirmed the important role of society and social organization in the psychological well-being of individuals. The connections Mayo failed to see, however, were the ones that Durkheim always made between social reality, religion, and morality. Durkheim's understanding of the divine was not a transcendent personal God but rather the spiritual and moral reality of relationships and social organizations. Mayo never addressed issues of morality in his research and writing.[41] Likewise, he did not consider that the social reality of work might have a religious or spiritual dimension that needed to be considered, but his conclusions were certainly leading in that direction.

Future management theorists and organizational psychologists have frequently expanded on the social dimension of work as well as the human needs of workers beyond a wage. Abraham Maslow argued that meaning in work was a characteristic that could be placed within a hierarchy of human needs alongside religion and spirituality.[42] Frederick Herzberg's study of the motivation to work distinguished negative and positive factors in workplace organization. While the negative (what he called "hygiene") factors like supervision, working conditions, salary, benefits, and job security were important, they alone were not sufficient to provide higher productivity. Herzberg argued that achievement, responsibility, advancement, and the possibility for growth were the real motivators for high productivity.[43] Other theorists have made similar claims, but the key is to note how psychology has become the primary science of work. Primitive forms of external motivation, either by economic incentives or fear, were supplemented or replaced by corporate efforts to create internal incentives for hard work based on the employee's desire for relationships, creativity, recognition, and inherent meaning in work. This was the hallmark of "human relations" as a form of management that emerged after Mayo's landmark study, and it also characterizes the face of welfare capitalism after World War II.

New Forms of Welfare Capitalism

The move into psychology set the stage for corporate sponsored personal development programs that emerged in the 1960s and continue today. Designed for and appealing especially to white-collar employees, personal development programs seek to foster personal growth and increase personal effectiveness. They tap into a desire for self-improvement that is part of American culture broadly, but they do so with the assumption that the personal improvement of employees will benefit the business. Usually offered by training departments or outside consultants, personal development programs can include challenging outdoor experiences like whitewater rafting or a ropes course, and they can also be conducted within the corporate office involving techniques such as meditation and visioning. Overall, personal development programs are distinguished by their lack of a direct link to specific job responsibilities.[44] For some workers, offering a Spanish class at work could be for personal development while for others it could be a prerequisite for a promotion or a new corporate initiative. Likewise, white-water rafting may not have a direct tie to corporate mission, but the teamwork and confidence it inspires may have measurable effects at work.

Use of the behavioral sciences as well as a growing distaste for the methods of Taylorism has also led managers and scholars to think of corporations as having distinctive cultures that effect how work is done and how decisions are made. These theories argue that corporations are communities with their own rules, policies, procedures, and etiquette. For example, when changing jobs, a person is able to recognize differences in corporate culture almost immediately. In some corporations all men are expected to wear dark suits and wing-tip shoes. In other organizations, a suit would be out of place, and in still others wearing a tie might identify someone as "stuffy" or out of character with the organization's casual atmosphere. People use different acronyms and tell inside jokes, which new employees fail to understand. But corporate cultures have deeper effects than these. In some corporations the culture is structured so that employees are highly valued; employees are trusted, and their opinions matter. In other organizations, employees are disposable, often abused, and not treated like human beings.

Behavioral regularities, norms, espoused values, a guiding philosophy, rules of acceptance, and the feeling or climate that a corporation conveys have all been named as aspects of corporate culture.[45] A corporate culture also can provide a corporation's conscience. In some, bending and breaking laws is a matter of course, but in others high ethical standards are expected, respected, and followed. The implication is that corporations are morally coherent social units where values and beliefs are held and taught. Corporately held value commitments lessen the importance of independent moral and spiritual agency since the group will, in many ways, guide decision-making and corporate goal-setting.[46] Those who do not fully adopt the corporation's values are thought to be undersocialized to the values of the organization, and a more complete integration into the corporate culture may be necessary.[47]

Since corporate culture has great potential as a means of control, corporate leaders and their consultants have sought to manipulate and shape corporate values to maximum advantage. Businesses want employees to accept and internalize corporate values, norms, and aims. In order to achieve this, the process may be as simple as learning through repeated social interaction with others already immersed in the culture.[48] In an interview, a candidate may be identified as a "good fit" based on an initial consideration of his or her qualities, mannerisms, education, or other factors. What follows is an "encounter" between the individual and the new culture. This is an immersion experience, which identifies contrasts and surprises between old cultures and new ones. New employees will seek to have certain values clarified as well as specific expectations communicated to them. Finally, an employee is assimilated.[49] Each of these stages may entail some sort of ritual or rite of passage to indicate that socialization to the corporate culture has progressed.

The reality of corporate culture has led managers and management theory away from seeing corporate leadership and institutional change as strictly a rational process. Cultures are often highly irrational even though they may intend to be efficient and well-structured. A corporate culture helps to determine and define corporate identity as well as to shape decision-making, and since no business is the same as any other, no corporate culture or corporate identity is the same either (although clusters of styles may develop). The consequence is that corporate managers with the exact same problem could reach radically different conclusions because their corporate cultures press them to interpret the data differently and thus to apply principles or to pursue common ends in distinctive ways. Different processes of decision-making, perspectives, and values often influence results more than the facts and problems themselves, and managerial experts increasingly interpret, as forms of myth and ritual, the activities and relationships that shape the culture. In this way, the corporate organization has an inherent mythic identity and spirituality that, along with moral norms, the organization seeks to propagate in order for workers to become part of the corporate culture. However, this same spiritual and moral identity can also be a force for employers to harness and use to manipulate and control workers.[50]

Old-style welfare capitalism has also reemerged in recent years with a new set of benefits. We now see corporate interest as well as employee support for benefits that harmonize one's work with other areas of life as well as corporate organizations that respond to deep psychic needs and desires. *Fortune* magazine reported this development in January 2001 when it proclaimed the rebirth of the company town. In new office complexes that are now "corporate campuses" and through growth in nontraditional benefits, the author Jerry Useem argued that we are seeing a reformation of the company town that is appealing to white-collar employees and employers who are increasingly strained for time and talent. As Useem writes,

> [The modern corporation is] where you can eat, nap, swim, shop, pray, kick-box, drink beer, run your errands, start a romance, get your dental work done. . . . It's where you can bring your whole self—mind, body and spirit—to work each day. Which is a good thing, because you'll be here, if not from cradle to grave like the old company towns, then certainly from dawn to dusk.[51]

The new company town tends to be more like a shopping mall than an old-fashioned city. Housing is no longer the centerpiece. Instead, the realities of dual-career families and longer hours have come together. Time is the most precious commodity for both worker and employer, and the convenience of multiple services and opportunities means that employees do not have to leave the office to meet other needs. Energy and think-time can be devoted exclusively to the enterprise and away from personal concerns.

As with the old company town, these benefits help to recruit and retain workers by providing services that meet basic needs, inspire loyalty, and promote increased productivity. One area of growth is in health-related services produced by companies in addition to traditional health insurance benefits. Wellness programs as well as "employee assistance programs" that provide counseling and assistance with substance-abuse problems have been added by many firms.[52] One of the distinguishing features of the Hewitt Associates' *100 Best Companies to Work for in America* is the presence of health facilities at the workplace and/or subsidized or discounted health club memberships, because this is such a desired perk.[53] Although there is a well-documented link between physical fitness and personal job advancement, companies themselves expect a financial return from wellness programs since they produce healthier, more productive employees.[54]

While wellness programs focus on the mental and physical health of employees, a rapidly expanding concern in recent years has been for a balance between work and family life. Attention to this area has grown especially in the last twenty-five years with the large number of women now in the workforce and with the resulting reality of two working parents. In most cases, the relationship between work and family has been understood as a trade-off with time spent in one role taking time from the other, but companies and employers have increasingly sought to reconcile their various needs. Certainly, a parent does not stop worrying about his or her children when they are on the job. As a result, creating peace of mind about family life is now seen as a legitimate business concern because stress from family life can easily spread into the work sphere. Companies are now trying to create win-win situations in which family needs and company objects are both met simultaneously.[55] Common benefits include maternity leave and "flextime" (i.e., the opportunity to work the same number but more flexible hours). Smaller numbers of companies also offer paternity leave, on-site day care or day care assistance, and elder care for aging parents. In one of the most expansive approaches, Ford Motor Company established thirty Family Service and Learning Centers across the United States at its various plants and facilities. Open twenty-four hours a day, these centers will provide care for sick children who otherwise might not be able to attend day care (meaning the employee would have to miss work), after-school tutoring for the children of employees, summer camps, and services, such as computer classes, for Ford retirees. Although these initiatives are part of a contract Ford negotiated with the United Auto Workers, the programs are available to both white-collar and production employees. Ford is convinced that the new centers will produce financial results as they enable the company to attract and retain quality employees while relieving them of some family-related stress.[56] The family–work connections have gone so mainstream that the *Wall Street Journal* has a regular "Work and Family" column that helps both employers and employees navigate such issues.

The diverse services provided by American corporations (everything from child care to personal development programs to fitness centers) seek to re-create holism in an employee's life—but on corporate property. The company becomes the new οἶκος—except that you do not sleep there (except possibly for a nap in a company provided "nap tent" or meditation room). The most basic and even very intimate tasks can be accomplished through employer-provided concierge services; this includes everything from car repair to buying birthday cards for family members.[57] Employers are now concerned about all areas of a worker's life. "While employee assistance programs, wellness centers, leadership training and family care programs may look widely different . . . they share a common goal of enabling workers to improve their work effectiveness and performance through the development and improvement of personal abilities."

The whole human person and economic productivity are thus joined in a symbiotic relationship.[58]

Being Explicitly Spiritual at Work

The move from later forms of welfare capitalism to an explicit concern for spirituality has not been a major leap. In many ways, it has simply been a matter of semantics as certain benefits have been repackaged and reinterpreted as being part of an employee's and employer's spiritual identity. But as we read earlier, this change in language has also required some precision in words as well. Most companies focused on spirituality (except for the evangelical Christians described in the next chapter) actively avoid direct connections to "religion" and religious traditions in order to be more ecumenical, engaging, and noncontroversial. Since employers and employees want to maintain a clear distinction between religion and spirituality in the workplace, the result is a very general definition of spirituality. As management professor Judith Neal defines it,

> Spirituality in the workplace is about people seeing their work as a spiritual path, as an opportunity to grow personally and to contribute to society in a meaningful way. It is about learning to be more caring and compassionate with fellow employees, with bosses, with subordinates and customers. It is about integrity, being true to oneself, and telling the truth to others. Spirituality in the workplace can refer to an individual's attempt to live his or her values more fully in the workplace. Or it can refer to the ways in which organizations structure themselves to support the spiritual growth of employees.[59]

Author and consultant Martin Rutte refuses to even define spirituality since he fears that doing so will alienate rather than invite; instead, he claims that spirituality should be a question or inquiry into meaning in life and work rather than an answer that compels agreement.[60]

Within the corporate organization, the manifestation of spirituality most often occurs through a set of shared values and practices, which are understood as spiritual in character. An interest in spirituality may lead corporate leaders to talk about creativity, inner wisdom, happiness, relationships, service, and ethics as a seamless unity tied to an eternal (or deeply personal) source. Use of the word "spirituality" in itself can be an important marker in the process since many business organizations, business education, and the rationality of the business ethos influenced by "scientific" management have been resistant to such terms. Coupled with the changing vocabulary is a values shift whereby managers may consider that profits are not the primary focus of business but are instead a means to measure the quality of relationships built between customers, workers, communities, and the environment. Overall, advocates of spirituality in business desire to change the very values that drive enterprise, but they do so with a Gandhian sense that the only way to bring about a true and lasting change in action and behavior is to simultaneously bring about a spiritual transformation.

The use of the word "spirituality" as well as the invocation of spiritual values is also directly tied to the quest for wholeness that is articulated by both workers and corporate leaders. Many workers want to be recognized as holistic beings, and companies believe that the full potential and creativity of an employee requires holistic happiness as well as holistic dedication to corporate work. The corporate embrace of holism has now been classified as an expression of spirituality. Family-friendly policies and fitness rooms can thus be an expression of a company's spirit as well as the firm's openness to the spirituality of workers when this term is defined as harmony among all aspects of life. The system of values found in self-described spiritual companies can focus further on a wider understanding of corporate stakeholders that values relationships between workers, customers, and suppliers, seeing them not as competitive or antagonistic but as cooperative and synergistic. Firms may have an enlightened or environmentally conscious approach to growth, which does not assume that more is better. They can also affirm the proper role of business in society while not challenging capitalism but making capitalism and the individual company subordinate to the common good.[61] Support for these values and the new sought-after ethos is often found by engaging a variety of resources and practices. Some are recognizable as tied to ancient faith traditions while others are novel or a recasting of the secular into the sacred.

An often utilized practice of spirituality in corporate life is storytelling. This can take a variety of forms, including reading and discussing existing stories from a source outside the group, or by telling personal stories and engaging in dialogue about them. Many of the books written about and for workplace spirituality are now sources for the practice of storytelling. By far the most well-known example is *Chicken Soup for the Soul at Work*, a collection of 101 stories about life at work. The authors of this book (one of a growing collection on almost every conceivable topic) have even developed a guide for readers to use in establishing a "Chicken Soup Group" in the workplace. The steps focus on group organization, but they also prompt personal reflection and awareness of feelings as stories from the book are read in the group. They also "ask participants if they want to make a commitment to do something this week that will make a difference at work."[62] Other books and essays affirm the value of storytelling or provide a forum for the author to share his own story of triumph, failure, and enlightenment. Still another genre of books uses fables to communicate a message about business management; these include *Leading with Soul* by Lee Bolman and Terrence Deal, Robin Sharma's *The Monk Who Sold His Ferrari*, and Ellen K. Rainineri's *Wisdom in the Workplace*.

Storytelling as a practice shares many of the values named as attributes of workplace spirituality such as community and compassion, and it can demonstrate the close tie between forms of spirituality and theories of corporate culture. Telling stories creates an intimacy, fosters stronger relationships among the conversation partners, and socializes new employees into the group. Since many of the stories may not be directly work related, storytelling can demonstrate how the organization honors the holistic character of life. From the individual's perspective, telling about a sick parent, a divorce, or some other seemingly "personal" matter *at work* makes the workplace into a space and set of relationships where the whole self is welcomed and valued. From the organization's perspective, the management theorist Peter Senge has argued that dialogue fosters creativity and builds relationships of trust that enable additional dialogue to take place. Development of skills for dialogue is essential, according to Senge, because it allows the work group to access a higher level of thinking and creativity than can be done individually.[63]

In 1994, the poet David Whyte published a book titled *The Heart Aroused: Poetry and the Preservation of the Soul in Corporate America*. He now makes a living reading poetry at corporate meetings and encouraging business leaders to write poetry as a stimulus for creativity, change, and spirituality in their work. Whyte contends that storytelling, including poetry, can evoke the spiritual forces that are necessary for corporate happiness and well-being. As he describes it,

> The corporation, in calling for a little more creative fire from their people, must make room for a little more soul. Making room for creativity, it must make room for the source of that fire and the hearth where it burns—the heart and the soul of the individual.[64]

For Whyte, poetry and storytelling are "kindling" for this creative process. He uses such classics as Beowulf, the Gaelic myth of Fion, and Samuel Taylor Coleridge's poetry to connect with the soul—what he defines as the "indeniable essence of a person's being and spirit."[65]

But others have identified and used methods and practices other than storytelling for similar purposes. At Xerox Corporation, three hundred employees were involved in a Native American "vision quest" that included twenty-four hours of isolation in remote environments. *Business-Week* reported that Xerox employees "from senior managers to clerks" participated in the program as a means to spark new ideas and creativity for product development. Such activities seek to make a connection to "inner wisdom" that can be heard only when much of the "noise" of our modern culture has been silenced or escaped. To promote creativity through dialogue, Xerox has utilized Native American talking circles to facilitate meetings. In these events, a "talking stick" is shared among participants to encourage deep listening to the one person speaking. *Business-Week* reported that the results of these practices were the development of a highly profitable new copier-fax-printer as well as inquiries about similar programs from corporate giants like Nike and Harley-Davidson.[66] Using a more traditional approach to spirituality, the Ford Motor Company has operated a training and retreat center located in a Roman Catholic monastery outside of Detroit since the 1980s. Some employees visit the center twice a year for workshops that include an "awareness hour" and "creativity building exercises." [67] Rick Gutherie, the former director of the center, developed a program that combined the latest in management theories about communication, team-building, and creativity with a climate that has "value boundaries" derived from the Bible and defined as faith, love, and truth. Gutherie and Ford call this synthesis "self-organizing leadership," and it is the very opposite of Taylorism and the Fordism of the early twentieth century. The paradigm developed at this monastic retreat "provided a new business structure for making decisions based on agreed upon principles. This eliminated the need for top-down control and unleashed the creative power of our spirit."[68]

The range of companies that seek to embody forms of spirituality is great, and the expression of a desire for more holistic and spiritual workplaces has taken many forms. At Lotus Development Corporation, a large software manufacturer now affiliated with IBM, a "soul" committee was formed in 1994 to study employee morale and how it could be improved.[69] In 1992 the World Bank in Washington, DC, sponsored a discussion group on workplace spirituality that continues today. What began as a small lunchtime discussion group around brown-bag meals soon became a major employee organization at the bank known as the Spiritual Unfoldment Society; fifty to sixty people attend weekly meetings, which are a "safe forum for the exchange of beliefs and ideas that promote spiritual awareness."[70] The group's leader, Richard Barrett, has since left the bank and is now a speaker and advocate for corporate policies that link "the well-being and survival of their employees to the well-being and survival of the company."[71]

A smaller company that can be said to embody forms of workplace spirituality is Tom's of Maine. Founded by Tom Chappell, Tom's of Maine is a personal-care products company that specializes in natural and environmentally friendly products. As the CEO and majority owner of the company, Chappell almost single handedly transformed Tom's of Maine into a company with a spiritual focus. Facing a spiritual crisis of his own, Chappell enrolled in Harvard Divinity School, and he was soon bringing Harvard professors as well as the books they assigned to corporate board meetings and employee gatherings. Chappell understands workplace spirituality to be a deep sense of connection, service, and commonality. For example, Tom's of Maine seeks to build partnerships with sales outlets, involving meetings between the marketing and community relations departments of both companies, so that values and relationships replace deals and competition. As the owner and CEO, Chappell has also sought to let people engage the company's spirit on their own terms and with their own language. This means that biblically rooted terms like "tithing" are replaced by alternatives like "giving back" to the community and the environment.[72]

A whole collection of new entrepreneurs like Chappell have sought to create a similar spiritual ethos in their businesses. The well-known Ben Cohen and Jerry Greenfield of Ben & Jerry's Ice Cream founded their company as a socially responsible organization that refuses, in their words, to operate under the "absurd" belief that "because spiritual connection is intangible or quantifiably immeasurable, it does not exist."[73] Howard Schultz has told a similar story about the values, spirit and explosive growth of Starbuck's Coffee in *Pour Your Heart Into It: How Starbucks Built a Company One Cup at a Time*. Interestingly, the founders of all three companies have written books that share their management philosophy and the connection to spirituality and values. Chappell's *The Soul of a Business* has made him a popular speaker on the subject of integrating spirituality and work, and Cohen and Greenfield wrote *Ben & Jerry's Double Dip* to advance their business philosophy and spiritual vision. Other self-proclaimed spiritual or enlightened entrepreneurs who have told and sold their stories include Mel and Patricia Zigler and Bill Rosenzweig in *The Republic of Tea: Letters to a Young Zentrepreneur*, and furniture maker Herman Miller's Max DePree, who wrote *Leadership is an Art* and *Leadership Jazz*.[74]

On the "supply" end of workplace spirituality, there appears to be a growing interest in spirituality by organizational consultants. Attending conferences on workplace spirituality, it is impossible not to notice the large numbers of professional consultants, especially in the area of organizational development. Also present are feng shui advisors who practice the ancient Chinese art of spiritual alignment for workplace organization. A dissertation by Katja H. D'Errico at the University of Massachusetts at Amherst considered the impact of spirituality on business consultants, including the "tools" it provides for consulting work as well as the level of openness there is to explicit consideration of spirituality in organizational consulting. The consultants interviewed noted that:

> bringing a spiritual focus to their consulting work enhanced the team work of their clients. Fostering positive attitude and creating win/win situations allowed teams to build positive energy and experience synergy. These participants felt that such synergy enhanced group motivation and productivity.

Yet there was still some hesitance among the consultants interviewed to mention spirituality directly or use the language of "spirit" and "soul" even though the consultants admitted that their work was inherently spiritual.[75]

Specialty consulting firms now provide psychic services and astrologers to assist employers find employees that will be the right fit. Adopting what some would consider a spiritual practice, a few employers also use enneagram readings, a form of personality identification and transformation that reports results via a nine-pointed star. Advisor Associates, a consultant in New Jersey, offers companies psychic readings of potential employees that claim to tell an employer how the applicant will relate to other employees, whether they have psychological problems or addictions, their level of honesty, and their dependability.[76] It seems likely that increased interest in spirituality by workers and corporate leaders, combined with promises of enhanced productivity, will create an expanded market for consultants who use spirituality explicitly or implicitly. Already, companies like Boeing, AT&T, Lotus, TRW, Pacific Bell, and Proctor and Gamble have used spirituality consultants.

Consultants who address spiritual themes have a variety of origins. Some are religious practitioners of some sort (like the feng shui advisors or Christian ministers) who now address issues related to work in a fee-for-service arrangement. Others have emerged, not surprisingly, from organizational psychology and previous consulting work in organizational development, which was attentive to issues of corporate cultures. The question raised is whether consultants can "use" spirituality like any other aspect of corporate culture as a technique for organizational change. Consultant Krista Kurth argues that organizational development consultants "should not formally teach or make specific, traditional, [organizational development] interventions when dealing with spiritual issues in organization."[77] But it is doubtful that a prohibition against the instrumental use of spirituality can be sustained if it is seen as a successful method to higher profits.

Overall, the move to address issues of spirituality in work should be understood as a confluence of an expanding welfare capitalism and the demise of Taylorism in forms of white-collar work. Yet by no means has Taylorism completely disappeared. In fact, Taylorism has become the strange bedfellow of organized labor. Unions have always been most successful in industries and workplaces that still rely on scientific management. According to Sanford Jacoby, "the new industrial unions pragmatically constructed their regulatory systems around the division of labor wrought by the Taylorists."[78] Union contracts thus reinforced and protected certain forms of job design sometimes in spite of technological advances that made specific tasks obsolete. The likely foundation of this odd partnership is that both unionism and Taylorism relied on the same assumptions about "economic man" and external work incentives.

The Underside of the Holistic Workplace

In the face of Taylorism and various forms of dehumanizing work now encountered, many workers have welcomed the move toward a more spiritual workplace, and practices of workplace spirituality have responded to the basic fact that the spiritual and religious dimensions of life are very real and even foundational to a vast majority of people. Most significantly, workplace spirituality trends can allow individuals to honor their deeply held beliefs and practices while on the job rather than "checking" that part of their identity at the door when they arrive. Yet thankfulness and appreciation for more openness to spirituality at work should not lead either the workers or commentators to avoid careful scrutiny and serious critique of these practices. Several problems may be present, including the commodification of spirituality, the overreaching of authority and independence of spiritual leaders, and the risk of an all-consuming holism that makes the workplace into the defining and controlling institution of life.

The commitment to holism is a major attraction of corporate spirituality, but it also raises many of the biggest concerns. In their book on holistic trends within human resource management, Frank W. Heuberger and Laura Nash ask whether we *want* the corporation to be holistic. Do we want to offer and even subordinate everything that we are to the corporation? Philip H. Mirvis fears the company that becomes a "total community" and is able to exploit, coerce, and manipulate workers because of that intimate relationship.[79] More abstractly, Michael Walzer raises related issues in his book *Spheres of Justice*, arguing that different spheres of life and their institutions deserve their own autonomy. As Walzer states it, "Different social goods ought to be distributed for different reasons, in accordance with different procedures, by different agents." Such autonomy is necessary for freedom and human flourishing. This was the basis of the Enlightenment's separation of church and state, and it may argue for a contemporary need for a distinction between corporation and soul.[80]

As we have seen, the creation of a holistic lifestyle grounded in the business enterprise was the very purpose of the company town. It certainly had a major effect on how life functioned and how faith was manifested in Gaston County, North Carolina. When, in 1929, workers at a Gaston mill went on strike in protest of low wages and poor working conditions, this holistic social fabric was tested, and the lack of distinctiveness led to predictable results. The mainline, so-called respectable clergy in the county remained silent or aligned themselves against the strike—and often in favor of the mills' management.[81] However, the less respected ministers of the Church of God and Holiness churches, who were never supported by mill owners, tended to support the strikers and workers despite their almost "exclusive focus on personal sin and heavenly salvation." According to the sociologist Liston Pope, "Only preachers who stood largely outside the economic and religious privilege of the Gastonia community, as then organized, supported the strike in any way," and this was a very small group. The four ministers in the Loray mill towns themselves gathered soon after the strike and began to implement a strategy of opposition. Their counsel to congregants was to seek different means to express their grievances. They also sought to divert the attention of indigenous strike leaders by hosting a series of revivals in the towns while the strike was in progress.[82]

There may not have been a direct relationship between the financial support of clergy and their opposition to the strike, but Pope argues that these financial arrangements were part of a larger symbiotic relationship that existed between economic and religious institutions within the community. His conclusion is that "the church tended to pass from a dynamic force for social change to a static sanction of the change effected." All the ministers who opposed the strike saw the economic development of Gaston County through textile mills as a positive development above criticism, and they often saw the mill town as a means not only to facilitate a good economy but also as a way to develop good people. While Pope warns against a simplistic Marxist analysis that would make religion in Gaston County "the opiate of the people" and the clergy the enforcers of the capitalist's will, clergy did serve a primary role in acculturating workers to the church–mill symbiosis, resulting in a loss of prophetic responsibility by the clergy as well as prophetic resources for social change.[83]

The question today is whether allowing the corporation to take greater responsibility for spirituality as well as for family life may invest the economic sphere with too much power and thus invite tyranny. While day care centers, elder care, concierge services, and spiritual storytelling may be appealing company benefits, they may also mean that spirituality and family life are treated like commodities, produced and distributed according to economic rationality rather than by their own respective spheres. This is the great lesson of the company town: by design it sought to bring all of life under the realm of economic production and efficiency.

Managerial and spiritual leaders can also be intertwined and confused in the pursuit of holism. In the company towns of Gaston County, ministers assumed the role of managers, and managers took on the responsibilities of religious leadership, teaching Sunday school and serving in other capacities. While forms of business spirituality today are in many ways remarkably different, the connection between business leadership and spiritual and/or moral leadership remains. Today, the CEO, owner, or manager serves not only as a boss who supervises, coordinates, and hires or fires employees; she can also serve as spiritual mentor and guide. The position of corporate leader is then transformed into that of guru (or parent), and the manager has the opportunity and perhaps even the responsibility to serve as a leader for multiple areas of the employee's life. This can include an Aetna executive who teaches employees the personal benefits of meditation or a Xerox official who encourages participation in a vision quest for the good of the company.[84]

The use of paid spiritual leaders in corporate settings raises similar issues of expanding corporate control and the potential manipulation of employees. As the field and profession of organizational development continues to focus on corporate culture, ethos, morale, and teamwork, it also appears that it will continue to draw upon or directly use spiritual resources. This might include meditation techniques, yoga, or stress management exercises as well as more overt appeals to spirituality, spiritual language, and spiritual practices from Native American and Asian traditions, whether feng shui or talking sticks, that are a particular focus in today's workplace. Yet employing spiritual leaders in business corporations can further commodify religion and spirituality, making spirituality into a corporate benefit on par with good life insurance or a fitness center. We are probably already at the point when some employees are picking and choosing companies to work for based on their provision of spiritual resources in some form. But the buying and selling of spirituality is problematic; subordinating it to the cold market logic of utility can easily undermine the values of spirituality that attempt to mitigate against market excesses in the workplace and that make spirituality attractive to workers in the first place. To return to Walzer, spirituality cannot maintain its own dignity and autonomy as a sphere of human life if it is subordinated to the economic sphere and the laws of supply and demand.

Questions must also be raised specifically about the effects of workplace spirituality on employees and whether intentionally or unintentionally it has become a means to manipulate or control workers. Is the corporate effort to help employees find meaning in their work a way to extract more time at work? Certainly, the drive for holism encourages them to feel at home in the work environment and may even encourage workers to regard fellow employees as family. However, it is difficult to tell whether the emphasis on holistic environments is a response to the real needs of workers or a rhetorical strategy by corporations that need to justify their demands for additional time and creative effort by employees. Perhaps it is a combination of both. Regardless, spirituality has the potential to be an abusive tool to keep employees in line and discourage protests because the company and the team environment are seen as a sacred space and relationship.

The definition and meaning of spirituality that is used in much of corporate America can create misunderstandings and difficulties. In many cases it arises out of a New Age metaphysics while embracing an eclectic mix of resources. New Age spirituality can connect terms of Asian religions like the Taoist *yin* and *yang* to quantum mechanics and advanced ideas about the nature of energy in the universe while at the same time embracing Freudian, neo-Freudian, and Jungian psychology.[85] The focus on holism also has connection to New Age spirituality in its focus on the integrity of the human body and nature as well as the embedded existence of the individual, nature, and society.[86] This may lead to a stance that is against materialism and supportive of environmental sustainability. Furthermore, this holistic focus may reject older Cartesian and Newtonian worldviews (and the spiritualities they foster and support) in favor of the omnipresence of energy (and thus spirituality) in a worldview grounded more in quantum physics then order of nature.[87]

The potential difficulty with such a worldview is that it can lack a sense of transcendence and, as a result, be more easily co-opted. As Max Stackhouse has described it,

> [it] presumes[s] that there is one whole in which everything exists; the whole is animated by a primal energy that can be found within each person . . . if we would only allow ourselves to come into contact with our inner resources, we will become integrated, energized, effective and able to live up to our profound potential in natural harmony with others and the cosmos.[88]

Without a transcendent reference, notes Stackhouse, it is virtually impossible to "impose moral constructs on natural human impulses to material security."[89] In other words, despite lofty claims to values and social responsibility, spirituality may become a means to bless corporate actions that do harm to corporate stakeholders. In a different way, this is the point made by Liston Pope with respect to the ministers and mills in Gaston County. A sense of transcendence—whether through a personal God or an ideal community—can lend to spirituality and religion a prophetic vision and voice, but the symbiosis of minister and mill and the embrace of spirituality by the modern corporation have the potential to compromise that voice when the corporation mediates the divine or becomes the ideal community itself. Even Matthew Fox, perhaps the epitome of New Agers, faults New Age spirituality for its excessive optimism, which "feeds the status quo and offers legitimization to the privileged at the expense of the less privileged."[90]

The coercive character of workplace spirituality can also extend to including direct challenges to an employee's current beliefs and worldviews. For example, do employees at Tom's of Maine or Xerox truly feel empowered to opt out of the latest spiritual experience or speaker? Spirituality advocates argue that appeals to the soul and spirit of employees transcend denominational and religious boundaries. Nonetheless, many employees might feel awkward in a business meeting that invoked a spirit that was not their own personal vision of God or the divine. The argument of religious neutrality in workplace spirituality fails the degree to which Eastern, New Age, Native American, or even Christian practices are invoked because these expressions are not "generic" but forms of spirituality plucked from coherent theological systems, traditions, and worldviews. Even more, authentic practitioners of Native American or Eastern religious traditions may be offended by commercial syncretism that exploits their deeply held convictions.

Spiritual but Not Exploitive

It is because of the potential for religious coercion that careful distinctions need to be made between spiritual practices and resources provided and encouraged by the businesses themselves, and spiritual practices initiated by workers and allowed by employers. Unfortunately, much of the literature and journalistic analysis of workplace spirituality fails to consider this difference. Many companies provide space for lunch-hour Bible studies, allow online prayer groups, and/or accommodate the religious or spiritual practices of employees (including holidays and dress). The theologian Ron Theimann notes that "the workplace is a middle ground, between specific religious beliefs held by employees and an older view that everything in the workplace must be purely secular." He counsels employers to allow employees to express their religious or spiritual views and values just as they would allow other forms of expression.[91] For Theimann, corporations can make room for spirituality and religious expression as a means to recognize the integrity and wholeness of employees, but this need not include a fostering of spirituality in pursuit of holistic business goals. In

Religion and the Workplace, Douglas A. Hicks has similarly argued for a sharp distinction between what he names "religion and spirituality *in* the workplace" versus "religion or spirituality *of* the workplace." While the former designates respect for the diverse religious and spiritual practices of individual workers, Hicks faults the latter for imposing "generic" spiritualities that deny religious and spiritual difference.[92] Both Theimann and Hicks agree that an imposed secularism in workplace is inappropriate, but they also agree that an imposed spiritual or religious identity can be equally problematic.

Yet making the workplace into a spiritually welcoming yet neutral place for individuals to live out their personal convictions may still be insufficient. What Walzer, Theimann, and Hicks see as liberating autonomy, many workers may understand as fragmentation and a source of a divided self. The desire for a shared workplace vision or purpose in work beyond material ends alone can lead to the creation of a rich corporate culture where spiritual meaning is simultaneously found and generated. Meaningful corporate cultures and expressions of workplace spirituality seek to humanize work (and capitalism), but it is a challenge to be spiritual while not being exploitive. Disbelief can never be entirely suspended because the same source of meaning and spirit can also be a new means for control.

Leaders and advocates of workplace spirituality too often ignore the risks because they believe all potential problems have been mitigated through nomenclature. By rejecting "religion" for "spirituality," individual autonomy and choice are thought to be affirmed against religious dogmatism. Thus, by the very definitions used, spirituality cannot be abused or exploited because it is totally individualized. But as Neal's definition of workplace spirituality states, the term also includes how "organizations structure themselves to support the spiritual growth of employees," and there can be a fine line between "support" and "use" whether it is religion or spirituality that is invoked.[93]

3

The Making of a "Christian Company"

In a small region of the Tembrius River Valley in Asia Minor, twelve obscure burial stones have for decades puzzled archeologists and historians of the ancient world. By style, all appear to be from the same stonecutting workshop, and all are dated from the middle of the third century to the beginning of the fourth. The stones carry the standard inscriptions from burial monuments of that period, the name of the deceased and the giver of the monument, but they also include something unique. Towards the bottom of the stone, in Greek, are carved the words "Christians for Christians" (Χριστιανοι Χριστιανοις).[1]

Theories abound about the meaning and source of these words, but Gary J. Johnson has proposed that these monuments may be products from "the earliest known Christian business."[2] Other scholars have argued that Christian stonecutters may have made the monuments, but Johnson goes further by claiming that the "Christians for Christians" formula was a workshop signature that identified the Christian identity of the cutters and their primary customer base. While evidence exists that the stonecutters sold to non-Christians, monuments appear to have been prefabricated with Christian symbols and words, anticipating a regular clientele of Christians.[3] This may have been an important service to fellow believers, but it may also have been a successful market niche.

This anecdote from early Christianity is interesting because it resembles a contemporary movement by some American evangelicals to establish and operate businesses that are explicitly "by Christians" and often "for Christians." This chapter considers in depth a model of workplace spirituality that evangelical Christians are creating today and how self-avowed "Christian companies" understand their business mission to exist along side a commitment to service and evangelism. With the growth in these firms, they have increasingly been organizing into parachurch groups, and other efforts are being made to encourage Christians to shop and buy from other Christians with targeted marketing and advertising. Together, they form an alternative approach to workplace spirituality compared to the more ecumenical ones describes in the previous chapter.

Evangelicals in the Marketplace

Much attention has been paid to the growing political significance of evangelicals in the past twenty-five years. While they avoid easy definition, the term "evangelicals" refers to Christians who emphasize personal conversion and the authority of the Bible. During the 1976 presidential campaign, candidate Jimmy Carter professed to the nation that he was "born again," moving evangelicals and evangelicalism into the mainstream of American politics. *Roe v. Wade* and the Equal Rights Amendments in the 1970s were especially significant for mobilizing conservative religious groups. In the 1980s, the Moral Majority and then the Christian Coalition in the 1990s exercised considerable influence in local, state, and national elections.[4] Overall, evangelical involvement in Republican politics has made the party more conservative and more attuned to social issues like abortion and "family values."

The popular image of evangelicals has often focused on ministers such as Oral Roberts, Pat Robertson, and Jerry Falwell, all of whom developed large TV ministries in the 1980s, and evangelicals have become distinguished by their frequent use of commercial media for evangelism and outreach. According to historian George Marsden, "in the 1980s the most modest estimate is that about thirteen million Americans watched these shows regularly; but other estimates claimed that up to sixty million Americans were at least occasional viewers."[5] Many of these television ministries continue today, and despite several scandals they have been vehicles for massive fund-raising as well as name recognition and political outreach. Pat Robertson turned his television notoriety into a credible presidential candidacy in 1987/88 despite never having been elected to public office before.[6]

The use of commercial media for evangelism was quite natural for modern evangelicals because commercialism has never been frowned upon in evangelical history. In fact, the emergence of the evangelical style of Christianity is directly linked to the marketing appeal of revivals and other religious methods that emerged in the United States in the late eighteenth century during the Second Great Awakening. Charles Finney became nationally famous for his revivals in the early nineteenth century, but what distinguished him most was his assertion that revivals are rationally planned events with clear cause-and-effect relationships. Finney did not trust saving souls to the movement of the Holy Spirit as much as to the careful planning and execution of a set revival program. Finney's *Lectures on Revivals* stated clearly what efforts should be made to promote revivals (marketing), how they should be facilitated, and what should be done as follow-up (customer service).[7] Although Finney often spoke against the predatory practices of industrial capitalism, he practiced a religious revivalism that was analogous to free market economics.

As it developed in the twentieth century, evangelical theology and practice has established intimate connections between capitalism, anticommunism, and patriotism. In addition to his showmanship, the preacher Billy Sunday combined patriotism with Christianity by extensive use of the American flag in his revivals and lambasting the godlessness of Germany during World War I.[8] Sunday was undoubtedly the most well-known and popular religious figure at the turn of the twentieth century, combining patriotic showmanship with classic revival religion and a large organization, rare then but now common in revivalist enterprises. Sunday himself is quoted as saying, "I am not a preacher but (a) businessman [and] I endeavor [to] bring (1) system and organization, (2) business principles, [and] (3) common sense" to revivals.[9] The *New York Times* noted on April 10, 1917, that "Sunday and his helpers made it clear that they were going after souls as a successful corporation goes after sales."[10]

Fears of "godless communism," beginning at the end of World War I coupled with the Russian Revolution, continued throughout most of the twentieth century among American evangelicals, and evangelicals countered this fear with more determined efforts at evangelism as well as theological defenses of capitalism.[11] Most evangelicals continue to be apologists for the divine character of capitalism.[12] Jerry Falwell defended capitalism as "'clearly outlined in the Book of Proverbs in the Bible' [while] other evangelicals quoted the advice of the apostle Paul to the Thessalonians: 'If any would not work, neither should he eat.'"[13] While more liberal Christians have frequently lifted up the supposed socialism of the early church in the book of Acts and the frequent criticism of wealth in the New Testament, evangelicals see within capitalism and its institutions the intention of God and the source of divine blessing. The evangelical focus on free will and the all-important choice necessary for salvation easily correlates to the choice made in the marketplace for goods and services. Many evangelical pastors, even when associated with denominations, operate as something like entrepreneurs with great independence and little hierarchy because of their "free church" traditions. Today, evangelicals are quietly creating new business paradigms that are distinctive in the way they draw upon evangelical theology and practice in their forms, function, and sense of mission.

Characteristics of Christians Businesses

One of the most interesting among these models is the explicit effort to align business practices with Christian principles. A growing number of companies describe themselves as "Christian businesses" or otherwise warrant the moniker by their self-professed efforts to be guided by the Bible, prayer, and a strict Christian code of ethics. The model of the Christian company is so well known that it has been featured in the *Wall Street Journal* (1985), *Fortune* (1987), *U.S. News and World Report* (1995), and *Time* (2005). Each of these publications has recognized that evangelicals are increasingly flexing their economic strength. Bob Reese, an evangelical and president of a Dallas manufacturing firm, told *U.S. News and Word Report* that "support of Christian business is one area where we can [regain control of] our culture, and politics is another."[14] In that same article, *U.S. News* reported that almost half of the small business owners in the United States describe themselves as evangelicals.[15]

With the increasing prominence of evangelicals in business and rising numbers of Christian companies, parachurch organizations have been formed to provide support, networking, and resources. One organization, Fellowship of Companies for Christ (FCC), was formed specifically for owners and chief executives who understand their business leadership/ ownership as an act of Christian stewardship—their unabashed goal is to change the world for Christ, one company at a time. FCC offers workshops and training events for CEOs and company owners; they support local groups for study, prayer, and fellowship; and they produce a variety of books, manuals, and magazines for use by Christian business leaders in their own companies. FCC claims that company leaders serve a special function in the Body of Christ, and Christian owners and CEOs must understand themselves as stewards of the companies that God has entrusted to them. The organization has both national and regional offices with programs available at each of these levels and across denominational lines.[16] An older but similar parachurch organization, The Christian Business

Men's Committee, has been in existence for more than sixty years and appeals to a broader group of business professionals (not just owners and CEOs) with similar programs and a regular magazine.[17]

In a 1991 study published in the *Journal of Business Ethics*, four business professors used a survey of FCC members to describe the distinctive characteristics of Christian companies. The authors sought to determine if a Christian identity affected the companies' relationships with key stakeholders—customers, employees, communities, and suppliers—and the degree to which practices varied among Christian companies in different economic sectors (services, manufacturing, finance, etc.). By using open-ended survey questions, the researchers were also able to document the specific practices of companies with respect to the identified stakeholders.[18]

According to the study, customers and employees are the two stakeholder groups with whom the Christian identity of firms is most readily apparent. In relation to employees, many firms offered on-site religious activities, and others emphasized the manager's responsibility as a role model.[19] Seventy-three percent of the companies reported that they sought to proselytize customers. According to the authors, these efforts to evangelize customers included:

- Distribution of Christian books and gospel literature
- Inviting customers to meetings where Christian testimonies are heard
- Displaying Christian principles in a prominent area, such as the company's reception area or lobby
- Enclosing biblical quotations in product containers, packaging, invoices, stationery, monthly statements, or customer order forms
- Inviting customers to church, to worship together
- Giving Christian gifts to customers, such as Christian calendars and bumper stickers
- Using Christian symbols, e.g., a cross or a fish in company logo
- Conducting "friendly Christian" conversations with customers
- Ministering to clients from the scriptures
- Distributing company brochures and literature with biblical messages
- Praying with customers, inviting customers to pray together on an ad hoc basis
- Printing biblical verses on restaurant menus

- Witnessing
- Playing church music on company premises[20]

Customer satisfaction was also highly regarded, with 78 percent of all firms stressing things like honest dealing, high quality products, promise keeping, and the quick resolution of customer complaints.[21] Obviously, some of these evangelism techniques are more active than others, but each conveys a sense of the companies' identity.

In terms of community relations, Christian companies frequently supported both Christian and secular organizations, but as might be expected a higher percentage of companies gave to Christian organizations and charities. Like customers, suppliers too were subject to proselytization with 48 percent of the companies reporting activities such as witnessing to and praying with suppliers. Other efforts were more indirect such as writing inspirational notes and Bible verses on invoices, purchase orders, and checks.[22] While each of these features would seem to distinguish the firms, the authors rightly note that their study did not contrast the Christian businesses with others.

Other analyses of Christian businesses have noted how the Bible is the essential business guidebook in these firms. While not all evangelicals are biblical literalists, the authority of the God's Word is primary and this necessarily displaces some of the authorities that might guide other business leaders. In their book *A Spiritual Audit of Corporate America*, Ian Mitroff and Elizabeth Denton argue that biblical authority often leads Christian businesses to see beyond quarterly profit reports, and it can foster a unique sense of hope and optimism.[23] Since God is recognized as the CEO and owner of the business, this often causes reflection on the purpose and actions of the company that are not normally found in other enterprises.[24] Owners of Christian businesses have a sense of stewardship that is broader than profits and short-term gains. The FCC also encourages applying the popular "what would Jesus do?" approach to corporate management, but obviously this leads them back to the authority of scripture in that discernment.

Unfortunately, talk about "Christian companies" is sometimes dismissed as oxymoronic, and these companies are often the butt of unfair prejudice. Mitroff and Denton classify Christian companies as "Religion-Based Organizations" in their business spirituality typology, but they also use words like "extreme" and "dark" to describe them. In a very superficial use of James Fowler's stages of faith development, Mitroff and

Denton label this type as "primitive" in its level of faith development.[25] To their credit, they note that not all Religious-Based Organizations are fundamentalist, yet they express a business concern that "homogeneous workplaces and organizations function best in extremely stable and invulnerable environments." Since they find this context to be extremely rare, their implied doubt is whether such organizations are economically stable.[26] This concern may be warranted since the vast number of Christian businesses are quite small, most small businesses are economically unstable by definition, and most will also fail. But as the examples in the next section demonstrate, this need not always be the case, as some Christian businesses have proven to be very successful in their respective economic sectors.

Profiles of Christian Businesses

Examples of Christian companies include many prominent retailers and other firms in the United States today. The trucking company Covenant Transportation offers Bible studies at its corporate headquarters and displays pro-life messages on every truck.[27] Touch1 Communications, a small telecommunications company in southern Alabama, has used its marketing literature to proclaim the Christian message and thus accentuate the Christian orientation of the company, including what that means for customer service. While employment discrimination based on religion is illegal, the alignment of Christian faith and for-profit businesses is clearly possible. The profiles of three different companies in diverse industry areas bring together Christian ideals, values, and messages to the business in diverse ways.

Chick-fil-A

With more than 950 restaurants in thirty-four states, Chick-fil-A has been a restaurant success story over the last forty years, and it is an interesting example of a Christian company. It was founded by S. Truett Cathy in Atlanta after World War II, and the firm remains privately held, which allows it to manifest Cathy's deep Christian beliefs and values. The company's signature product has been a fried, boneless breast-of-chicken sandwich sold originally in mall food courts, but has expanded to include free-standing restaurants and other restaurant concepts.[28] In 2000 the company surpassed $1 billion in sales for the first time.[29]

The most distinguishing mark of Chick-fil-A is that it is closed on Sundays. This was a pattern established by Cathy the first weekend his first restaurant opened in 1946. Cathy has noted that this initial decision to close had less to do with his Christian ideals than it did with his sheer exhaustion at running a twenty-four-hour diner. However, since that time, being closed on Sunday has distinguished Chick-fil-A and represented Cathy's beliefs as a Baptist and a Sunday school teacher. Cathy is convinced that it has also allowed the company to prosper—even without Sunday sales. In his words,

> As a Christian, I was taught that Sunday was the Lord's Day, a time for rest, worship and family togetherness. Keeping all of our Chick-fil-A restaurants closed on Sundays has allowed our restaurant employees to spend time with their families and to refresh themselves physically, mentally and spiritually each week. This policy also has enabled us to attract people who appreciate these values, and I feel our people are more productive as a result.
>
> Critics often tell me, "Look at all the business you're losing." As a Christian, I respond that I have honored God by adopting this principle. As a businessman I point out that, in many cases, our Chick-fil-A restaurants generate more sales per square foot in the same setting in six days than many other restaurants do in a full week.[30]

Cathy has also stated that being closed on Sunday is not something that he has particularly emphasized, but others have noted it because the practice seems so foreign to the fast food industry.[31] It is, however, stated on the corporate website that "in keeping with the Christian faith of the founder and his family, the 960-plus-restaurant chain maintains a 'closed-on-Sundays' policy."[32] Cathy also notes that he has been accused of hypocrisy because he and his family eat out on Sunday even though his own restaurants are closed.

Being closed on Sundays has been frequently cited as one of the aspects of corporate culture that makes Chick-fil-A a good place to work. Turnover at Chick-fil-A is very low compared to the average in the fast food industry, averaging at 40 percent compared to the 300 percent in the industry as a whole. Huie Woods, vice president for human resources at the company, stated that Cathy's religious convictions permeate the company. Corporate employees receive good pay, frequent perks, and no one has ever been laid off.[33] Individual stores are operated as a partnership with the local owner, who needs only $5,000 to start. After a rigorous screening process, Chick-fil-A will build a new store; the local manager is guaranteed a salary of $30,000, and then the manager must split the profits with the company 50/50 after paying Chick-fil-A 15 percent of gross revenues.[34] Any employee at a Chick-fil-A store is also eligible for a $1,000 college scholarship.[35]

The more explicitly Christian characteristics of Chick-fil-A, besides being closed on Sunday, are not usually seen by visitors to the company's restaurants. At the corporate headquarters in Atlanta, albeit behind the scenes, the evidence is more apparent. In 1987, *Fortune* described a Monday morning corporate meeting at Chick-fil-A like this:

> To the strains of a recorded gospel song, top managers and their staffs intently watch slides of an evangelical mission in Poland. The music stops and the lights come up. Several of the 75 or so members of the audience take turns praying aloud. One woman asks God to watch over a friend's hernia operation, another prays that a co-worker's eye surgery will succeed.[36]

Next to this description, in this normally hard-hitting business magazine, is a picture of S. Truett Cathy with his head bowed in prayer. The article also describes Chick-fil-A's corporate campus in Atlanta as a place with nature trails that "feature plaques bearing quotations from the Bible."[37]

In several publications, Cathy has noted that 1982 was a pivotal year in the company's history, and it was also a time when the company's religious foundation was more explicitly affirmed and announced. After a period of sluggish sales, top managers met with Cathy at a retreat to plot the future course of the company, and this included a philosophical reflection on "why we are in business." In his book *It's Easier to Succeed Than to Fail*, Cathy notes that this conversation soon turned to the Christian faith shared by all the top executives who were gathered. According to Cathy, "We all decided that our purpose in being in business needed to reflect the belief that God plays a major role in our lives." The resulting corporate purpose stated that the company existed:

1. To glorify God by being a faithful steward of all that is entrusted to us.
2. To have a positive influence on all who come in contact with Chick-fil-A.

This decisive meeting closed with the commitment to share these statements of purpose to all store operators but not to make shared faith a requirement for joining the company.[38] Nonetheless, Chick-fil-A was clearly transformed not only into a "work family" but also into a "family of faith."

Cathy believes that "loyalty begins with trust," and he seeks to follow God's own example by entrusting employees and local operators with assets and opportunities. Because he believes that God has entrusted Chick-fil-A's assets to his care, he does not seek to micromanage their use.[39] By recognizing that the assets are not really his but only entrusted to his care by God, Cathy has found the type of freedom that allows others within the organization to be truly creative.

It is somewhat unclear what the corporate purpose's commitment to religious (or nonreligious) inclusively means since new stores are "dedicated" in a ceremony that closely resembles Christian worship. In *It's Easier to Succeed Than to Fail*, Cathy reprints the script from a dedication ceremony as well as the prayer of a local minister who presided over the event. Cathy's own words at the event are illustrative:

> Two things are central to life: physical food and spiritual food. Ours, too, is a divine business—that of providing physical food for physical needs. We want to dedicate this Unit to the honor and glory of the Lord and ask His blessing on us. May this be an asset to Him in this area of ministry, and may we recognize Him from whom our strength and power come.[40]

The minister's prayer also closed in the name of Christ, making the Christian character of the business readily apparent to all those who might have attended the event or read Cathy's book.

While Cathy has not sought to advertise Chick-fil-A as "chicken for Christians," he has also not shied away from sharing his faith commitments and their manifestation in the company. As he states it, "I don't want people coming to Chick-fil-A just because we sometimes talk about God." Nonetheless, he has also credited the company's turnaround since 1982 to something like divine intervention. Cathy feels that much of their problem in 1982 was competition from other fast food companies offering new chicken sandwiches, but according to Cathy, improved marketing and a corporate organization only explain part of the company's future success. Cathy has stated, "I also feel that God honored our commitment to Him."[41] Cathy has also attributed to prayer and conversations with his family an earlier decision not to sell out to the Morrisons cafeteria chain.[42] These assertions as to the power of prayer seem to be connected to Cathy's overall philosophy, which could be described as a gospel of success.

Open evangelism of customers has never been a concern for Chick-fil-A, but the company has offered unique promotions that have an affinity with Christianity. The use of prizes and toys in children's meals is widespread in the fast food industry, and it is hard to imagine a G-rated movie that does not also have a corresponding promotion through McDonalds or Burger King. Chick-fil-A, perhaps due to its smaller size, has not followed this commercial track in its children's meals, but it has partnered with other products that are consistent with its corporate values. The company has sought to make its children's meal distinctive by offering toys and prizes that foster knowledge and character development. Currently, the company "offers eight or more series of collectables every year under the theme "Growing Kids Inside and Out." Chick-fil-A has also been recognized nationally for its children's meal by *Restaurant Hospitality* magazine.[43]

An example of this practice was Chick-fil-A's partnership with Big Idea Productions and Thomas Nelson Publishers to feature books with the popular Veggie Tales characters. What made this partnership unique was that the books offered by Chick-fil-A did not include any of the Bible stories or Christian messages for which Veggie Tales are known. Instead, the books used the popular Veggie Tale characters (Larry the cucumber and Bob the tomato) to teach secular subjects like opposites, the alphabet, counting, and colors. The only hint of a Christian message in the "prize" is a foreword in the book by the president of Big Idea Productions that affirms, "We believe that children are a gift from God and that helping them learn and grow is nothing less than a divine privilege." Chances are that a child would never read these words, but an introduction to Bob and Larry may later lead the child to request a book or video that has a more explicit Bible message. While not the same as handing out children's Bibles, it is an interesting way to promote a product with a mission compatible to Chick-fil-A's corporate identity. The company has also offered minibooks associated with Bill Bennet's *The Book of Virtues* (long before the revelation about Bennet's gambling habits), and overall its children's toys are more educational than entertaining.

Now in his eighties, S. Truett Cathy still works forty hours per week at Chick-fil-A and for its many philanthropies. His children have now assumed the senior management positions, and a new generation will soon be entirely entrusted with Chick-fil-A. Perhaps the greatest tribute to Cathy is his children's commitment to his own values and the mission of Chick-fil-A as a privately owned and certified company. In January 2000, his children presented to Cathy a document they described as a "covenant" with each other and with their parents as to the future of the company. Not only did they affirm their personal faith in Jesus Christ, but they also pledged themselves to continued support of the company's charitable efforts and also the business values of their father, including being closed on Sunday.[44]

ServiceMaster

The headquarters of The ServiceMaster Company is unique among large corporations in the United States because it includes an eleven-foot-high statue of Jesus washing the feet of a disciple.[45] As the corporate name indicates, the company is in the service business, but the name also communicates a dual message that the organization seeks to be the "master of service" and to provide "service to the Master."[46] Unlike Chick-fil-A, ServiceMaster is a publicly traded company with its stock available for purchase by individual and institutional investors. But despite its public status, the company has charted a distinctive course because it claims that its first objective is "to honor God in all we do."[47]

The company that would become ServiceMaster was founded in 1947 by Marion Wade.[48] Like Cathy's Chick-fil-A, the company's Christian identity reflected Wade's personal faith, but for Wade it was also the result of a profound personal crisis. Wade was injured when his chemicals exploded while mothproofing a closet. This prompted him to reconsider how his rug-cleaning business related to his faith, and he committed himself to a more seamless integration between the two after studying Joshua 24:15, "Now if you are willing to serve the Lord, choose this day whom you will serve."

I told the Lord I would turn everything over to Him. I said: "I don't expect any miracles. I don't intend to sit back and expect You to run everything, but I want You to tell me how to run things and send my way the men I will need to do the job. I realize that all I have to know is in the Bible and I will seek it, but I will need Your help to understand it. I choose to serve the Lord, but You will have to show me how."[49]

When a nun suggested an expansion of Wade's business into cleaning hospitals, a new opportunity resulted that became the major area of the company's earning growth.[50]

Today, ServiceMaster is a $3.5 billion company with a diverse set of business enterprises in the service industry. The company manufactures no products but instead provides services that homeowners and other businesses would prefer not to do themselves. Famous brand names and products in the ServiceMaster family include Terminex, TruGreen-Chemlawn, Merry Maids, Rescue Rooter (plumbing), and the ServiceMaster Clean brand of cleaning supplies for rugs, upholstery, and fire damage. The company serves over 10 million homes and has more than 5,400 franchisees who market the company's services as independent operators.

In further fulfillment of his prayer, the men who joined Marion Wade at ServiceMaster brought with them the same Christian commitments as did the founder. The three most prominent men in the company's success have also been graduates of Wheaton College, the evangelical flagship located only a few miles from ServiceMaster headquarters. To attract potential employees with the same faith and value system, Wade placed an advertisement in the Wheaton alumni magazine stating, "If you feel God is calling you in business, get in touch with Marion Wade," resulting in several new hires and long-term employees.[51] Wheaton graduates Kenneth Hansen and Kenneth Wessner were Wade's earliest partners and succeeded him when he died in 1973. Like Wade, Wessner has declared his own commitment to bringing together faith and work: "Our company recognizes God's sovereignty in all areas of our business. . . . Our objective is to apply consistently the principles, standards and values of the Bible in our business attitudes and actions."[52] But by far the most prolific spokesman for ServiceMaster and its faith-based orientation has been C. William Pollard. A former professor and administrator at Wheaton, Pollard joined the company in the 1970s and served as CEO from 1983 to 1993 and again from 1999 to 2001; he was chairman of the board from 1990 to 2002. During his corporate leadership and continuing today, Pollard has been an aggressive advocate for the ServiceMaster vision, and most of the writing and reflection on ServiceMaster's values has come from his hand. In 1996 Pollard published *The Soul of the Firm* to tell the "ServiceMaster story."

What ServiceMaster and Pollard recognize is that the heart of any service business is the employees who work for it. No product is produced
at ServiceMaster, so the employee and the product are indistinguishable.
When analyzing ServiceMaster, management guru Peter Drucker told the
board of directors that the real business of the company is "provid[ing]
dignity and profit through improved productivity."[53] Wessner said simply,
"We are in the business of training people."[54] This is a corporate purpose
and mission that transcended the distinction between employees cleaning carpets, killing bugs, fixing plumbing, or dusting houses. The emphasis
on dignity is one that Pollard relates directly to the corporate objective "to
honor God in all we do." Pollard asserts that ServiceMaster seeks to recognize the image of God in every employee, and this results in a recognition of the employee as an individual worthy of dignity and respect. In the
service business that is a hard thing to do, and many service providers at
the "front-lines" are used to being ignored or demeaned for pushing a mop
or providing necessary but low-level service work. Pollard argues that God
and business mix at ServiceMaster because people are what bring the two
together. It is also this same conviction that allows Pollard and Service-
Master to welcome those who may not believe in God or Christ because
of their respect for others' inalienable dignity. What Pollard rejects is that
corporations must be belief-free to be open and diverse; instead he asserts
that diversity of all sorts can be welcomed by a Christian value-center that
affirms all people.[55]

Pollard's vision of workplace spirituality is a full-scale rejection of the
Taylorism of the early twentieth century. He mocks Henry Ford's question, "Why is it that I always get a whole person, when what I really want
is a pair of hands?" arguing instead that companies always have the whole
person, and this is what gives a soul to a company.[56] The corporate objective that follows honoring God is "to help people develop." This means
more than development of skills for specific purposes. Pollard claims that
it goes so far as to include making employees "better people."[57] Through
this vision, the company has been successful in reducing the turnover of
employees well below the industry average; the company has fostering
self-esteem and a sense of personal responsibility even in the lowest level
employees.[58] The firm's focus on personal development gives it an almost
Aristotelian character as a place where virtues are fostered first and profits
are a secondary result or by-product.[59]

The image of Christ washing the disciples' feet symbolizes for Service-
Master the value of "servant leadership." As Pollard defines it, servant

leadership is a role model, a risk-taker, a promoter of others, an initiator, a giver, a listener, and someone who can be trusted. Regardless of official role, title, or salary, Pollard lifts up the example of Jesus, who demonstrated that true greatness is realized in service. As Pollard describes it,

> Servant leadership is part of our ethic, and it means that the leaders of our firm should never ask anyone to do anything they are unwilling to do themselves. The leader exists for the benefit of the firm, not the firm for the benefit of the leader.[60]

At ServiceMaster, this becomes a reality in regular "we serve" days in which managers and corporate office staff work with employees, providing direct service to customers. Pollard's own training when he joined the company included cleaning and mopping a hospital where ServiceMaster had a contract.[61] Although he makes no mention of it in his book, Pollard's notion of "servant leadership" is rooted in the vision of Robert Greenleaf and his landmark essay "The Servant as Leader." Greenleaf argued that the best leader is a servant first who seeks the growth of those served.[62] This is largely the vision that Pollard articulates as well, and it has special meaning in a company where service is the enterprise itself and not merely the means by which a product is manufactured or delivered. Having an attitude of service is critical for prospective employees at Service-Master, and community service and charity work have been important for applicants.[63]

Hobby Lobby

Those who live near a Hobby Lobby store may have seen one of the company's Christmas or Easter advertisements. Since 1997 the company has placed full-page ads offering a devotional message on these Christian holidays. Each ad reaches more than 35,000 readers, and an affiliated company has placed similar ads in *USA Today*. The 2002 Easter message was a black-and-white drawing of an empty tomb and a bright light. The caption read,

> You choose your beliefs, your neatly tied package of what can and cannot be. With these beliefs we weave the fabric of our religion. But what if God refuses to be defined by what we consider believable? What if truth is not something we create, but something we discover and embrace?

What if God is actively and aggressively looking for you? What if He really desires to spend eternity with you? What if he rose from the dead to prove it?

All of the messages include the Hobby Lobby name, a scripture passage printed in full, and the statement: "If you would like to know Jesus as Savior and Lord, call the Need Him Ministry at 1-888 NEED HIM (1-888-633-3446)."[64]

David Green, the founder of Hobby Lobby, is the son and sibling of ministers, and the only member of his family who is not a pastor.[65] Green, however, says that he was called to serve in a different way—through Hobby Lobby. "Hobby Lobby is basically a ministry. As owners we feel like we have the right and freedom to express our views and run the company with the biblical principles as best we can."[66]

Compared to both Chick-fil-A and ServiceMaster, Hobby Lobby is much more evangelistic and unabashed in its Christian identity. The newspaper ads, the company website, and charities that the company supports all embody Green's leadership and Christian faith.

Hobby Lobby is a major retail outlet for individuals interested in crafts and home decorations. The company began in 1972 and now has more than three hundred stores in twenty-eight states with sales exceeding $1 billion.[67] Competing against companies such as Michaels and Jo-Ann Stores, the company has succeeded in a highly competitive industry by using large stores and by creating a set of affiliated companies that supply 10 percent of the merchandise sold by Hobby Lobby. This vertical integration gives Hobby Lobby a leg up on its competitors, but it is still the number three company in revenues compared to its two major competitors.[68] Green also states that "our Christian convictions affect the kind of merchandise we carry and don't carry." No ash trays, shot glasses, or risqué greeting cards can be found on the shelves at their stores.[69]

Like ServiceMaster and Chick-fil-A, Green claims that the company's Christian identity greatly affects how employees are treated. "We have to be people-oriented, to be truly concerned about them, their family and their work hours." The company's statement of purpose echoes ServiceMaster's dedication to employee development. The company commits itself to "company policies that build character, strengthen individuals and nurture families."[70] Similar to the forms of workplace spirituality described in chapter 2, Hobby Lobby seeks to be holistic, but they find the source for their policies in distinctively Christian ideals. Hobby Lobby stores are also closed on Sunday, which the company regards as an employee benefit since it allows time with family. The company's Sunday policy has evolved over time. In 2000, only 70 percent of its stores were closed on Sunday, but by 2003, all were.[71]

The move toward a company-wide policy of Sunday closing raises interesting questions about how Christian companies define and live that identity. The first company purpose at Hobby Lobby is "Honoring the Lord in all we do by operating the company in a manner consistent with biblical principles."[72] S. Truett Cathy would also identify with this commitment, but he made a decision from the very beginning of his restaurant operation to close on Sunday. Green's move to closing on Sunday may indicate his developing understanding of what it means to be consistent with biblical principles, or more cynically, the company's growing financial success may have provided the opportunity to honor the Sabbath in this way.

Nine years after founding Hobby Lobby, David Green started an affiliated store for Christian books. Mardel Christian and Educational Supplies now has nineteen stores with an expected growth of three to five stores per year. Run by Mart Green, David Green's son, Mardel is even more explicit in its ministry objectives. The company's vision is "to see the products we sell and donate provide people with the hope of eternal life through Jesus Christ our Savior and Lord." The company also donates 10 percent of pre-tax profits to providing Bibles throughout the world, and it is a major supporter of Wycliffe Bible Translators.[73] Mardel provides the Green family with an entree into the enormous Christian book market (see chap. 4). It also is another business opportunity that allows the family to connect their Christian faith to economic life.

Marketing for Christian Businesses

The larger connection between Christianity, marketing, and evangelism is a complex one. Many churches are using traditional marketing techniques as a means of evangelism, and Willow Creek Church—the granddaddy of the megachurches—was founded based on a marketing survey. With respect to self-styled "Christian companies," the connections move in the opposite direction. Christian companies are marketing their products and services in ways that support both their evangelical mission and their business mission. They seek both to build up their business and to build up the Kingdom of God.

To understand this phenomenon, some historical and sociological context is helpful. As we read in chapter 1, the famed sociologist Max Weber explored the connection between Christian belief and business in *The Protestant Ethic and the Spirit of Capitalism*. Looking at the New England Puritans in particular, Weber argued that a distinctive theology of election compelled Puritans to work hard, live ascetically, and build capital in order to demonstrate their membership among the elect. Less well known, however, is a much smaller essay by Weber that makes the connection between Christianity and capitalism in a different way. Following a visit to the United States, Weber wrote about a diverse group of Christians in "The Protestant Sects and the Spirit of Capitalism." With its focus on conservative Methodists and especially Baptists at the beginning of the twentieth century, there are important parallels and insights into contemporary Christian businesses, their evangelical owners, and the marketing strategies they employ.

While in the United States, Weber visited many locales, and in "The Protestant Sects" he describes a visit to his Baptist relatives in the backcountry of North Carolina. He attended a worship service involving full immersion baptism, and Weber quizzed his relatives about the service. In particular, he was surprised that his relative knew in advance that a certain person would be baptized. When Weber questioned how this was known, the relative replied, "Because he wants to open a bank."[74]

It is the connection between membership in a Christian "sect" and its relationship to business ownership, as well as credit worthiness, that Weber considered in the essay. He argued that the rigorous standards for admission to a Christian "sect" included not only a doctrinal but also a moral examination of the candidate. As a result, "Admission to the congregation is recognized as an absolute guarantee of the moral qualities of the gentleman, especially those qualities required in business matters."[75] Although joining a Christian sect did not mean that the congregation would assume responsibility for the member's debts or contractual obligations, the rigorous admission requirements by a congregation were a signal to others in the community that a person could be trusted in the marketplace.

Weber's great insight from this experience was to offer a typological distinction between membership in a "church" versus a "sect." As Weber described it,

Affiliation with the church is, in principle, obligatory and hence proves nothing with regard to the member's qualities. A sect, however, is a voluntary association of only those who, according to principle, are religiously and morally qualified.[76]

In a church membership, Weber asserts, people are born into it because of their parents or region and practices like infant baptism; there is also little if any grounds for expulsion or discipline. In contrast, membership in a sect is personally chosen, and the sect imposes moral and doctrinal standards for access to membership and extensive procedures for disciplining members who vary from those standards in the attempt to guarantee that conversion is not simply a short-term event. For this reason, Weber concluded that membership in a sect was a sign to all who would do business with that person. As a seller, he will be honest and fair in all dealings. As a buyer, she will be worthy of credit and a prompt payer of debts. In small communities it was not necessary to advertise one's sect membership because it would be widely known anyway. If it was not known, an inquiry was relatively easy, and Weber notes how frequently Americans (as opposed to Europeans) inquired about religious membership and worship attendance.[77]

Weber argued that certain business practices, most notably fixed prices, were common to Christian sectarians. Today many of us bemoan the process of haggling when we buy a car, but negotiable prices were a common feature in most enterprises during the nineteenth and early twentieth centuries. The danger with this arrangement is that those with the least power and social status tend to pay higher prices, and there is also the possibility of gauging a customer if you know the degree of need the person has for the product you are selling. For sectarian adherents, fixed pricing was a requirement because it was impossible to ask two different prices for the same item and then claim to be fully honest in one's dealings. Methodists, Baptists, and Quakers all prohibited their members from haggling.[78] John Wanamaker, the famed Baptist merchant from Philadelphia, became well known for his use of fixed pricing, and he grew prosperous, in part, because of it. While Quakers, Methodists, and Baptists might not fit our definition of a sect today, for Weber they qualified because they were willing to make fixed pricing a standard for religious membership and grounds for congregational discipline.

Among American Lutherans a similar religious attitude led, in the early twentieth century, to the creation of mutual insurance companies that were distinctively Lutheran. Fearing that confessional Lutherans in the Midwest might join deistic and synergistic secret societies (Masons, Odd Fellows, and the like) for their inexpensive insurance and fraternal benefits, Lutherans established their own insurance enterprises. The two largest to emerge were Lutheran Brotherhood (historically Norwegian) and Aid Association for Lutherans (historically German). While a recent merger between the two created a company named Thrivent Financial for Lutherans, even today agents of the $58 billion company may sell insurance only to members of Lutheran congregations.[79] Lutherans certainly buy insurance from other sources, but Thrivent remains distinctive in both its clientele and by directing its philanthropy exclusively to Lutheran congregations and Lutheran institutions such as colleges, schools, and camps. In this way, the members of the denomination continue to care for their own through the organization. The founders of Lutheran Brotherhood even quoted from Galatians 6:2, "Bear ye one another's burdens, and so fulfill the law of Christ," as an argument for caring for one's denominational brethren and not abandoning them to seek support from heretical lodges.[80]

While Weber's distinction between church and sect may have made sense at the beginning of the twentieth century, today it would be difficult if not impossible for the average person in the marketplace to use the same criteria to identify people who are truly honest in business. Fewer religious groups have such exacting moral standards for membership, and denominational identity has also eroded, making denominational labels less appealing and reassuring (as indicated by the name "Thrivent," which has no immediate Lutheran connection). The sheer size and complexity of the U.S. economy offers another reason for difficulty. Christian businesses, however, are still seeking to distinguish themselves, but they are now openly advertising their theological convictions through organs like *The Shepherd's Guide*—a type of Christian yellow pages. Begun in 1980, *The Shepherd's Guide* is now published in more than 125 metropolitan areas in the United States and Canada.[81] Like any other yellow pages, the guides include advertising from many different types of businesses, including attorneys, physicians, car dealers, contractors, and mortgage companies. Also included is a complete list of churches in the area covered (including Roman Catholic), inspirational messages, quotes from the Bible, and the same steps for being saved found in a religious tract all interspersed with the ads.[82]

While it may be the largest of these Christian yellow pages, *The Shepherd's Guide* is not the only resource of this sort. Some are limited to certain regions, and others are only available online. What they share is some sort of religious and moral standard that all the advertisers must uphold. For *The Shepherd's Guide*, potential advertisers must affirm that:

> I have received Jesus Christ as my personal Savior, and my desire is to live for His Glory. I have been born again according to John 3:3 which states " . . . except a man be born again, he cannot see the Kingdom of God." I pledge to hold the highest Biblical code of ethics in my business transactions. It is my ambition to treat my clients with the utmost respect and integrity.

The *Christian Yellow Pages* (CYP) in the Dallas-Fort Worth area promotes its greater accountability:

> All of the businesses and professionals that are in the CYP directory have been pre-screened and pre-qualified. You will see the church where they attend as part of their listing and in some cases even the missionaries and ministries they support.[83]

By stating this information, the CYP provides a possible means to ascertain the seriousness of the person's religious and moral convictions as well as their orthodoxy from the consumer's perspective.

Advertising in more mainstream and "secular" sources can also include distinctive markers that indicate the identity of a Christian company. Using verses of scripture is one example, but the most common of these is the ancient Christian fish symbol.[84] With a history dating back to the second century, the fish has long been a marker of Christian identity. Its business advantage is its subtlety (compared to a cross), because it is likely only other Christians will recognize it as a Christian symbol. This highlights the difficulty of marketing to Christians since a desire to solicit business from other Christians is often coupled with a desire not to alienate customers who may not be Christian (or evangelical). David A. Lehrer, an attorney for the Anti-Defamation League of B'nai B'rith, has cautioned Christian business owners that "your intentions may be quite noble, but if you're wearing your religion on your sleeve, others will feel that they're not welcome." But this may be precisely the point for such businesses. The use of Christian symbols or even advertising in distinctively Christian outlets like *The Shepherd's Guide* is often described by business owners not as a crass marketing tool but as a statement of faith and method of evangelism.[85]

A Jewish Business Network

Evangelical Christians are not alone in the formation of economic subcultures, but other religious groups can be more hidden either because of the faith-based products they sell or the size and relative isolation of the religious community. In 2007 the *New York Times* reported on a variety of businesses in Israel that cater to the distinctive needs of ultra-Orthodox Jews. Perhaps the most interesting product described was the cell phone service that blocks sex-related numbers, provides a discount for calling other ultra-Orthodox numbers, and charges more than 2600 percent more if calls are made on the Sabbath.[86] In the United States too, it is not hard to imagine that religious minorities of all sorts could develop faith-based businesses to serve distinctive consumer needs. Kosher foods—and meat, especially—are another example within Judaism since they fulfill unique dietary needs. While those outside the Jewish tradition might also have an interest in kosher meat products as either healthy or exotic alternatives, the primary wholesale and retail market for kosher meat will be Jews, and ensuring that the products are prepared in accordance with Jewish laws will require Jewish workers or supervisors, creating opportunities for Jewish businesses up and down the supply chain.

Products that allow or support obedience to distinctive religious laws and customs are a natural place for faith-based businesses to develop among religious groups, but it is more interesting when religious identity provides a religious minority with a competitive advantage over the majority or other groups. As Weber described it, for evangelical Christians this advantage resulted from other evangelicals and the wider culture associating evangelicalism with honesty and hard work. For Jews, several scholars have noted that the wholesale diamond industry in New York City exhibits similar characteristics. The New York diamond district trade is more than 95 percent Jewish, as Jews have a centuries-old tradition of work in diamonds. Among the brokers and cutters, diamonds are frequently shared on consignment with only the most minimal paperwork—if any at all.[87] The process depends upon a system of trust, and the high levels of trust provide those in the diamond district with an advantage over potential competitors who would require complex security, insurance, and contracts to protect against fraud and theft.[88]

While the Jewish subculture itself offers a high degree of trust via the homogeneity of the business network, Judaism as a faith tradition also permeates the diamond business both within individual firms and in the trade network. Anthropologist Renee Rose Shield describes diamond broker offices with Jewish decorations, pictures from Israel and, for the Hasidim, pictures of important leaders.[89] But more important than individual offices is the Diamond Dealers Club (DDC) that operates as a combined brokerage, social club, and philanthropic organization.[90] Although a small percentage of its members are non-Jews, the ethos of the DDC is thoroughly Jewish with its own *Beit Midrash* for Torah and Talmud study, a business calendar that honors the Jewish Sabbath and all Jewish holidays, kosher food, and an atmosphere where Yiddish is the primary language.[91] Most importantly, the DDC offers its own system of contract enforcement, legally understood as mandatory arbitration, that in practice is most like a *Bit Den* or Jewish religious court. According to the ancient rabbis, turning to arbitration rather than legal measures was to be the preferred method for conflict resolution among Jews.[92] Because as a religious tradition Orthodox Judaism depends upon communal life and relationships, it is a religious impossibility to either leave the community or face its disapprobation, making arbitration a highly effective and nearly ironclad means to resolve disputes. When an Orthodox diamond cutter was asked why he did not steal the diamonds entrusted to him, he responded with all seriousness, "Where would I go?" He would not be able to return to his particular religious community, and no other community—religious or otherwise—would be acceptable.[93]

The economist Barak D. Richman, echoing Weber, argues that a competitive advantage can result when compliance with contracts is more than business and is itself a religious act. In addition to a personal desire to remain religiously obedient, for Orthodox Jews religious institutions provide a supplemental contract enforcement method. The enforcement is not punishment as much as a loss of honor in the community. Richman reports that one means of punishment is to deny the offender the blessing of reading the Torah during the Sabbath service; denying the sixth of the seven readings is especially significant because the sixth reading is the greatest honor due to its correspondence with the sixth day of Creation when God made humans.[94]

Because they operate on a wholesale level and because complete knowledge of the trust networks is limited to community insiders, Jewish diamond brokers and cutters would likely find little benefit in a Jewish equivalent to *The Shepherd's Guide* that markets their faith-based business to a wide audience (Jewish and otherwise). The competitive advantage to Jews in the New York diamond trade exists only at the brokerage and cutting levels. While a network for retail marketing can offer an advantage to many Christian businesses, an arbitration and contract enforcement system is what makes a network valuable to Jews working in diamonds. Neither type of network is better or worse, but the presence of different types and forms of faith-based business networks demonstrates that affinities between types of enterprises, levels within the supply chain, and particular religious beliefs will vary according to the religious and economic advantages the affinities are able to offer.

The Division over Christian Business Ethics

The hallmark of a self-styled Christian business is that its owners and operators see it as an enterprise with goals broader and higher than monetary gain. The Christian business is a ministry, serving customers, employees, and other stakeholders, but most importantly being faithful to Jesus Christ in a certain, evangelical way. Unlike the uniformity that may characterize Jewish ethics in the diamond trade, old divisions within Christianity reveal themselves in the way different Christian groups understand the character of Christian commerce. For some Christians, personal piety, fair dealing with employees, customers, and suppliers, and charity define the ethical obligations appropriate for a Christian business, but for other Christians a move beyond "personal ethics" and toward "social ethics" is necessary.

The roots of Christian social ethics stretch back more than a century to the emergence of "Christian sociology" as a distinct area of study and classification of theological literature. As the ethicist Max Stackhouse described it, "the newer social sciences provided the analysis of the empirical situation [and] a distinctive understanding of the teachings and principles of Jesus provided the normative orientation."[95] Theologians such as Walter Rauschenbusch and Washington Gladden specifically attacked the laissez-faire capitalism of the early twentieth century often associated with social Darwinism and the will of God in nature. They used tools like class analysis but also insisted that the teachings of Jesus transcended personal relationships and personal salvation to include the very structures of social and economic life. Rauschenbusch addressed this theme explicitly when he titled one of his books *Christianizing the Social Order* (1912) in which he specifically addressed the "unchristian" economic practices of capitalism.

By the 1910s there was open hostility between some evangelicals and proponents of what was being called "the Social Gospel." A key factor was the association of social Christianity with theological liberalism and modern biblical scholarship. Both were anathema to conservative Christians. While evangelicals saw social concern as a response to personal salvation, liberal theology and Social Gospel advocates appeared to the evangelicals to make social activism more important than individual repentance and receipt of God's grace.[96] Advocates of the Social Gospel, like Rauschenbusch, also began using early forms of social analysis as part of the Christian ethical task, but evangelicals failed to see the importance of this new science, for right Christian living.

A clear example of this conflict can be seen between Gladden, a leading advocate of the Social Gospel, and the revivalist Billy Sunday. In 1912 when Gladden was serving a Congregational church in Columbus, Ohio, a group of area ministers invited Billy Sunday to hold a revival there. Sunday had been leading revivals throughout the Midwest since 1896, but Columbus was his biggest city thus far. Gladden failed in his effort to keep Sunday out of Columbus and was rebuked by his fellow clergy when he published an article that was critical of him. By numbers alone, Sunday's visit was a huge success, and he used his time in Columbus to attack Gladden's social concern as "a lot of tommy rot."[97]

Ironically, during the nineteenth century, evangelicals (including pietist and holiness Christians) were leading advocates of social change in prisons, slavery, and urban poverty.[98] The historian George Marsden argues that during the later half of the century, evangelicals moved away from seeking political and social reforms even though they remained committed to personal charity. Marsden sees this "great reversal" as a "shift from a more Calvinist to a more pietistic view of politics."[99] No longer were evangelical Christians concerned about creating the biblical "city on a hill" of the Puritan vision. Writing in the *Journal of the Evangelical Theological Society*, Frank E. Gaebelein states that evangelicals have tended to hold the position that Christians should "just preach the gospel so that people are born again and then changed people will bring about the needed social change."[100] While Gaebelein finds this position problematic and even contrary to good evangelical theology, he readily admits that it is a widespread view that has led to a slow response by evangelicals on such important issues as the civil rights movement and poverty.

As an example of this divide in business practices, Chick-fil-A as a Christian company has largely ignored or at least been unaffected by the Christian and secular critics of the poultry industry. In the best-selling book *Fast Food Nation*, author Eric Schlosser described in detail many of the problems with poultry production and the meat processing industry in the United States. According to Schlosser, the poultry industry has been transformed by the widespread use of chicken in fast-food industries like Chick-fil-A. Large poultry processors exercise tremendous control over the production of poultry and have created a system of poultry production that closely resembles sharecropping in its manipulation of local farmers.[101] A variety of Christian voices have been heard recently speaking against the conduct of the poultry industry. The National Interfaith Committee for Worker Justice has inaugurated a "Poultry Justice Campaign" to advocate for the largely Latino immigrants who work in processing plants and who have been threatened or fired for complaining about unsafe working conditions.[102] In November 2000, the Roman Catholic bishops of the South issued a pastoral letter on the poultry industry that expressed concern about the plight of both poultry growers and the immigrant poultry processors. Drawing upon the tradition of Roman Catholic social teaching, including Pope Leo XIII's *The Condition of Labor* (*Rerum Novarum*), the bishops called for dialogue and justice on behalf of those adversely affected by the expanding poultry business.[103]

Because the worldview of evangelicalism does not emphasize moral responsibility beyond the personal, even in the midst of Christian criticism, the silence and inaction of Cathy and Chick-fil-A is easily explained. Cathy has stated explicitly that "there's no such thing as 'business ethics,' it's personal ethics."[104] For some Christians, however, demanding that a supplier treat employees fairly and with the utmost concern for safety would seem to exhibit the love of Jesus much more than a Bible verse on a purchase order. Using the same form of social ethics, Cathy might demonstrate Christian love in his business by setting rigorous policies for his suppliers, perhaps even requiring them to adhere to the same high standards that he demands in his restaurants; he might also concern himself with the waste generated by his stores, and he could guarantee that workers in all Chick-fil-A franchises have adequate health insurance. All of these might be worthy criticisms, but they depend upon a moral perspective that thinks these are important issues and sees them as the moral responsibility of businesses and their owners. For most of those in the Christian business model, the issues of social ethic are indeed "tommy rot," unimportant or inapplicable to their business practices.

The rise of the "Christian business" model can be interpreted then as a form of workplace spirituality and as an evangelical subculture in economics. Importantly, it is a subculture grounded in the personal rather than the social Christian ethical tradition and does not challenge the larger capitalistic system in which it functions. If anything, evangelicals and Christian business owners may be more enthusiastic about the free enterprise system than other economic actors. The historian Randall Balmer has compared the larger evangelical subculture to the utopian communities of the nineteenth century, but in economic terms it is hard to imagine either the capitalist evangelical or the socialist utopian recognizing the similarities.[105] Yet they may find agreement in the social organization of work, and in this way the Christian business model is also related to the New Age and corporate developments described in the previous chapter. With Christian businesses, the definition of spirituality is clearly more confessional, but they share with New Age enterprises a desire to create a holistic workplace that welcomes, honors, and even furthers faith. Similarities with the human relations movement in "regular" corporate America are present too, but the value of community and the value of individuals stems from the Christian understanding of *imago dei* (image of God) present in each employee as well as each customer and supplier. Evangelical theology takes this yet further by insisting that loving someone compels Christians to witness to them and seek their conversion and salvation in Jesus Christ. By owning and working in a Christian business, the opportunity for evangelism is much greater and more accepted than other enterprises would allow.

However, for the many Christians who work in publicly held companies or secular nonprofits and government, the Christian business model of workplace spirituality is not a viable model at all nor is the model of Jewish diamond brokers and cutters in New York. An employee at John Deere or Microsoft does not have the same opportunity to connect faith and work as a small business owner does. Some devout Christians might argue that Christians should work only in settings where it is possible to be a 100 percent Christian all of the time (and certainly this is the same argument made by some Orthodox Jews) since work in a secular setting could require a radical segmentation of the worker's life in which faith and work never connect. Yet Christian businesses and marketing strategies "for Christians by Christians," while supporting an evangelical subculture and the realization of "personal ethics," do little to engage the larger world of economic life. What is unknown about the further development of the faith-based business model is whether it will move beyond the personal to include social ethics in its theological and moral vision not unlike the engagement of the evangelical subculture in American politics. The related issue is whether the model can be replicated in extremely large enterprises with global reach. While politically evangelicals define social problems in their own way and with their own emphases, few if any observers would argue that they are still withdrawn from American politics and public affairs. We have yet to see the same level of economic power by the Christian business model, but perhaps it too will become a transforming influence on American life through business culture and economic practices.

4

Jesus as a Management Guru

With the striking title of *Jesus, CEO* (1995), Laurie Beth Jones concisely yoked religious and business symbolism in a way never done before. Over the next ten years Jones's book became a best seller, was translated into four languages, and sparked several sequels. It also marked the beginning of a new emphasis on Jesus as a teacher of business and management techniques. Prior to her career as a writer, Jones was the founder of advertising agencies in El Paso and San Diego. While she had dedicated her advertising agencies to God's glory, Jones increasingly wondered whether she was fulfilling that promise, and at the same time she longed to write a book—especially a book about Jesus. Working at a retreat center in the desert, Jones wrote *Jesus, CEO: Using Ancient Wisdom for Visionary Leadership*, making Jesus and herself into management gurus.[1]

In his life and ministry, Jones writes, Jesus demonstrated "the strength of self-mastery, the strength of action, and the strength of relationships." While many leaders may have one or two of these characteristics, Jones's assertion is that few have them all like Jesus.[2] Even more, Jones is convinced that these strengths are techniques that "can be applied to any business, service, or endeavor that depends on more than one person to accomplish a goal, and can be implemented by anyone who dares," and through short, two- to four-page chapters, Jones explains how.[3] Although the format varies, chapters usually begin by explaining how Jesus exemplified a certain trait (such as delegating authority), followed by an example from Jones's personal life, perhaps a contemporary story or a reference to another biblical figure such as David, Elijah, or Esther, and finally a few sentences of advice about how to implement the technique of Jesus into the reader's own life and work.

In one typical chapter, Jones begins with the title "He had a plan." After a quick quote from a friend, Jones describes how Jesus was a leader with a plan:

He gave clear instructions to his staff members regarding how they could attain their desired results. He also had received a plan that he was working on implementing. He spoke often about how something was either part of or not part of the plan. He did not claim to know all the details, but he certainly saw the big picture and acted on a day-to-day basis according to his inner convictions.[4]

In a similar way, Jones describes in another chapter how Jesus "guarded his energy," protecting against "energy leaks" that can distract and drain the "tremendous amount of energy" required by leaders.[5] Jones ascribes to Jesus certain characteristics of good management and demonstrates how he exemplified good management in ways that can be adopted by anyone. Even more, they can be learned without direct engagement with the scriptures since Jones provides the valuable service of separating the wheat from the chaff for the needs of successful business leaders.

Jones's particular success may be due to her ability to combine biblical proof-texts, generic God-talk, and easy-to-swallow management advice. The book uses a distinctive vocabulary, repeatedly referring to Jesus's disciples as his "staff members." She refers to Jesus, God, and a Higher Power; the latter two are clearly synonymous for her, but it is not clear if her Jesus is divine. Perhaps most striking is Jones's claim that she realized many years before writing the book "that Jesus had many feminine values in management," which place greater value on personal relationships.[6] Jones also notes that her use of scripture in the book often relies on her own paraphrases of English translations.[7] In *Jesus, CEO* she casually tells stories about female pastors that she has known, and she, at times, even mentions evolution without any apparent recognition that such a sentence may be controversial to some evangelical readers. Clearly, it would be hard to label Jones with fundamentalist stereotypes. Yet she is faithful in her repeated turn to scripture, regardless of how elementary her application may be, making 136 direct references to verses in addition to other references focused on biblical figures.

Jones has replicated this format in four other popular books. *Jesus in Blue Jeans* (1997) departed from the focus on business and leadership to offer "a practical guide to everyday spirituality," with chapters formed around the themes of poise, passion, power, and perspective. In *Jesus, Inc.* (2001), which was later issued in paperback as *Jesus, Entrepreneur*, Jones describes the traits that made Jesus the greatest "spiritreneur," which she defines as those who "fully integrate their soul in a workplace enterprise."[8] *Teach Your Team to Fish* (2002) follows the *Jesus, CEO* formula to offer the techniques of Jesus for working in groups, and her most recent volume, *Jesus, Life Coach* (2004), offers Jesus as a coach for personal and career success.

"Jesus Books" and the Religious Marketplace

While the popularity of *Jesus, CEO* and its sequels is interesting in itself, it also exemplifies a "do-it-yourself" approach to workplace spirituality, which is growing in popularity and most often found in local bookstores. While the idea of a calling has remained prominent in Christian theology, in practice, however, Christians in the United States report a growing gap between faith and work. More specifically, they report that churches and clergy fail to nurture and support a vibrant connection between spirituality and work. One survey of five hundred business leaders indicated that if faced with "a serious business decision," 82 percent would speak with a colleague, 74 percent would pray, 65 percent would speak with a spouse, and 60 percent would meditate alone. Only 33 percent would speak to a spiritual or religious leader.[9] A decade ago, the sociologist Robert Wuthnow found similar results from a large quantitative and qualitative study of faith and economic life. Wuthnow's research into middle-class American Christians is striking because it revealed not only the irrelevance of active church membership in economic life but also the sense that churches did not have anything to say about business matters. For example, Wuthnow reported that church members and nonchurch members were equally likely (43–44 percent) to deal with job stress by shopping.[10] Wuthnow argued that many in the middle class were in a spiritual dilemma. They turned to the church to help with their workplace problems and stress, but the churches were not "making much difference in middle-class lives." A key problem, said Wuthnow, was that "middle-class churches are built on the premise that their members have enormous quantities of unfilled time," a premise that seemed to be increasingly doubtful.[11]

There is often a sense by pastors that their church members do not want them to "meddle" in personal issues like work and finances, but the true issue may be mutually perceived incompetence. Churches and clergy have focused almost exclusively on the family and family metaphors that create a disconnection with work as a sphere of life and faith.[12] A study by Laura Nash and Scotty McLennan titled *Church on Sunday, Work on Monday* also revealed that most clergy view work in a capitalist system as morally suspect, and seminarians in the same study reported that the best way for clergy to make a link between work and faith is to "change the way businesspeople think."[13] Among clergy there is little if any interest in being a resource for everyday life in the workplace with its frequent moral ambiguities, and that likely renders them irrelevant to the workplace faithful.

If Christians are unable to make a connection between faith and work in their churches, they frequently are able to find what they want at a Christian bookstore. In some of these larger venues, there are even business and money-management sections with a whole variety of titles. Bill Anderson, president of the Christian Booksellers Association (CBA) puts it this way: "We're a nation of people who believe in God, but we are biblically illiterate. What the Christian bookstore does is supplement what people should be getting from the pulpit and Sunday-school classes."[14] In economic terms, Christian bookstores provide the supply to an unmet demand.

In 2001 Christian books and other Christian resources were an industry worth more than $4 billion.[15] Even in the 1980s, the Gallup Organization predicted that through 2010 religion and spirituality books would see the largest sales increase of any category.[16] Many Christian books are now mainstream; titles are carried at more traditional bookstores and Wal-Mart. In fact, *Newsweek* reported in January 2005 that mainstream retailers have increased their sales of "Christian products" by $100 million, forcing some Christian bookstores out of business because they are unable to compete against the discount and big-box stores.[17] Outside of Christianity, Phyllis Tickle has remarked on the remarkable growth of New Age books and publishing, noting that their success led them to form a trade organization—New Alternatives for Publishing, Retailing and Advertising (NAPRA)—with its own trade journal.[18]

If, as sociologist Wade Clark Roof has argued, America is a "spiritual marketplace," then the main entrance may be the bookstore. Bringing together unlikely comrades in search of spiritual guidance and enlightenment,

> bookstores function as the virtual synagogues of spiritual instruction. These stores have large sections labeled Bible, Christianity, and Judaica . . . [and] alongside them now are even larger sections devoted to

books on Eastern religions, New Age religion, and self-help philosophies (often extending over into either the management or leadership sections). These section headings overlap considerably.[19]

Mass media and corporate power have brought together evangelical Christians and New Age devotees in a way no ecumenical dialogue or council could have imagined. Not only do diverse spiritual adherents wander the same aisles, but we also see the eclecticism in the books themselves. *Jesus, CEO* and its heirs are successful because many of them are able to appeal to self-identified Christians who seek to follow the path of their Lord Jesus Christ and to New Age adherents who seek guidance from the Jesus who is a great teacher of wisdom. Roof contends that despite their significant differences, evangelical Christians and New Age purveyors of spirituality "frame questions and answers in ways that are often quite consistent." The common denominator of the spiritual marketplace is the spiritual consumer, for whom personal choice and privatized faith are axiomatic.[20]

The idea that "the customer is always right" makes sense with hamburgers or cars, but it is challenging when applied to faith, religion, and spirituality. Yet the idea of consumer sovereignty in spirituality is simply the next step after affirming the primacy of the individual in one's own spiritual life. Privatization easily leads to commodification.[21] Individuals can and must "cobble together a religious world" from the great diversity of sources they find available.[22] And what is or is not available as a spiritual resource is largely determined by what is commercially viable as opposed to what religious traditions and religious leaders offer.[23] The explosion of books on religion and spirituality is thus one manifestation of a rapidly expanding spiritual marketplace. Christians or any other spiritual seekers who have an unmet desire to connect their faith and work may indeed be able to find helpful books to bridge this gap.

To meet the diversity of demand, the number of published spiritual and religious books is enormous, but the variety of best-selling books is quite narrow. According to Tickle, religion editor for *Publishers Weekly* (the publishing industry's trade journal), there are really only four types of religion best sellers. The first, those that focus on angels and other paranormal phenomenon, and the second, religious fiction like the Left Behind series, are important but not of primary concern here. The other two categories, ancient wisdom and self-help books, have far more bearing on books like *Jesus, CEO*.[24] Self-help books are easy to understand, and

Tickle rightly connects them to the self-help movement, which includes books for and about Alcoholics Anonymous groups and other twelve-step programs. These books are meant to be personally useful in improving life.[25] "Ancient wisdom" books serve a similar purpose by retrieving some kernel of knowledge that was "lost" to previous generations or by offering a new insight that makes a historical event or figure somehow more accessible. Wisdom that may have been "time-bound" can then be "timeless."[26]

Books that connect work, business, and faith easily blend both ancient wisdom and self-help, especially if self-help is expanded beyond the therapeutic to embrace success and advice literature. The subject headings given by the Library of Congress are illustrative. We now have books under subject headings such as Management—Religious Aspects, Business—Religious Aspects, Jesus Christ—Leadership, and Executive Ability—Biblical Teaching. Jones's *Jesus, CEO* includes three subject headings: "1. Success, 2. Success in business, [and] 3. Jesus Christ—Leadership," and it appears that *Jesus, CEO* was the first use by the Library of Congress of the heading "Jesus Christ—Leadership." The Library of Congress seems reluctant to do what Christian book publishers have done already—that is, link Jesus directly to business or management. There currently are no subclassifications under "Jesus" that make a tie to business or management, but the connection to leadership ranks Jesus alongside winning coaches, successful CEOs, and heroic political and military figures.

The stream of books in these categories is never-ending. Jesus may be the most popular biblical figure in the titles, but the business wisdom of the House of David along with other biblical patriarchs has also been explored. A short sample of titles includes:

The 25 Most Common Problems in Business and How Jesus Solved Them (1996)
The Leadership Wisdom of Jesus (1998)
Leadership Lessons of Jesus (1997)
More Leadership Lessons of Jesus (1998)
The Management Methods of Jesus (1996)
Moses on Management (1999)
The Wisdom of Solomon at Work (2001)
What Queen Esther Knew: Business Strategies from a Biblical Sage (2003)

While all of the books are in some way distinctive, they have a common pattern that is not unlike the format of the books by Laurie Beth Jones. All attempt to glean nuggets of wisdom from the teaching and example of Jesus or other biblical figures and then make connections to modern economic life and workplace issues. What varies most dramatically is their direct engagement with the Bible and specific biblical texts. Charles Manz's *The Leadership Wisdom of Jesus* is full of scripture verses followed by more detailed discussions of management theory and practice. In *The 25 Most Common Problems in Business*, author Jim Zabloski paraphrases scripture and moves quickly from Jesus to business practices, devoting most of his attention to practical tips and examples that have only a loose connection to Jesus. *The Leadership Genius of Jesus* by William Beausay II strays even farther from direct biblical references, beginning with an issue or personal story followed by a version of "Jesus was like that" or "Jesus did that." Since he seldom quotes scripture and uses few biblical citations, Beausay takes some liberties in how Jesus is constructed. In contrast, in *The Leadership Lessons of Jesus* and *More Leadership Lessons* of Jesus by Bob Briner and Ray Pritchard, the authors walk through the Gospel of Mark (chapters 1–6 in the first book and 7–10 in the second), gleaning from it what people can learn from Jesus's actions, and as a result, these books have a more devotional tone.

The "Jesus in business" movement is not limited to books alone. Laurie Beth Jones has moved from being an author to corporate trainer and consultant. Her website, www.jesusceo.com, describes the full range of services she offers that build on her insights into the relationship of Jesus to the workplace. Jones's books after *Jesus, CEO* highlight many of her encounters as a consultant. The "Lead Like Jesus" celebration, which premiered through a national video conference in November 2003, is a similar phenomenon. Led by Ken Blanchard, co-author of *The One-Minute Manager*, and Rick Warren, author of *The Purpose Driven Life*, "Lead Like Jesus" is a multimedia effort, combining books, videos, study guides, and local "Leadership Encounters" with an organizational base in Blanchard's Center for Faithwalk Leadership.[27]

Analyzing the quality of biblical interpretation in these works is problematic because it reveals the wide divide between Christian theologians and businesspeople. From a theological perspective, the books might be judged universally deficient because they pick and choose texts with no clear rationale, use texts out of context, and use texts simply as vehicles to communicate the business ideas of the author. Christians interested in a "social ethic" like that described in chapter 3 might also find fault with the books for avoiding texts such as the story of the rich young ruler, Jesus's statement about serving God and mammon, or the parable of the rich fool. But if Anderson is right and Christian books like these teach a biblically illiterate church, then their education will introduce them to a Jesus who leads in very similar ways to the management theories of our time (teams, "walking around," etc.). Jesus, in these books, is not so much the Son of God or even a charismatic religious leader as a skilled business practitioner.

From their research, Nash and McLennan argue that the differing worldviews of theological leaders and businesspeople inevitably lead to different understandings of Jesus plus different readings of scripture as a whole. Businesspeople often see God at work in the marketplace while clergy and theologians are frequently suspicious about this idea. For businesspeople, Jesus may be a workplace role model who is "supportive but decisive." For clergy, Jesus exemplifies values of humility, self-sacrifice, and disinterest in material reward—traits that are sometimes the opposite of those needed for workplace success.[28] In interviews conducted by Nash and McLennan, "One banker noted that the God of the Old Testament, who ordered society and provided sustenance, shelter, and justice, was really 'a banker.'"[29] Likewise, a similar reading can be made of Esther, Joseph, David, or Solomon. The Bible and its characters become mirrors in which one's values and the best attributes of one's profession may be magnified. To be fair, clergy and theologians are not necessarily exempt from this charge when they see in Jesus traits such as humility and self-sacrifice, traits that they themselves think they exemplify.[30] Nash and McLennan also contend that businesspeople are naturally attracted to wisdom traditions that allow for application in daily life.[31] Wisdom literature and other biblical stories can also be expansively interpreted, thus allowing people in the workplace to find a personal link with God and Jesus.[32]

The Man Nobody Knows

The current interest in Jesus as a source of business guidance is not without historical precedence. Both fiction and nonfiction works manifested this same goal during a flurry of media activity between 1890 and 1930. Like *Jesus, CEO,* Bruce Barton's *The Man Nobody Knows: A Discovery of the Real Jesus* became a runaway best seller with more than 250,000 copies sold in 1925 and 1926 alone, translations into several languages, and even a silent movie of the same title.[33] Barton's Jesus was a business leader who "built the greatest organization of all," demonstrating success as a salesman, a supervisor, and master of his own destiny.[34] Like Jones, Barton was also able to capitalize on the success of *The Man Nobody Knows* with several sequels, including *The Book Nobody Knows* (about the Bible), *The Man from Galilee* (which offered more pictures than text), *What Can a Man Believe?* (which argued that Protestantism was too focused on creedal distinctions), and *He Upset the World* (about the book of Acts and especially St. Paul).[35] Barton's corpus, combined with other nonfiction works like *The Businessman of Syria* (1923) and the fictional *In His Steps* (1897) established a pattern for business books even though they frequently offered remarkably divergent descriptions of Jesus.

Barton, the son of a Congregational minister, worked regularly as a journalist and a writer in his early career. Like Laurie Beth Jones, Barton was also in the advertising business. In 1919 he and several partners founded the Batten, Barton, Durstine, and Osborn firm, which nine short years later became one of the largest and most influential advertising firms in the United States.[36] Like his father, Barton embraced liberal Christianity, but he saw religion and Jesus especially as a source of personal inspiration rather than a basis for social reform.[37] In that sense, like *Jesus, CEO*, Barton's *The Man Nobody Knows* was clearly a "success manual" rather than a religious or devotional book.[38] The result was that the book fell prey to a two-pronged attack by critics and reviewers. Religious conservatives, faulted the book for its failure to affirm Christ's divinity and basic tenets of Christian theology. From more liberal Christians came criticism for using Jesus to bless capitalism and the business practices of the day.[39] *Christian Century* attacked the book for making Jesus into a mere "efficiency expert" (a new Taylor?), falling prey to the sin of every biographer of Jesus in making him into a reflection of the current age. The *Century* even longed for the robber barons, stating,

The frank scorn of the nineteenth-century business man for religious principles and Christian ethics is preferable to the unconscious insincerity—for it is only rarely conscious—of the modern captain of industry who veils the most predatory practices of industrial and commercial life with phrases of moral idealism.[40]

Unfortunately, the current editors of the *Century* have printed only a brief announcement of *Jesus, CEO* in the "No Comment" section, offering little serious engagement or critique of the work.[41]

Yet a reading of Barton's *The Man Nobody Knows* reveals a depth unknown by Jones's *Jesus, CEO* and its sequels. Although they certainly follow a similar design, Barton explored Jesus in more depth and with fewer outside examples. He was also willing, at least at times, to consider some of the more critical passages related to wealth and success (toward the end of the book, Barton even retells the story from Luke 12 of the rich fool). Defining success in business as much more than the accumulation of wealth, Barton faulted the rich fool for using his "business as nothing but a means of escape from business." The "true" business of life as well as success necessarily includes generosity and self-sacrifice, and for that reason the subject of the parable rightly suffered.[42] At the same time, Barton drops names and examples of the major industrialists and financiers of the day, such as Henry Ford and George Perkins of the New York Life Insurance Company, but his book avoids Jones's personal anecdotes. Barton also uses quick summaries of Jesus's attributes and actions that can be readily imitated, and the God he describes is "a happy God, wanting His sons and daughters to be happy."[43] Barton asserts, for example, that Jesus exemplified three main attributes that lead to success: "blazing conviction"; seeing the best traits in others; and "unending patience." These sound remarkably like the three traits of Jesus that Jones names in *Jesus, CEO*. [44]

A contemporary critic of Barton, James Rorty, also found fault in Barton's union of business and faith, but Rorty offered a more psychological explanation of the work. He argued that Barton was "selling" the profession of advertising to the nation, to himself, and perhaps to his clergyman father as advertising was previously associated with the snakey salesmen of patent medicines and the promotions of P. T. Barnum. By linking Jesus and capitalism, Rorty concluded that "in *The Man Nobody Knows* [Barton] accomplished the *reductio ad absurdum* of the 'Protestant ethic.'"[45]

Other critics of Barton (and those like him) were more crafty, pulling out the biblical support for his claims from under him. Not surprising given its almost universal use at the time, Barton repeatedly quoted from the King James Version (KJV) throughout his book, and it provided Barton with an important turn of phrase since he frequently points to Jesus's statement in Luke 2:49, "Wist [know] ye not that I must be about my Father's business?" In the 1950s, the Revised Standard Version (RSV) phrased it as "I must be in my Father's house." Both the New International Version (NIV) and New Revised Standard Version (NRSV) maintain the same translation as the RSV, but the NRSV adds a footnote indicating that the verse could be translated as "be about my Father's interests." While the Greek text does not clearly use a word for "business," the connection to "house" is nowhere in the verse and must be understood as a translator's interpretation based on earlier verses that describe Jesus in the Temple. In fact, "business" was not a bad English translation. When a revised edition of *The Man Nobody Knows* was issued in the 1950s, Barton made several alterations, including acknowledgment of the alternative translation for the earlier KJV's Luke 2:49. However, he added that the "'essential remains the same': Jesus 'offered his life to men.'"[46] Nonetheless, the punch is lost in the new translation, requiring Barton to make the direct connection himself. What seems more intriguing is the possibility that a negative reaction to Barton's use of "business" precipitated the use of alternative translations that could not be so easily appropriated for the endorsement of commerce.

Given his context and background, Barton was clearly influenced by the Social Gospel tradition and its interest in the teachings of Jesus. The late nineteenth and early twentieth centuries had witnessed great economic and social change through industrialization and urbanization, and as ethicist Max Stackhouse describes it, "the primary moral response to these developments . . . [was] to apply the teachings of Jesus to economic structures."[47] The focus on the "historical Jesus" by biblical scholars at the time made this a logical development. Thus, higher biblical criticism (as compared to lower criticism, which deals with recovery of original texts) directed attention to the message of Jesus as a prophet and sage while liberal theologians of the period became interested in the Kingdom of God as a theological vision and as the central theme in Jesus's teachings. Social Gospel advocates like Washington Gladden and Walter Rauschenbusch turned to these themes repeatedly. Using a devotional study form, Rauschenbusch himself explained the relationship of Jesus to practical issues like leadership and business in *The Social Principles of Jesus*, published in 1920. What divided liberal Protestants was not the centrality of Jesus and his teaching for economic problem-solving but whether Jesus was an ally of the poor and working class or a businessman.[48] For Rauschenbusch it was clearly the former, but Barton went the other way. Still others, such as the University of Chicago's Shailer Matthews, argued that Jesus was neither capitalist nor socialist.[49] What these commentators held in common, however, was the belief that the life and teachings of Jesus were decisive in guiding Christians in economic life.

The significance of Jesus and his teachings were seen not only in theology but also in fiction. After the Civil War, a whole category of literature emerged (perhaps modeled after Harriet Beecher Stowe's *Uncle Tom's Cabin*), which focused on social reform. The Social Gospel novel sought both to entertain and prompt social action by introducing characters whose worldviews were shattered by exposure to poverty and other social ills. The actions of the novels' characters in seeking change then provide the moral example for readers to follow.[50] According to William C. Graham, these novels "did not simply promulgate the movement, but helped to form it." Graham places the approximately one hundred authors of Social Gospel novels alongside theologians in the development of Christian social ethics.[51] Of course, as with the theological writings, the novels also focused on the life and teachings of Jesus, and they must be viewed as influences on Barton. The most famous of these with a focus on commerce was Charles M. Sheldon's 1897 *In His Steps,* a runaway best seller of the time with a reported 30 million copies sold worldwide.[52]

First given as speeches at Sheldon's church, then serialized, and finally published as a book, the novel tells the story of a middle-class pastor, Henry Maxwell, who challenges himself and his congregation to ask "what would Jesus do" in all aspects of life. The novel then follows Pastor Maxwell and several of his congregants as they seek to follow this model. Many of the examples are related to business and wealth, including the practices of a newspaper publisher, a small shopkeeper, and a brother and sister with inherited wealth. The novel moves from its small-city origins to the metropolis of Chicago where Maxwell partners with a former bishop and others to start something best described as a settlement house in the slums. Although critical of many economic and social practices of the day, Sheldon still focused on individual reform and change in order to bring social reform.[53] Temperance is a repeated theme, including the individual citizen's need to support prohibition but also the need of the individual who drinks to refrain from liquor and the property owner to refuse rental to a saloon. Sheldon was bold in his calls for leaders in business to pay better wages and show concern for the poor.

Nonetheless, a writer such as Barton could easily read *In His Steps* and later write a book like *The Man Nobody Knows* because individual reform and a focus on success remained consistent. The fictional Pastor Maxwell was a hero to be admired, not unlike the characters in a Horatio Alger rags-to-riches story or the industrial icons of the period, such as Andrew Carnegie, Harvey Firestone, Thomas Edison, and Henry Ford. Although not without sacrifice and hardship, the main characters of Sheldon's novel become successful following "in His steps."[54] This is precisely the outcome Barton desired for the readers of *The Man Nobody Knows*. Oddly, nothing like a Social Gospel novel has reappeared in current Christian fiction (although recently there was renewed interest in the "what would Jesus do" phraseology, including bumper stickers and rearview mirror danglers), and thus there is no fictional parallel to *Jesus, CEO*.

Management Gurus

A connection that does exist, however, is between Jesus and the multitude of business experts who function as "management gurus." While the term "guru" has roots in India with respect to spiritual wisdom and guidance, today we use the term loosely to describe almost anyone with expertise, but use of the term still conveys "a mystical dimension which implies that the expertise has been gained by other than conventional means."[55] Management gurus serve a similar role. They offer expertise but, more importantly, unique wisdom and guidance. They see the world, the marketplace, and institutions in a different way than does conventional wisdom. Several sources name Frederick W. Taylor as the first business guru since his development of scientific management was a radical new way of thinking about management and was widely popular at the beginning of the twentieth century, leading to expansive sales of his books and his employment as the first high-priced, celebrity consultant. In 2003 Thomas Davenport and Laurence Prusak developed criteria to rank the top ten business gurus of our time, using Google hits, citations in the Social Science Index, and mention of the names in business and popular media. The list included Tom Peters (co-author of *In Search of Excellence*), Peter Drucker (the guru of business gurus), Dan Goleman (author of *Emotional Intelligence*), and Michael Porter (professor at Harvard Business School and author of *Competitive Advantage*).[56] But it is important to note that there really are no objective criteria for business guruhood other than popularity, and their popularity does not tell us anything much about the quality of their work.

Rather than trying to understand the basis of guruhood, another means to grasp the phenomenon is to classify those who are recognized as gurus. Using this approach, Andrzej Huczynski argues that there are three "schools" of gurus: academics, consultants, and hero-managers. Academic gurus are those such as Michael Porter, with formal ties to academic institutions, while consultant gurus like Tom Peters have neither corporate nor academic ties.[57] It is the hero guru, however, who deserves the closest attention with respect to the Jesus books. According to Huczynski,

> The hero-manager's approach is not based on research, study or consultancy experience. It is developed from learning-from-experience. Its authority comes directly from success. By distilling the essence of what successful managers do (irrespective of context) it is believed that the secrets of success can be revealed.[58]

The main vehicle for the hero-manager is the business biography or autobiography, a genre of English literature that stretches back to the nineteenth century. In the early twentieth century, this genre took on a new meaning with the great industrialists like Henry Ford, Andrew Carnegie, and Alfred Sloan all writing autobiographies. Today and in the recent past we might point to books by and about Bill Gates of Microsoft, Lee Iacocca of Ford and Chrysler, and Jack Welch of General Electric.[59]

Jesus books on leadership and business (along with other biblical figures) largely follow this hero-manager model, but they are even more closely aligned with other hero-managers drawn from history—Machiavelli, Sun-Tzu, Attila the Hun, and General George Patton have all recently been made into leadership and management experts. Among religious figures outside the biblical traditions, the most popular hero-manager has been Siddhartha Gautama, usually known simply as the Buddha. Demonstrating the ecumenical reach of a good, spiritually connected hero-manager, Ken Blanchard, the founder of Lead Like Jesus, wrote the introduction to *What Would Buddha Do at Work? 101 Answers to Workplace Dilemmas*, praising it as a work "rich with words of wisdom for people in organizations both large and small."[60] *What Would Buddha Do at Work?* follows a similar format to other books of hero-inspired management wisdom, asking how the Buddha would answer common business problems, offering a short quotation from such Buddhist literature as the Dhammapada, and providing a short two- to four-paragraph response. *Enlightened Management: Bringing Buddhist Principles to Work* focuses less on the wisdom of the Buddha and more on the positive effects of Buddhist-inspired meditation techniques—no doubt a form of wisdom in and of themselves. Perhaps one of the most ambitious books of the genre is *Business and The Buddha*, written by Lloyd Field with a forward by the Dalai Lama. Field's work engages the Buddha's wisdom at both the micro- and macro-levels of business life, considering potential Buddhist correctives to the capitalist economic system and the ideas of Adam Smith as well as concrete business decisions that can be guided and improved by the Buddha's teachings.[61]

Even fictional characters have received the honor of being hero-managers, with two new books extolling the leadership philosophy of Tony Soprano. As Hucznski notes, the key to being a hero-manager guru—whether historical, contemporary, or fictional—is SUCCESS. However, the guidance of any hero-manager will need to transcend the particularities of specific products and corporations. If GE's Jack Welch can provide good guidance for a small deli owner, then it is not too much of a stretch to imagine that Attila the Hun may be a worthy guru for a manager in a highly competitive industry. Jesus fits this criterion and so does the Buddha, but the success of religious figures usually needs to be defined differently, and this is precisely what Laurie Beth Jones does in *Jesus, Entrepreneur*. According to Jones,

> Jesus wanted more than anything to be successful. He said it was what drove him, what haunted him. He had such a yearning for it that he was willing to give up everything to get it. Jesus' definition of success was "to do the will of God."[62]

Broadly speaking, all followers of Jesus might claim this standard of success, but it is also difficult to understand how this can be an analogy for the market leadership of one's product or substantially increasing shareholder value.

Success Literature and the Gospel of Wealth

Unlike academic and consultant gurus who offer techniques to their readers, audiences, and clients, hero-managers are more focused on character and personality traits. Jack Welch may offer techniques, but successful management strategies in one industry may not always be successful in another. Character traits are more easily transferable, and attention to personality and character are more important in business than ever. Undoubtedly, this idea is related to Stephen Covey's *The 7 Habits of Highly Effective People*. Published in 1989, it has consistently ranked on the business best seller list, and Covey himself has become a management guru (of the consultant variety). The thesis of Covey's book is that management books for most of the twentieth century were focused on techniques for business success such as Total Quality Management (TQM) and corporate re-engineering. The problem, says Covey, is that true success is not gained by structures and techniques but through integration of principles and habits into a person's "basic character."[63] Covey contends that the barriers to success are not "out there" but internal to the personality and character of the individual.

In *The 7 Habits* and in several follow-up books, Covey explains how certain, universal "principles" guide happiness and success in work, family, and life in general. Although he does not use the term directly, Covey's reference is to "natural law" as well as to a related wisdom tradition that transcends time and culture. The clearly spiritual bent of Covey's work is frequently noted as well as its connection to self-help programs and literature.[64] Critics contend that Covey's focus on individual transformation ignores social and structural realities, but for an employee following Covey's model, the only workplace problems that merit concern are individual ones. "Within Covey's framework, the individual employee is urged to deflect the blame for things that are happening . . . away from senior executives onto him- or herself." The individualistic tone of his program taps into the American fascination over self-help programs while at the same time advancing business interests by putting exclusive focus on the individual employee.[65]

One of the best-known of Covey's recommendations is the development of a personal mission statement that reflects an individual's values, hopes, and dreams. Covey likens it to a personal "constitution," which, like the U.S. Constitution, will guide an individual and represent to others what those values are.[66] Laurie Beth Jones has taken this idea of a personal mission statement and developed it into an entire book of her own. In *The Path: Creating Your Mission Statement for Work and for Life* (1996), she provides guidance and a workbook for writing a personal mission statement that is more explicitly religious than Covey's, invoking Christian language and prayers at several points in the guided process. The contemporary boom in Jesus books closely followed Covey's publication of *The 7 Habits* in 1989, and, like Covey, these books are also focused on individual transformation and neglect structural or social concerns that may be barriers to happiness and success. They differ in tone only because Covey is less explicitly spiritual.

Whether or not Covey's "seven habits" are the best character traits to emulate may be debatable, but his concerns over the success literature of the last century are entirely sound. He refers to them as "superficial."[67] But in fact they represent a long tradition among success writers, a tradition that stretches back well into the nineteenth century. Richard M. Huber argued in *The American Idea of Success* (1971), that there are three main traditions of success writing: the character ethic, the personality ethic, and mind power. Covey conflates the first two, which according to Huber are related yet distinct, but it is the focus on "mind power" that draws Covey's ire and represents most of the religious thinking about success in the last century.[68] At their heart, "mind power" philosophies hold that, "the route to riches was not strength of character . . . it was not a winning personality . . . the way to wealth lay in the self multiplied." In other words, it was the tapping of a latent energy available to all. For the religious, the ultimate source of this energy is God; for the secular, the source is the human mind.[69]

Religious proponents of mind power trace their roots to the various New Thought movements of the nineteenth century, including Mary Baker Eddy's Christian Science. In the logic of New Thought, God equals spirit, and spirit equals mind. Ergo, God and mind are one. One's individual power is directly related to unlocking the power of the mind, in attitudes, and in using the mind effectively.[70] Two common techniques of mind power are visualizing success and autosuggestion, which consists of using repetition to stimulate and prompt the powers of the unconscious mind.[71] An excellent contemporary example of these practices is Anthony Robbins, whose infomercials and books, like *Awaken the Giant Within* and *Unlimited Power*, are precisely the type of success literature that Covey finds to be so vacuous.

The two most well-known advocates of religious mind power in the United States have been the Reverend Norman Vincent Peale and his spiritual heir, the Reverend Robert H. Schuller. Through books such as *A Guide to Confident Living* (1948) and *The Power of Positive Thinking* (1952) as well as *Guidepost* magazine, Peale made mind power a part of mainstream Christianity.[72] *The Power of Positive Thinking* offers a format similar to *Jesus, CEO*; it is full of stories and anecdotes from the Peale's personal experience coupled with scriptural quotations. Yet Peale's work still uses typical mind-power techniques. In *The Power of Positive Thinking*, he tells readers to employ visualization by "formulat(ing) and stamp(ing) indelibly on your mind a mental picture of your life succeeding," and he encourages autosuggestion by the frequent repetition of such scriptural passages as Philippians 4:13 ("I can do all things through Christ which strengtheneth me" [KJV]) and Romans 8:31 ("If God be for us, who can be against us?" [KJV]).[73] Likewise, prayer is a "method through which you can stimulate the power of God to flow into your mind."[74]

Robert H. Schuller, pastor of southern California's Crystal Cathedral and host of the *Hour of Power* on Sunday television, learned from Peale but with some distinctive differences. From humble roots in Iowa, Schuller migrated to California and began his ministry in California style with a drive-in church at a drive-in movie theater, which eventually lead to the ten thousand-member Crystal Cathedral. Comparing their words alone, Peale and Schuller have only subtle differences since what Peale described as "positive thinking" Schuller renames "possibility thinking." The key distinction, however, is that while Peale stood clearly within the bounds of liberal Protestantism from his pastorate at New York City's Marble Collegiate Church, Schuller effectively allied himself with American evangelicalism. Although Schuller is not a typical evangelical preacher, he has been endorsed by Billy Graham and other evangelical icons who have spoken at the Crystal Cathedral. Self-help and success already had a well-established heritage within evangelicalism, and Schuller tapped it effectively. Within evangelicalism, faith healing is but one example of mind-God power, and other evangelicals, like Oral Roberts, have easily combined a focus on "health and wealth" with evangelical theology and practices.[75]

The latest popularizer of Christian mind power is Joel Osteen of Lakewood Church in Houston. Lakewood has over seven thousand members and a worship space that looks more like a convention hall than a traditional church, but Osteen's advocacy of visualization in his sermons, in an expansive television ministry, and in a recent book, *Your Best Life Now: 7 Steps to Living Your Full Potential* (2004) make him worthy of attention. The titles of Osteen's sermons and sermon series reflect the same positive or possibility thinking of Peale and Schuller. Osteen has preached sermons with titles such as "Winning the Battle of the Mind," "Enlarge Your Vision," "Never Lose Your Hope," and "Do All You Can Do to Make Your Dreams Come True."[76] In *Your Best Life Now*, Osteen endorses a form of religious visualization—what some critics of religious success literature have called "name it and claim it" theology:

We have to conceive it on the inside before we're ever going to receive it on the outside. If you don't think you can have something good, then you never will. The barrier is in your mind. It's not God's lack of resources or your lack of talent that prevents you from prospering. Your own thinking can keep you from God's best.[77]

Like New Thought a century ago, Osteen is teaching his flock how to access God's immense power and generosity by the right attitude and clarity of mind, and the results will be both spiritual and economic.

If Osteen is a contemporary purveyor of visualization, Bruce Wilkinson is the most recent advocate of autosuggestion. Wilkinson is the author of *The Prayer of Jabez*, a best seller with more than four million copies sold and several weeks on the best seller lists. *The Prayer of Jabez* draws upon the petition of an obscure biblical character from 1 Chronicles 4:10, but as Wilkinson packages it, prayer is essentially a form of autosuggestion coupled with petitionary prayer. In the Bible, Jabez prays, "Oh, that you would bless me and enlarge my border, that your hand might be with me, and that you would keep me from hurt and harm!" Wilkinson advises others to follow in his footsteps and pray this prayer repeatedly, tapping into "unclaimed blessings waiting for you"(NRSV).[78] He also connects the prayer to one's calling, equating "territory" and "border" with a vocation—whether business or motherhood.[79] To encourage repetition, Wilkinson counsels readers to pray it every morning and tape it to the bathroom mirror or calendar.[80] Critics have faulted Wilkinson for replacing the communal Lord's Prayer with the highly individualist prayer of Jabez and, even worse, for making God into a version of Santa Claus.[81] Yet, like Robert Schuller, Wilkinson's conservative theological credentials and the long-standing practices in Christianity (and evangelicalism, especially) of petitionary prayer for material needs and benefits make *The Prayer of Jabez* mainstream. In fact, Christian critics of Jabez have been faulted for their discomfort and doubts about the power of petitionary prayer.[82] As a result, mind power's autosuggestion for success has been fused with repeated prayer in ways that evangelical Christians may not even recognize nor be able to untangle.

Covey was certainly right that the vast majority of success writing has focused on mind power (although he does not name it as such), and for theologies of success this is even more true. Covey's corrective in *The 7 Habits* is to retrieve what he calls the "character or personality ethic," but the character ethic and the personality ethic, while related, are not synonymous. A concern for character almost always included at least passing reference to personal appearance and representation. But unlike a deeper focus on character, "the personality ethic dangled a cluster of psychological principles, easily learned, immediately productive, and with no necessity of deep transformation in our hearts and minds."[83] The personality ethic made these techniques supreme with the key point always being communication and with no need or place for religion.[84] Covey recognized the distinction as well, separating his seven habits into two main parts. The first three habits, what he describes as "private victories," really are in the classical model of the character ethic since they focus on the internal change that brings success. The second set, what he describes as "public victories," are largely communication strategies consistent with the personality ethic.[85]

To make sense of books like *Jesus, CEO* as expressions of workplace spirituality, we must view them within these multiple context and histories. As a contemporary publication genre, they meld both the personality ethic and mind-power traditions of success literature to another tradition of popular management advice and business exemplars (which can also be rightfully called success literature). The result is that these books are full of techniques, quick fixes, communication strategies, new attitudes, and paths to undiscovered strength. What is lost is any moral concern about success itself. From its roots deep in Puritanism and Calvinism before that, a focus on character was not about material or financial success as much as "true success" that was tied to the fulfillment of one's calling.[86] Writers on the character ethic asked whether material success, even if it was a by-product of a virtuous life, would hurt one's character and even one's very salvation. Personality and mind-power advocates include cautions against greed, but they only fault it as the ultimate motivation for success. Covey cautions against money, work, possession, and pleasure "centeredness," but he condemns them only as the core values.[87] He never asks whether wealth or possessions, in and of themselves, might lead one astray. Management guru books may contain only a few personal moral scruples; perhaps it is obvious, but "success literature" cannot question—even when Jesus is the model—whether worldly achievement is a bad idea.

5

The Spiritual Education
of a Manager

In the small Iowa town of Fairfield, Maharishi University of Management's Indian-themed architecture is a sharp contrast to typical midwestern styles. At first glance, the curriculum Maharishi offers seems like other colleges in the region with degrees in several disciplines and a large focus on business management at both undergraduate and graduate levels. What distinguishes Maharishi, however, is its founder, Maharishi Mahesh Yogi, upon whose philosophy the university is based. Looking deeper, the curriculum of the university is premised on the Vedic philosophy advanced by Maharishi, and the university claims to be a center for "consciousness-based education." In the heart of the Bible Belt, David Lipscomb University in Tennessee is an older institution with a 106-year pedigree and a spiritually oriented business curriculum as well. In September 2007, incoming business students at Lipscomb participated in a weekend "BASIC Training Camp" with BASIC standing as an acronym for "Business Administration Students Imitating Christ." The weekend retreat served as the introduction to a new business course at Lipscomb: The Foundations of Business—A Christian Perspective.[1]

While miles apart in distance and theological perspective, these institutions are just two examples of efforts to make the business curricula of colleges and universities into means for spiritual education and formation. As workplace spirituality has gained prominence in corporate offices and American life, business faculty have taken notice. This chapter describes the various ways spirituality has become a part of the business curricula at public, private, and religiously affiliated colleges and universities, and it proposes a four-part typology for these efforts as a means of classification, analysis, and critique. Relatedly, a new scholarly organization is providing an overarching professional framework for all of these types and is playing an important role in making workplace spirituality a mainstream academic area.

The Early Years: Religion and Business in Higher Education

Taking a long, historical view, it should not be any surprise that spirituality and religion have a place in the business curriculum. From its earliest history, the relationship between higher education and religion in the West has been closely intertwined, with the universities that arose in Europe during the Middle Ages licensed by the Roman Catholic Church to grant degrees. The great European universities were also important in the professional education of the time, including faculties for theology, law, and medicine in addition to those in the liberal arts. Although the subjects of the university included Greek and Roman philosophy and wisdom outside scripture and church teaching, the universities framed these more secular subjects within the Christian context. The academic day began and ended with Christian worship; clergy were frequently the teachers in multiple areas of study beyond theology; and the faculty had the opportunity to interject Christian teachings into every subject.[2] The university was a bulwark of Christendom, and education was fully integrated with faith.

The Protestant Reformation established an even stronger connection between faith and learning by emphasizing the priesthood of all believers and the theological concept of vocation. A university professor himself, Martin Luther insisted that schools and education were absolutely essential to the life of a community, and establishing and maintaining them was a Christian responsibility because God had entrusted young people to the community's care.[3] Luther advocated study of the liberal arts, and he dismissed the arguments—even then—that an education was a waste of time and money.[4] It was valuable, Luther said, because it prepared young people for service in a variety of roles, as well as for the general responsibilities of good citizenship. Unlike Luther, John Calvin was not an academic, but he too held education in high regard. He founded an academy in Geneva that included secular disciplines and ancient philosophers in its curriculum, and with Luther, Calvin affirmed the vocation and calling of every Christian in a way that honored all the professions and not just the ministry.[5]

When the Puritans in America founded Harvard College in 1636, there was great continuity with the European models in terms of faith and learning, and in the purposes of education in serving God and community through vocations. This became the standard as other colleges were founded in the colonies over the next two hundred years of American history. What pragmatic Americans frequently modified was the sectarian character of their colleges, which were originally denominationally founded, and they replaced confessional identity with what historian George Marsden calls "Protestant nonsectarianism."[6] Market forces sometimes dictated the nonsectarian impulse as colleges competed for students from outside their own sects. But intellectually, Enlightenment values led to a reinterpretation of faith and learning with strong confessional commitments understood, as opposed to the universal values of both Christianity and science. While practices like mandatory chapel would continue, their substance was less confessionally rigorous and focused instead on service, morality, and a general belief in God that was greeted with widespread acceptance.[7] Certainly, some colleges held to their confessional identity more than others, but a cultural Christianity held considerable sway. Chapel was still compulsory at many state universities, including at preeminent institutions like the University of Michigan, until the late nineteenth century. Leading educators argued that this form of Christianity was appropriate, even at public institutions, because it served the national interest by inspiring character and advancing Christian civilization.[8]

Business as an academic subject was, however, largely absent from the curricula of colleges and universities during this period due to its late emergence as a profession. While being involved in trade and commerce was nothing new, a class of professional managers came into being for the first time in the nineteenth century. As the corporate form of economic organization produced large enterprises like banks and railroads, the American economy experienced a shift from both mercantilist capitalism, which was state dominated (think of the British East Indies Company), and from entrepreneurial capitalism, which was family-centered (think almost any small business), toward a new "managerial" capitalism.[9] In large corporations, ownership was held by a diverse group of stock holding individuals and other corporations. It is in these large, highly capitalized corporations that the responsibilities of the manager became much broader. The manager's authority was almost absolute, and management became a "defining characteristic" of the modern business organization.[10]

Traditionally, those involved in trade, production, and other forms of commerce learned their work through apprenticeship. Able youth would attach themselves to an established merchant to learn the trade, perhaps staying as a partner or eventually leaving to found their own enterprises. In later years, the firm itself would provide for education and skill development. Schools in the American colonies (and then states) would sometimes offer courses in specific mathematics practical to business (sometimes referred to as "casting accounts"), but it was not until the mid-nineteenth century that private business schools began to offer an alternative to the apprenticeship model. As a training for bookkeeping and other clerical functions, the new business schools claimed that they could offer the same knowledge and skills that could be gained through apprenticeship but at a faster pace and without the cost of a long, subsistence-level apprenticeship. Some business schools operated as chains with multiple locations; the Bryant-Stratton Business College, for example, had more than fifty locations in the United States in 1863.[11] At traditional colleges and universities, though, there was still little attention given to the academics of business. A survey in 1871 by the U.S. Commissioner of Education (a predecessor to the Department of Education) counted only twenty-three colleges and universities that offered any commercial subjects.[12]

The Later Years: Religion and Business in Higher Education

Ten years after the survey, the University of Pennsylvania established the first school of business at a traditional college or university. With a $100,000 gift from Joseph Wharton, the eponymous Wharton School's purpose was to prepare young men for careers as professional managers in the new economy, yet even the school's benefactor questioned whether a college education in business was necessary for success. By 1900 business schools had been established at the University of California and the University of Chicago, and ten years after that, business programs were offered at the University of Wisconsin, New York University, the University of Michigan, Dartmouth College, and Harvard. By 1920, sixty-two colleges and universities offered business education, and in 1916 the American Association of Collegiate Schools of Business was established, offering the first professional organization for this field in higher education. By 1928, 7 percent of all undergraduate degrees were in business.[13]

The introduction of business education into the nation's colleges and universities reflected several changes occurring in higher education more broadly. In 1862, the Morrill Act created land grant universities to serve the nation through industrial and agricultural education as well as research in those same fields. Funds from the sale of public lands were to be used to support university studies in these practical areas; some states used the funds to supplement existing colleges and universities, while others established new ones. Four years earlier, advocating for a similar bill, newspaperman Horace Greeley argued for a "seminary which provides as fitly and thoroughly for the education of the captains of industry as Yale or Harvard does for those dedicated to either of the professions."[14] The idea that higher education could extend beyond the traditional liberal arts and historic professions was taking hold in the public mind and in the practices of higher education.

At the same time, higher education was changing because of the impact of the German research university and new expectations of what the university should be. In some respects, these developments were foreshadowed by the Morill Act and the emergence of colleges focused on practical research for farms and industries, but the German university also modeled a more fundamental shift that affected how both business as a discipline and faith, as both a practice and subject of study, should be regarded in higher education. Increasingly, American academics were including time in German universities where they came to value the research ideal, subjecting all fields to rigorous "scientific" analysis that was value free.[15] This was coupled too with a professionalization of the professorate. The doctoral degree became the sign of professional expertise, and every college, no matter how small or what its mission, wanted these research experts on their faculty.

In his reflections on religion in higher education, Mark Schwein points to Max Weber's "Science as a Vocation" as the clearest exposition of this transformation. Weber argued that the work of the academy was strictly rational with no places for values or ultimate concerns, and if a professor had such ascetic concerns, he must deny himself those values when doing academic work.[16] Marsden refers to this phenomenon as "methodological secularism." It was this idea, related also to emerging understandings of academic freedom, that allowed for any idea or question to be pursued, regardless of its subject or consequence. There were to be no sacred cows in the new academy, nor were there to be books like the Bible or church teachings that were immune from analysis or being placed in historical context. Significantly, most scholars, at public and private institutions alike, saw this movement as fully consistent with Christian ideals.[17] Liberal Christianity offered the academic equivalent of a civil religion that allowed value-free scientific pursuits in the spirit of a generic, nonsectarian, and moral religion. Scientific study would advance American society, and this was understood as fully in accord with Christianity because, they asserted, the United States was, indeed, a Christian civilization.

Forces outside higher education were also having an impact. Largely in an effort to prevent public support of Roman Catholic schools, many states passed laws attempting to end the public support of all religion in schools and other public institutions. New case law in the courts was also defining religious discrimination, and liberal Christianity's own opposition to discrimination of any kind, including religious discrimination, supported the nonsectarian impulse.[18] Seemingly positive developments like the Carnegie Endowment's retirement program for college teachers were also significant because Carnegie would support only those institutions that were nonsectarian. In order to be part of this valuable program, many church institutions reconstituted themselves.[19] But perhaps the most important outside development that quickly became an academic issue was early twentieth century fundamentalism. As it played out on college and seminary campuses as well in the courtroom of Tennessee's Scopes trial, fundamentalism was identified as backward, anti-intellectual, and a danger to scientific achievement, and *all* sectarian Christianity (meaning any form of Christianity that held to a specific creed or confession) was judged unfit for the academy.[20] In its own evolutionary advance, by the late twentieth century, "nonsectarian" increasingly meant "nonreligious."

Among Roman Catholic colleges, their strong religious identity was also challenged from within. During the 1950s, Catholic scholars themselves began to identify the weaknesses of their own institutions, including a failure to send their alumni in proportionate numbers to graduate and professional schools. A "ghetto mentality," perhaps from the immigrant character of Roman Catholic identity, was faulted for isolating their colleges and faculty from the intellectual mainstream.[21] The historian Philip Gleason reports that the response by the colleges was an "excellence binge" but one in which the models of excellence were the thoroughly secularized Harvard, Columbia, and University of California.[22] Faced with their own crises over academic freedom, legal challenges to sectarian identity and governance, and the endorsement of greater lay leadership by Vatican II, Catholic colleges and universities faced challenges not unlike their Protestant brethren.[23]

The same forces pushing for research and professionalization in the academy also created challenges for business. When business education became part of academia at the turn of the last century, these same challenges may have been present, but they were not really at home. The focus of business education was largely on business practice with courses frequently taught by local professionals. The business school was understood as a service to the business community and frequently more closely associated with them rather than to the other faculty.[24] Likewise, faculty in other disciplines saw their business colleagues as inferior because their claim to academic expertise came through experience rather than research. When the case method was introduced into business education early in the twentieth century, it was an attempt to be both practical and scientific, not only offering "real world" problems but also treating the cases as akin to scientific experiments to be resolved by rigorous analysis.[25] But by the 1950s, business professors were becoming fully integrated into the academy's scientific model, focusing on research that may or may not have had an impact on business practice.[26] And business education more and more was focused on rigorous quantitative disciplines, economics, and the behavioral sciences, just like medicine as a profession found its sources in biology and chemistry. The continuing problem in business education was that "a critique of business programs as intellectually shallow and academically second-rate [was] counterpoised to a critique of the schools as far removed from managerial reality, thus irrelevant to, or destructive of, good management practice."[27] This would be (and continues to be) an ongoing debate among business faculty, and it is a one that sometimes spills over into disputes with other academics and with business practitioners.

Of course, research on business in the early to mid-twentieth century would have revealed the ascendancy of rational business management. Methods of bureaucratic organization for the large firm coupled with practices of Taylorism (the epitome of rational and scientific analysis of human work) were even defined as "scientific management." Outside the firm, similar nonsectarian influences were also present, from new laws in the 1960s prohibiting religious discrimination to an overarching civil religion, which professed a generic belief in God and morality but avoided sectarian specifics. The new consensus was even larger than liberal Christianity, encompassing what Will Herberg named in his popular book as *Protestant, Catholic, Jew* (1955). Herberg noted that a religious ethos did more than uphold the state, it also supported the culture. A part of that culture was business, but because the religious ethos was present broadly, organizations like the modern business corporation could operate with their own form of methodological secularism.

Spirituality in the Business Curriculum

The preeminence of "scientific management" was increasingly challenged within the business world during the late twentieth century, and different forms of workplace spirituality arose within the new environment. In and of itself, this would likely lead business faculty to take notice because of their emphasis on the realities of business practice. But within higher education, changes were also occurring in the 1980s and 1990s that made spirituality and religion more prominent on college and university campuses and provided an opening for spirituality in the business curriculum. The postmodern critique, which gained more attention in some disciplines than in others, questioned whether the academic ideals of objectivity and value-free inquiry were possible, and spirituality joined race, gender, ethnicity, and sexual orientation as an academically valid perspective within scholarly disciplines. Without the constraint of objectivity, teachers and scholars were free to incorporate spirituality and religious convictions in ways that may have not been possible under the modernist hegemony. Simultaneously, many colleges and universities with historic religious affiliations were re-exploring these connections, sometimes with outside foundation support. Increasing recognition of religious diversity, in the United States and globally, also made religion more interesting.

From these developments, religion and spirituality now have new places in business curricula. Four individual types can be identified, each with a distinctive vision for how spirituality, faith, or religion relate to the business curriculum, and the terminology is indeed part of what distinguishes them. Some colleges seek to maintain a unique Christian identity in their curriculum, some have embraced a broad conception of Christian vocation, some have adopted a "spiritual but not religious" perspective, and still others are creating connections between business and other religious traditions beyond Christianity.

Type 1: Maintaining Christian Sectarianism

Like the Christian businesses described in chapter 3, one group of colleges and universities has resisted the tendency toward secularism and now offers a competing vision for the relationship of higher education and Christianity. This Christian identity is evident in their business curricula. Institutions of this type reject any dualism between faith and learning or faith and business. Instead, they are guided by a worldview that subsumes all forms of commerce under the Lordship of Jesus Christ. These schools also reject the premise that excellence in business or any field is impeded by a Christian worldview and a fully integrated Christian higher education.

Calvin College in Grand Rapids, Michigan, is often identified as a flagship for the integration of faith and learning. The college stands in the Christian Reformed denomination, which was organized by Dutch Calvinists in the late nineteenth century. Calvin College did not emerge as a baccalaureate institution until 1920, but it has been able to build from a tightly bound church community with strong ethnic connections fostered by a system of day schools and a fierce Calvinist faith. These particular roots lead the college to a full engagement with the world—but on its own terms. Because faith and learning must always be held together, the college requires that all faculty be members of the Christian Reformed Church or one of its ecumenical partners, and the faculty strive to make a Christian worldview predominant in every course in every discipline.

The Economics and Business Department at Calvin is no exception to this overarching vision. Of the four thousand students at Calvin, roughly five hundred are business and accounting students, making it the first or second largest major.[28] For recruiting new students, the department's website communicates the Calvin distinctiveness clearly, stating right below the masthead that:

> Today, more than ever, leaders in the world of business and economics need to bring not only skills but also a Christian perspective to their job responsibilities. At Calvin, we have consciously founded our economics and business education on Christian values. Business is more than the study of profit-seeking enterprises and profit-making activities. Business at Calvin is the study of how to live responsibly by actively making business decisions which further God's kingdom.

While many outside this model would likely reject any notion of teaching "Christian business" or "Christian management," the same website also proclaims that the department's "sixteen full-time professors teach from a Christian perspective."[29]

Perhaps more than others, the required management course in Calvin's business curriculum illustrates how the Christian perspective is pervasive. The course catalog describes the course as an introduction to management "based on God's revelation in creation and His Word." The course's objectives speak of identifying the Christian purposes of business, claiming a personal calling to work in the business field, and developing those virtues needed to serve effectively as a Christian in the business world. Course texts include a standard management textbook but also other texts that allow students to explore the Christian tradition and its relationship to commerce. The course also includes *The Soul of the Firm* (1996) by C. William Pollard, former head of ServiceMaster, indicating the connection between the Christian educational subculture at Calvin and the economic subculture of self-styled Christian businesses.[30]

Arising from Christian evangelical roots in the Free Methodist tradition, Seattle Pacific University is another example of a business curriculum—both undergraduate and graduate—that has sought to be countercultural by framing and infusing its courses and academic programs with a Christian worldview. A new track in the MBA program allows students to concentrate on the "theology of business," and a series of one-credit "Spirituality in Business" courses allows students to focus on this issue every term, with varying topics.[31] Four members of the business faculty at Seattle Pacific defined their vision of a theology of business in a 2007 article titled "It's Not Your Business: A Christian Reflection on Stewardship and Business." They argue that a Christian vision of business is grounded in the notion of stewardship and draws upon the important doctrinal foundations of Creation, Fall, and redemption. They say that the idea of Creation should lead business managers to be concerned about the products they produce, the environmental impact of their enterprise, and a vision of business that goes beyond profit and shareholder value; the Fall leads to doubts about the complete efficiency of the market, the potential for wrongdoing, and the value of governmental regulation; and redemption in Jesus Christ offers the opportunity to live out God's will in business, even though it still might not be done perfectly.[32] Most recently, the business school at Seattle Pacific has sought to communicate their distinctive identity (albeit without Christian language) through a new marketing tagline: "Another Way of Doing Business."

The BASIC (Business Administration Students Imitating Christ) course at David Lipscomb University offers a third example of this countercultural type. Founded as a Bible school and then college in the nineteenth century's restoration movement, which sought to "restore" church practices to those at the time of the early Christian apostles, Lipscomb is now affiliated with the conservative Church of Christ denomination and firmly grounded in America's evangelical subculture. BASIC is a weekend retreat that begins the new "Foundations of Business: A Christian Perspective" course. The course offers an entrepreneurial approach to business education with new students starting up and running their own businesses, but the course requires students to consider several moral dilemmas along the way and the retreat includes activities for students to discover "their God-given gifts."[33] In their own assessment, students reported some initial hesitation about the retreat but appreciated the opportunity to learn "what God has planned for my life" and to become "passionate about bringing others to Christ through business."[34]

Manifested most clearly in smaller, conservative, Christian colleges, this model offers a clear counter to secularizing tendencies in higher education and business. By maintaining a Christian worldview in their business teaching, faculty in this type shape new generations of business leaders in that vision where faith and business cannot be separated.

Type 2: Fostering Vocation

The Christian theological concept of vocation has had an important relationship to both workplace spirituality and higher education, but the connection to higher education has been strengthened and in some cases remade in the last seven years with support from the Indianapolis-based Lilly Endowment. If the Carnegie Endowment was a source for church-related higher education's more secular turn, the Lilly Endowment could be understood as a counter force, and its work provides the basis for the second type.

With assets over $8 billion (which is more than three times the current assets of the Carnegie Corporation), Lilly Endowment is a major force in American philanthropy and the most important foundation in supporting research on religion and American religious institutions.[35] Since 1990 its research and substantial support have focused on church-related higher education, but in addition to their support of research, the endowment has also funded several programs for church-related colleges and for the faculty who serve them to explore issues of faith and learning, whether through the more narrow lens of a particular denominational tradition or more broadly. In the 1990s, the Lilly Fellows Program in Humanities and the Arts was funded at Valparaiso University to support graduate student fellowships, conferences, and other programs in those fields, and later the Rhodes Consultation on the Future of the Church Related College created a larger consortium of ninety faculty from multiple disciplines at church-related colleges who were interested in fostering campus conversations about faith, learning, and denominational heritage.[36]

In 1999, the Lilly Endowment inaugurated their largest effort in higher education with major grants totaling more than $176 million to eighty-eight church-related colleges and universities, and it is in this new Programs for Theological Exploration of Vocation (PTEV) that we see the endowment making an impact on the business curriculum. Although the theme of these grants was "vocation," Craig Dykstra, vice president of Lilly's Religion Division, characterized the initiative as "an honest inquiry." It was not a pre-established program for colleges to adopt but rather a guiding concept for colleges to use as they developed their own programs and outputs. Dykstra likened Lilly's support to "Socrates' dialogue with Meno as to what virtue is and whether it can be taught," adding "we hope for a dialogue on what vocation is and how one comes to have a sense of one."[37] Within that mandate, colleges and universities had wide latitude in designing programs that not only fostered dialogue about vocation among students but also prepared faculty and staff for the task. Because each college or university with a Lilly vocation grant has had great freedom in structuring their program, there is great diversity across the eighty-eight institutions and also significant differences in the effects on business curricula. And as the endowment was exclusively interested in self-avowed liberal arts institutions, many of the grantees did not even have business courses.

Hosting speakers and conferences in support of vocational exploration has been one popular way for business departments to draw upon Lilly resources. Some departments have invited alumni or local business people to meet with business students and reflect on their own senses of vocation and their various professional journeys, and others have connected to the authors, speakers, practitioners, and advocates of spirituality at work who make up what can be described as a workplace spirituality movement. As an example of the latter, David Batstone, author of *Saving the Corporate Soul* (2003), spoke at Concordia College in Moorhead, Minnesota, and Po Bronson, author of *What Should I Do with My Life?* (2002) addressed students and faculty at Wartburg College in Waverly, Iowa. Established academic experts on business ethics, theology, and the professions, like William May of Southern Methodist University or Emory University's Jon Gunneman, have also been involved, participating in a Lilly-supported conference on "Religion and the Corporation" at Butler

University. At Samford University in Birmingham, Alabama, faculty from the business and law schools hosted a conference exploring the public purposes of professional education for other business and law faculty titled "Credentialed for What? Exploring Business and Law Education for Public Obligation."[38]

The impact of the PTEV program on the business curriculum of participating institutions has varied. What may be most common is a renewed focus on ethics and social responsibility, a key aspect of vocation but one that may or may not be divorced from deeper theological ideas. Catawba College in North Carolina and Dillard University in New Orleans both established ethics courses that are now required for business majors, and Catawba business faculty also collaborated with its PTEV leadership to co-sponsor a business ethics essay contest. More widespread has been the use of Lilly funds and faculty development opportunities to integrate service learning into business courses or to inaugurate specialized internships—especially with nonprofit organizations. As an example, Hope College in Holland, Michigan, established a separate "Internship for Vocation" program, which matched business students with Jubilee Ministries, an organization located in the city of Holland that helps ethnic minorities start small businesses. At Goshen College, Wartburg, and Samford, Lilly support has led the business faculty to develop new initiatives in the area of "social entrepreneurship," a developing field focused on creative nonprofit and for-profit solutions to social issues.

Some college faculty have developed new courses that are more distinctively Christian. Luther College's new course on conflict management emphasizes how "our Christian heritage calls us to serve others and to foster reconciliation in the world," and Simpson College's new business course links vocation, career, and life planning.[39] In St. Paul, Minnesota, St. Thomas University's new course "Christian Faith and the Management Profession: Engaging Finance and Christian Thought" is a capstone experience allowing students "to understand the theological reasoning behind the Christian tradition's understanding of work and leisure as the basis to faith-filled response to finance."[40]

While vocation is clearly a theological concept with deep roots in the Christian tradition, this model's focus on vocation leaves room for full Christian sectarianism on one end (the St. Thomas course) and a fully inclusive Christian liberalism with an ethics focus on the other (the Catawba course). Sometimes these diverse expressions can be present even within the same institution, but the Lilly Endowment's impact is significant, encouraging new spiritual and moral explorations in business curricula at mainline Protestant and Roman Catholic institutions.

Type 3: Being Spiritual but Not Religious

The third type occurs at a combination of public, private, and church-related institutions, but the curricula they each develop are founded on making clear distinctions between "spirituality" and "religion." This push for distinction of terms has been described in previous chapters, but business educators in this model, especially at public and secular institutions, feel added pressure to avoid accusations of religious discrimination and proselytizing. To do this effectively, the first part of any classroom discussion will involve a careful definition of terms. Sometimes this is done inductively, asking students to brainstorm ideas or concepts associated with the terms "spirituality" and "religion" along with terms that might fit both categories. Efforts are also taken to be inclusive toward those students who may reject both terms and concepts.[41] In a classroom example from the *Journal of Management Education*, students are asked to discuss personally known spiritual exemplars and their spiritual practices while avoiding "sharing their subject's religious affiliation unless they feel it is essential—because it is the spirituality of the person, not his or her religious affiliation, that is important."[42] By adopting "spirituality" rather than "religion," business faculty assert that they are avoiding traditional dogma and collective beliefs and are referring instead to a more universal concept than to a narrowly confessional "religion."

Advocates for spirituality in the business curriculum can point to the changing character of business and the explicit presence of spirituality in business life to justify it as a worthy object of study; from "green business" to promotion of corporate social responsibility, new attention is being given to contemporary movements for business to serve more than the materialistic interests of stockholders. A different but related rationale focuses on the individual student and future manager, claiming that good leadership requires authenticity, self-knowledge, and a holistic knowledge of others, which includes spirituality. By engaging spirituality and moving beyond mere "materialistic values," business educators also have research to support claims that future managers will be happier, healthier, and have better personal relationships.[43] A 2002 survey identified more than forty-four universities around the world that have courses in workplace spirituality or related programs.[44] Realistically, however, what may be most important is the desire of business educators to bring spiritual ideals and expressions to their own work in the classroom. Business faculty are thus following Parker Palmer's advice to "teach who you are" and exemplify their own spiritual values such as humility, compassion, simplicity, mindfulness, authenticity, respect, and trust.[45]

Like ethics in the business curriculum, spirituality finds a variety of expressions. Modules within existing courses are one approach but are a little harder to identify through standard course names and descriptions. One course that stands out is the introductory management class taught by Christopher Neck at Virginia Tech University. In chapter 4, Neck's co-authored *The Wisdom of Solomon at Work* (2001) was noted as a contribution to the many books on workplace spirituality, but as a seven-time winner of the "Students' Choice Teacher of the Year Award" who teaches more than one thousand students in his undergraduate management class, Neck's curricular impact is more significant. In an interview with *BusinessWeek* magazine, Neck describes how his goals are much larger than teaching management theory. He speaks instead of helping students to find their purpose and a "deep-level, professional development" that includes asking students, "How can you manage others if you can't manage your own life?"[46]

One way Neck does this is to supplement student reading of a traditional management text with *Mastering Self-Leadership: Empowering Yourself for Personal Excellence*, a book he co-authored with Charles Manz. This course text goes beyond traditional management theories, asking students to consider their purpose in life and to engage in visualization exercises for personal success that the authors title "mental practice." Emphasizing both a healthy mind and a healthy body, the book also includes a full chapter on the importance of personal fitness as an critical element of self-leadership and personal success.[47] Overall, the book provides the textual basis for Neck's holistic engagement with his management students and the course's spiritual ethos, which is manifested through concern for purpose, meaning, and personal empowerment.

In a second more easily recognizable form of this type, students enroll in a specific business course with spiritual themes. In the MBA program at the University of Notre Dame, students can choose from two courses with the word "spirituality" in their titles. Students in "Spirituality of Work" begin by studying "theological perspectives on work"; the course gives specific attention to Christian spirituality broadly and the Roman

Catholic tradition in particular. In and of itself, this might place Notre Dame in type one or type two (Notre Dame was the recipient of a Lilly vocation grant), but while "Spirituality of Work" is offered each spring, in the fall "Spirituality and Religion in the Workplace" is offered instead. In the fall, according to the university catalog, the course is "offered in the Judeo-Christian tradition, involv(ing) readings from the Jewish, Protestant, Catholic and Buddhist perspectives," and it is this eclecticism that identifies Notre Dame with this model.[48] Even more, by offering both courses annually, the university appears to affirm by default the individual character of spirituality since the course itself can be selected based on personal preferences. Among Christian traditions, however, Roman Catholic college and universities—and especially those associated with religious orders—have the unique ability to use the term "spirituality" in a generic way but at the same time allowing that expression to be part of an overarching Roman Catholic ethos and identity.

Stanford University's graduate business program offers a course on "Lives of Consequence: How Individuals Discern Paths to Meaningful Engagement." Through the lives of figures as diverse as Martin Luther King Jr. and Steve Jobs, the course uses biographies and methods of self-reflection.[49] This is a method used by other colleges and universities too. Video clips and case studies of exemplary and more spiritual CEOs offer the opportunity for students to consider for themselves and with peers what spirituality is and how a meaningful life is defined.[50] In addition to biography, students also have the opportunity to study novels and plays in "The Business World: Moral and Spiritual Inquiry through Literature." Taught by Scotty McLennan, university chaplain and co-author of *Church on Sunday, Work on Monday*, the literature course uses a "two-text method," which asks "students to examine their own personal stories with as much care as the stories presented in literature."[51] Pointing to the importance of narrative in workplace spirituality, professor David Boje in the Department of Management at New Mexico State University structures an entire course around storytelling as a skill for consulting and as a way to engage organizational mythmaking.[52]

Adjunct professor Srikumar Rao's "Creativity and Personal Mastery" is the most popular course for MBA students at Columbia University. While the course never invokes the word "spirituality," its focus on "discover(ing) your unique purpose for existence," invocation of various wisdom traditions, and use of exercises that combine spiritual practices and positive thinking techniques clearly places it in this model. In one type of visualization exercise, Rao encourages students to engage in "as ifs." For example, students act "as if" every person they meet during the week has only one day left to live, and then they monitor how they perceive other people differently and how they act differently in response.[53] Rao's course has been so popular that he has offered a full-semester version at the London Business School and a one-day version at the University of California's Haas School of Business. Rao has written that the course is meant to be the starting point for a lifetime "journey of exploration of growth," and it is a journey together in the class and afterwards since he claims that "Creativity and Personal Mastery" is the only business school course with its own alumni association.[54]

Another group of management faculty are distinguishing themselves by offering consulting services, training, and executive education in workplace spirituality. At the University of Scranton, a Jesuit Catholic institution in Pennsylvania, Jerry Biberman chairs the management department, publishes extensively in the area of workplace spirituality, and maintains a website for his consulting practice, www.workingwizdom.com. Biberman describes his work as "synthesizing his personal experiences of Jewish mysticism, the spiritual exercises of St. Ignatius of Loyola, meditation, yoga, tai chi, and spiritual traditions from around the world."[55] He offers seminars on topics such as "Creating and Sustaining a Spiritual Organization," organizational consulting, retreat design and facilitation, and personal coaching.[56] At another Jesuit institution, Andre Delbecq, former dean of the Santa Clara University's business school, created a hybrid model that pairs MBA students and CEOs in a shared course on "Spirituality for Business Leadership." While acknowledging his own Roman Catholic identity, Delbecq's course includes resources from many religious traditions, ranging from Lakota Sioux prayer and meditation to the Christian prayer method of *lectio divina* but using scripture from a combination of Christian, Jewish, Buddhist, Taoist, and Hindu sources. What may make Delbecq's course unique is its study of wealth and poverty from the perspective of multiple religious traditions and field experiences, which asked participants to explore the "mystery of suffering" by experiencing a form of suffering that the student feared most—from spending time with the homeless to visiting a facility caring for children with serious birth defects. Perhaps different from being "spiritual but not religious," Delbecq has created an ecumenically religious and spiritual experience for MBA students and CEOs.[57]

While wider ranging than even the previous type, the "spiritual but not religious" curriculum centers the experience of spirituality on the individual with some attention to the business organization as a culture. The model rejects spiritual-material dualism in favor of holism, but it also makes established religious traditions into backgrounds or the source of practices that can be sampled, adopted, or discarded the degree to which they are personally meaningful. Since most collegiate and graduate education occurs in public institutions, it is also likely to be the model with most potential for growth and the most long-term influence.

Type 4: Emerging Religious Educators

The diversity of the American religious landscape has changed from mere varieties of Christian denominations to an abundance of different religious traditions and sects, but this new religious pluralism has been slow to manifest itself in religiously affiliated higher education. The small group of institutions arising from non-Christian religious traditions makes up the fourth type. These are colleges and universities that were established with the purpose of offering higher education within a faith context, and they wanted to offer more than religious subjects alone. The business programs at these schools reflect these purposes as well, trying, as noted in the examples below, to make expressions of Judaism and Hinduism manifest in their business curriculum.

In New York City, Yeshiva University claims to be the oldest Jewish university in America. The early waves of Jewish immigration to the United States from Germany brought with them a high desire and degree of assimilation into the surrounding culture, and this included assimilation into the mainstream educational system. But for new Orthodox immigrants, primarily from Eastern Europe, assimilation in both culture and education was rejected. The predecessor of Yeshiva University functioned very much as an old-fashioned yeshiva, offering detailed study of the Torah and Talmud as it had been done for centuries before in Europe, but Orthodox students would frequently leave their yeshiva for unlicensed schools or even city colleges for afternoon and evening classes in English, which covered such secular subjects as science, math, history, and grammar.[58] There was considerable controversy among students and administrators (including a student strike) and among administrators and Orthodox constituents as to whether secular disciplines should be studied at all, much less in an Orthodox institution. However, by the 1920s, secular education was a part of the curriculum, and in 1928 with approval from the New York State Board of Regents, Yeshiva College, the undergraduate division of Yeshiva University, was given the authority to offer the Bachelor of Arts and Bachelor of Science degrees.[59]

Whether students study chemistry or business, a day at Yeshiva still begins with study of the Torah and the Talmud with the afternoon devoted to a standard college curriculum. This includes business, and while Yeshiva had offered business courses and majors for a number of years, in 1987 a $12 million gift to the university led to the establishment of the Sy Syms School of Business as a distinct entity. Following the Orthodox tradition, even the business programs is segregated by gender with male students taking classes in one location and female students in another.[60]

In 2007 Moses L. Pava, a professor of accounting and business ethics, provided a window to view spirituality in the business curriculum at Yeshiva in his article "Spirituality In (and Out) of the Classroom: A Pragmatic Approach," published in the *Journal of Business Ethics*. What may be most striking about both Pava's definition of spirituality and his engagement of spirituality in the classroom is that it is not exclusively Jewish in form or substance. In describing spirituality, he refers to the five themes: acceptance, commitment, reasonable choice, mindful action, and continuous dialog.[61] At the same time, Pava also shares the final assignment in his business ethics course that requires students to prepare a case study about their own moral decision-making. Describing how Judaism is important, he writes:

> Remember in class we talked about how Jewish ethics is about "interpretation." We said that interpretation is neither invention (anything goes) or discovery (only one right answer). But, somehow, interpretation combines the best of invention and discovery and ends up being something all together different.[62]

In this way Pava encourages the students to draw upon the methods of Talmudic study that they know so well as they engage an event or issue in their own lives. He also describes how the course uses a variety of sources to engage spirituality and values, from movies to the Bible, from literature to the Talmud.[63] Certainly, the course makes Jewish approaches to spirituality prominent, but they are not absolute. Perhaps this is even the goal of a Yeshiva University education with its clear division of religious and secular studies.

As we read earlier, in Fairfield, Iowa, a very different model of business education is grounded in a form of Indian philosophy. In the early 1970s,

Maharishi Mahesh Yogi, the Indian guru who introduced transcendental meditation (TM) to the Beatles and the world, bought the bankrupt campus of Parsons College, a former Methodist school. The 140-acre campus would eventually become the Maharishi University of Management (MUM), a fully accredited institution of higher education and a center for the transcendental meditation movement in the United States. While adhering to standard "nonsectarian" language of identity, the curriculum of the university is based around the practices of "consciousness education" and requires TM as part of its business training. Not unlike the medieval model of education that included Christian worship at the beginning and close of the day, MUM frames the day with TM in the morning and evening.

The founder of MUM, Maharishi Mahesh Yogi, emerged on the international scene in the late 1950s when he began to lecture widely on the benefits and techniques of meditation. Growing up in India, Maharishi had studied under an Indian guru, but at his guru's urging he also earned a degree in physics from an Indian university. His science background was significant because he repeatedly used science metaphors to describe TM, and MUM continues to do this with its emphasis on the "science" of consciousness and creativity as well as active research programs to demonstrate the effectiveness of TM. The science metaphors are also significant in understanding why Maharishi and his supporters adopted a Western structure of education—the university—to advance their ideas.[64] While MUM officials claim that TM is not a religion, Cynthia Ann Humes has argued that Maharishi's program, while complex and evolving, is best understood in relationship to Hinduism. Early in his encounters with Westerners, Maharishi denied the religious identity of TM and his movement, moving away from terms like "enlightenment" and any association of meditation with the desire to escape this world and its cycle of rebirth.[65] However, Hughes argues that while Maharishi sought to be universalist in the beginning by avoiding direct references and connections to Hinduism and the Vedic traditions, over time he began to incorporate more of these traditions into his teachings as strategic revelation of "true religion."[66] At MUM, the transition from "spiritual but not religious" to more openly Hindu can be seen in the curriculum but also in the campus architecture, its vegetarian cafeteria, and a spa with Vedic health practices.[67]

The fusion of Vedic philosophy and business thought is outlined in Maharishi's own book on the purposes of the university. In *Maharishi*

University of Management: Wholeness on the Move, Maharishi states in the introduction that his university,

> will create managers who will float in happiness, success, and fulfillment. They will command authority in the field of progress and dictate their terms to the environment. They will be the guiding light of the post-industrial era, and functioning through Nature's Principle of Least Action, initiating dynamism in silence, they will introduce automation in administration to create a stable, balanced economy. They will be the embodiment of positivity and harmony, in whose presence nothing can go wrong, and will raise management to a new, enlightened level of performance, which will nourish everyone and everything. They will bring the dawn of new fortune to any field they choose to lead and will usher in a prosperous, blissful time of progress, peace, and fulfillment in all fields of business management and public administration.[68]

The words are lofty, as with any statement of mission, but the book describes how MUM will teach managers how to align their own lives and their companies with the principles of "Natural Law," which is "the knowledge and experience of consciousness" and the "infinite organizing power" of all areas of management—from accounting to marketing to human resources.[69]

In addition to their mention of "Maharishi Vedic management" and "Maharishi Vedic science," the descriptions for business courses at MUM reveal a different tone. The subtitle of the basic marketing course for the MBA program is "fulfilling evolutionary desires by attracting, delighting and retaining customers."[70] For the BA students, the core economics course is no longer the dismal science but the means for "efficiently using resources to promote fulfillment of individuals and society," and statistics not only teaches math but "powerful techniques based on the underlying orderliness of Nature." Students in the course in human resources understand how Vedic science can better enable managers to attract, retain, and motivate employees, and in the entrepreneurship class, students focus on "harnessing Nature's infinite creativity to plan and start a small business."[71] MUM's overarching philosophy of "consciousness-based education" asserts that learning must attend to knowledge both internal and external to the human self, and by engaging the whole brain through TM, students come to understand how these sources of knowledge are all one.[72]

Because it continues to use scientific language to describe its philosophy, another unique feature of MUM is its faculty's many successful efforts to develop research projects and publications that support Vedic management. The university has been the recipient of millions of dollars in U.S. government support for research in the health sciences, and its research on the effectiveness of TM in the workplace has been published in several peer-reviewed business publications. MUM faculty studies, some funded by foundation support, have shown that practicing TM in the workplace reduces stress, improves job satisfaction, and enhances work relationships; other studies have pointed to the impact of higher states of consciousness for leadership and organizational development.[73] The faculty at MUM thus offer an education for spiritual managers but also provide a research grounding for one expression of the workplace spirituality movement.

Since the number of colleges and universities with non-Christian religious affiliation is limited, this model is also limited. However, increasing religious diversity in the United States from new patterns of immigration since the 1960s may produce new models of higher education, or as with Maharishi, a fascination with Eastern religious traditions by upper-class, white Americans may expand the availability of this type. Like the Christian sectarians of the first model, these schools offer a religious worldview to be applied in business and all of life that stands against the secularizing tendencies in both.

Professional Identity

At the same time different types of spirituality were being discussed and taught in the management classroom, business faculty were also developing active research programs on workplace spirituality as well as a scholarly infrastructure to support their work. Turning Max Weber on his head, these same faculty are also unafraid to affirm that a primary motivation for their workplace spirituality research is their own spiritual experiences, practices, and identity.[74] The demands for value-free inquiry and complete objectivity are breaking down in teaching and research on workplace spirituality, but at the same time, business faculty recognize that the scholarly "rules of the game" require certain academic structures for both mutual support and academic respectability.

The 1990s witnessed an explosion in popular books about workplace spirituality, and in a few cases, the spirituality in business books were themselves written by established academics. Not available at Barnes and Noble or local bookstores were other essays, books, and conference proceedings produced by scholars for other scholars. One study identified 115 refereed journal articles on work and spirituality in business publications between 1990 and 1999. The *Journal of Organizational Change Management* was the most prominent publication with sixty-eight articles from 1992 to 1999 mentioning spirituality and two special issues on the subject. This journal was a likely source given the relationship between the study of corporate cultures and the study of spirituality. Several other journals published special issues focused on workplace spirituality in the 1990s, including the *Journal of Management Education* and *Chinmaya Management Review* (a peer-reviewed, English-language journal from India).[75]

In 1997 important developments occurred in two professional associations for business faculty. In the relatively small International Academy of Business Disciplines (IABD), Jerry Biberman and a colleague from the University of Scranton, Len Tischler, inaugurated a "Spirituality in Organizations" track at the organization's annual conference with proceedings from the conference published in IABD's *Business Research Yearbook*. In the much larger Academy of Management (AOM), the organization's first conference session on workplace spirituality overwhelmed planners with its popularity. Lee Robbins, business professor at California's Golden Gate University, reported that the session "was scheduled in a small room which could hold about 35 seated and over a hundred people tried to get in with people in the hall jockeying for position from which they could hear the session." In 1998 a preconference workshop on workplace spirituality at the Academy of Management by Biberman, Robbins, and Judi Neal was also well attended, and in 1998 and 1999 several existing groups within the academy sponsored sessions on spirituality, including the Organization Development and Change section, the Management Education and Development section, and the Social Issues in Management section. Following a petition drive at the 1999 meeting, the AOM established a Management, Spirituality, and Religion group and elected Biberman as its first chair.[76] In 2006 this seven-year-old group claimed 680 members.[77]

While organizationally distinct from the AOM group, in 2004 many of the Management, Spirituality, and Religion group's same leaders established the first refereed journal in the field of workplace spirituality: the *Journal of Management, Spirituality and Religion*. In the introductory issues, the editors (who again included Biberman from Scranton) expressed their high goals for the publication, writing:

> The *Journal of Management, Spirituality and Religion* aims to become the first port of call for academics in this fast expanding scholarly area. The journal will provide a forum to scholars engaged in the study of work and organizations, and in particular management, on issues pertaining to spirituality and religion as these affect all and any aspect of management, organizing and work. The journal aspires to become a hub for the generation of knowledge and a forum for the exchange of ideas and debate; as well as an information base on pertinent events: new books, upcoming conferences, etc.
>
> The journal aims to serve these two large communities – business studies scholars and religious studies scholars – and to act as a meeting forum for the cross-fertilization of both camps. It wishes to encompass, without prejudging any belief, a multitude of interests and concerns – the sole criterion being academic rigor and scientific merit.[78]

The concepts of "academic rigor and scientific merit" take on somewhat different meanings in this expression compared to the old value-free ideals of the German research university, but the existence of the journal itself, as a peer-reviewed publication with an editorial board from a collection of public and private institutions, lends the academic study of workplace spirituality a high degree of respectability and professional integrity. However, the hope for cross-fertilization with religious studies scholars may not have been as fully realized since few theologians or religious studies scholars are on the journal's editorial board, and few have published in it. Workplace spirituality is now a legitimate field of academic research with all the professional accoutrements to prove it.

Teaching Both God and Mammon

Whether invoking God, spirit, mindfulness, or natural law, business professors are taking a lead in reversing the nineteenth- and early twentieth-century's secularizing trends in higher education. They are developing curricula that include spirituality and religion; they are seeking authenticity between their faculty work and their personal spiritual or religious practices; they are studying the impact of spirituality on business organizations and consulting with the same; and they are forming professional associations and publications that provide respectability, support, and forums for their work. In their pedagogy and research, they theorize about the definitions of religion and spirituality, and implicitly and explicitly they develop theories of spiritual development in business and all of life. The Gospels of Matthew and Luke record the admonition of Jesus that no one can serve both God and wealth, but business faculty in a variety of higher education settings are attempting to prove Jesus wrong—or at least reconfigure his wisdom so that God can be served in and by the work of business.

In consequence, workplace spirituality has found a practical and intellectual home in business schools and departments of American universities. This transforms academic programs, but it also creates an infrastructure for the long-term support of workplace spirituality outside the academy. From its beginning as an academic discipline, business faculty navigated two worlds—the academic world and the world of business practice—and today the business department or school is a part of the academy but also the training ground for the next generation of business managers and a reservoir of experts for corporate consulting and business books. Managers prepared in a business curriculum with a spiritual or religious focus will likely view workplace spirituality in the corporation with appreciation, and business faculty can serve as the intellectual core of the movement. It may even be fair to say that business education is rediscovering the master's responsibility for the holistic formation of apprentices—an education that includes professional knowledge and skills but also values and attitudes.[79] Medieval masters were responsible for their apprentices' religious upbringing, and many business faculty are now doing the same albeit in diverse and creative ways.

In the strangest of ironies, mammon is bringing God back to campus.

6

Team Chaplains, Life Coaches, and Whistling Referees

When the industrialists in Pullman and Gastonia hired ministers to serve employees and residents in their company towns, they began a tradition of workplace chaplains that continues today. But times change. Chaplains at work have taken several forms over the last century, and religious pluralism, which once meant diversity in Christian denominations, is now much more complex. Religious traditions other than Christianity have grown rapidly in the United States and so has a post-Christian populace who consider themselves "spiritual but not religious." This chapter describes how workplace chaplains have both evolved in mission and grown in number amid these changes, but it also analyzes "life coaches" as an emerging category of spiritual leaders who help individuals address questions of purpose and meaning at work and elsewhere without direct religious content or labels. If not through a book or a traditional religious community, identifying who will help individuals (as well as entire places of business) explore faith on the job is crucial for understanding the workplace spirituality movement, and there is definitely not one answer. The spiritual marketplace offers a host of options, each with a price—financial and otherwise.

The reaction to workplace spirituality has also been diverse. In many cases, churches and other faith-based organizations are trying to provide their own form of workplace spirituality, reasserting the significance of Christian theologies of vocation and attempting to be relevant. Individuals have responded by asserting their rights to be religious at work, and others have asserted their rights not to participate in corporate-sponsored spirituality, together resulting in a dramatic rise in civil-rights complaints related to religion in the workplace as well as the emergence of workplace spirituality as an area for "risk management." Not all responses are serious, however. The comic strip *Dilbert* has taken a satiric look at workplace spirituality as another business fad, and writers and comedians have pushed different forms of workplace spirituality to the extreme for comic effect. Chaplains, coaches, and religious organizations are offering encouragement for workplace spirituality, but others are crying foul or shaking their heads and chuckling in disbelief.

Workplace Chaplains Revisited

The chaplain at Pullman was essentially a parish pastor with all the normal responsibilities of ministry yet in an environment that was owned, operated, and structured around the Pullman Palace Car Company. The company town environment called for a certain type of spiritual programming and leadership, but the "new company town" of modern welfare capitalism involves another. In these days, a chaplain serves a new type of workplace where frequently workers are no longer "employees" but "associates," and the employer is no longer a "boss"—but employer and employee together are part of the corporate "team," working toward common goals. Observing Europe and the United States over the last century, several other forms of workplace chaplaincy were possible—from the French worker-priests to the British and American industrial missions— but chaplaincy in the U.S. workplace never strayed too far from the company town and the pre-established patterns of welfare capitalism.

In France, the relationship to religion in general and Catholicism in particular is too complex to recount, but the intense secularism of the French republic during World War I required that Catholic priests be included in the military draft, creating a model of chaplaincy in which the priest served alongside the common soldier, literally "in the trenches," but not in a hierarchically defined priestly role. Following a similar pattern, during World War II French priests volunteered to go to Germany to work alongside conscripted French civilians laboring in Nazi factories.[1] At the same time in Paris, small yet similar experiments with worker-priests took form in French factories, and the number of worker-priests grew even larger after the war. The Roman Catholic hierarchy at first supported the worker-priests as a means of evangelism to workers, but the priests saw themselves not as clerical representatives but as partners with the workers, creating a new way of being the church by sharing the workers' life and future.[2]

In Britain, a similar impulse was guiding ministry with workers. Largely due to class divides, residents in highly industrial areas were thought by church leaders to be irreligious and in need of evangelism, but at the same time there was a desire to embrace workplace ministry as a means to transform the church and make it more responsible to contemporary society. Beginning with ministries to migrant workers between the world wars and then in the industrial city of Sheffield, organizations for industrial mission emerged. Ecumenical but always Anglican-dominated, teams of ministers served as chaplains within industries and were welcomed by owners and trade unions.[3] The chaplains sought authentic dialogue with the workers, offering pastoral care and a listening ear so that the church might learn from the workers' experience of life.[4] In the United States, industrial mission projects grew in Detroit and Chicago, while projects focused on white-collar workers were developed in Boston and New York.[5] Although the French worker-priests were an intentional ministry of a parish or diocese, industrial missions varied in form and organization with most more closely resembling the ecumenical mission societies of the nineteenth century, which, independent of denominational structures, sent missionaries around the world.

Ecclesiastical sponsorship for workplace chaplaincy had some following in the United States in contrast to the developments in France and Britain, but most chaplaincy has had a characteristically American free-enterprise bent in the spirit of the company town and American welfare capitalism. The industrialist R. G. Letourneau is often identified as the leader in American workplace chaplaincy; beginning in the 1930s he employed chaplains in his manufacturing plants and in the contracting work his company did for the Hoover Dam project. The R. J. Reynolds Company also employed chaplains after World War II, and many companies followed.[6] While the daily work of the chaplain was much like that of industrial missions, the corporate model of direct employment of a chaplain changed it from the ministry of the church to a benefit provided by the employer, and this has been the significant difference. On a large scale, Tyson Foods employed more than 120 chaplains in seventy-seven different production facilities in 2007. More often, however, American employers have chosen to outsource, contracting with a company that provides chaplaincy services much as they contract with firms providing other types of employee assistance programs. Founded by Gil Strictland, a retired military chaplain, Marketplace Chaplains USA (formerly

Marketplace Ministries, Inc.) employs somewhere around two thousand chaplains under contract to three hundred companies in forty-six states, making it the biggest workplace chaplaincy organization in the country. A smaller firm, Corporate Chaplains of America, employs one hundred full-time ministers.[7]

The heart of workplace chaplaincy in its corporate form is pastoral care to employees, offering spiritual counsel, conversation, and assistance in personal crises. Proponents argue that the "demand" for corporate chaplains is based on the fact that a much larger percentage of Americans say they believe in God than are members of religious communities with their own spiritual leaders. This need is met by the chaplain who even occasionally presides at special events such as weddings and funerals for employees and their families.[8] The chaplain can also complement an employee assistance program for mental and emotional health by making referrals for counseling, alcohol, and drug treatment, and other types of psychological aid and even assisting laid-off employees or employees who have been arrested.[9]

When interviewed, one chaplain had a difficult time defining succinctly the differences between his work and the secular counselor in his firm's employee assistance program; he stated that his work was "spirit guided," addressing existential issues and those that arise from "deep levels of despair"—issues that a mental health professional might feel uncomfortable addressing.[10] From the company's perspective, as with any employee assistance program or other employee benefits, there is hope that workplace chaplaincy will result in improved business performance through greater company loyalty, decreased absenteeism, enhanced morale and lower employee turnover.[11] In 1996 an article in the *Journal of Pastoral Care* cited a study reporting that for every dollar spent on workplace chaplaincy, an employer recouped four dollars because of reductions in absenteeism, accidents, psychological and medical treatment, and costs associated with drug and alcohol abuse.[12] Welfare capitalism has always been about enlightened self-interest, and workplace chaplaincy fits this pattern by adding a faith dimension. Critics of contemporary chaplains make the same complaints that were made of pastors in Gastonia's mill towns, fearing exploitation and the use of faith as a means to an economic end. But advocates claim that it is one of the best ways to respond to employees as whole people who value spirituality as a dimension of life or as an entire worldview.

What stands in contrast to Gastonia is the new concern over serving a much larger range of religious diversity. Chaplaincy has been and continues to be primarily Christian but not exclusively so. The majority of chaplains at both Marketplace Chaplains and Corporate Chaplains of America are Christian, but they provide chaplains of other religious traditions— Buddhist, Muslim, and Jewish—at an employee's request.[13] Following its founder's background and training, Marketplace Chaplains emphasizes that its workplace chaplains adhere to the same model of chaplaincy in the U.S. military, offering a "neutral, always available caregiver—which focuses on helping employees and families better manage basic personal life and work issues" and noting especially that its activities are "not an organized religious program."[14] Diana Dale, a chaplain and president of the National Institute of Business and Industrial Chaplains, a nonprofit group that certifies workplace chaplains, also stresses the care aspect of workplace chaplains against the fears that chaplains are primarily Christian evangelists.[15] When a group of Muslim employees, for example, requested accommodation for their required prayer times, Tyson chaplains arranged for the plant to do so.[16] Like most other aspects of an employee assistance program, the services of a chaplain are optional, and chaplains are explicitly theological only when asked. Their pastoral care approach allows them to be "spiritual but not religious," or in the words of Princeton University's David Miller, "faith-friendly" rather than "faith-based."[17]

However, other motives may inspire the employer. When requested, Marketplace Chaplains will include an "evangelism report" among its anonymous contact reports that documents how many employees have come to faith in Jesus Christ.[18] Certainly, the primary business rationale for workplace chaplaincy is increased morale and productivity, but many employers may hire chaplains with the motive or hope that "back door" evangelism will take place in the employee-chaplain relationship. In fact, Corporate Chaplains of America even includes this hope in their mission, stating that "our mission is to build relationships with employees, with the hope of gaining permission to share the life-changing Good News of Jesus Christ, in a non-threatening manner."[19] This changes the employer-employee relationship as well, fostering the type of religious paternalism critiqued in chapter 2.

Perhaps the best-known form of workplace chaplaincy thrives in the world of professional sports where players can be found in Bible study and worship before the big game. Until the 1960s, pro team locker rooms were more associated with foul language than prayer, and Billy Sunday abandoned his own professional baseball career because he found it incompatible with Christian faithfulness. But a quiet transformation occurred through the leadership of several devout players and coaches along with outside support by organizations like the Fellowship of Christian Athletes (founded in 1957) and evangelists like Billy Graham who began featuring prominent Christian athletes at his crusades.[20] In the 1970s, Bill Glass, a born-again sports writer, partnered with Bowie K. Kuhn, the commissioner of baseball, to start "Baseball Chapel" in every major league and eventually most minor league clubhouses. Today, in addition to team-specific faith leaders, a combination of chaplains associated with groups such as Motor Racing Outreach (NASCAR), Professional Tour Chapel (golf), Hockey Ministries International, and the Christian Surfing Association serve almost all professional sports.[21] A different set of organizations, including Pro Athletes Outreach, Athletes in Action, and Champions for Christ, offers regular faith-based conferences and events, organized by sport, exclusively for professional athletes and their families.[22] While it would still be hard to confuse professional athletes with angels, fans cannot ignore the public religiosity in much of today's sports, and this religious fervor is supported by chaplains employed (or voluntarily enlisted) by both team owners and collaborating parachurch organizations. And like other criticism of workplace spirituality, all of the God-talk by professional athletes and teams may be yet another attempt to use the divine for good workplace results, but in this case the worksite is an athletic field rather than a cubicle.[23]

Put in the Coaches

While workplace chaplains offer religious professionals to employees for evangelism, pastoral care, and employee assistance, the previous two decades have also witnessed the rise of "coaching" as a different form of helping profession in and outside the workplace. The idea of coaching is usually connected to the athletic field or gymnasium, but this new type of coaching is a highly individualized form of professional consulting. With "internal coaching," a firm hires or employs a coach to motivate, counsel, and develop an employee, working on tasks such as listening or assertiveness skills, navigating a difficult decision (like layoffs), and setting priorities. Sometimes referred to as executive coaching or business coaching, this was the fastest growing field of consulting in the 1990s, offering a convenient, one-on-one training session for the busy professional.[24] As with many forms of human resources training, the activities of executive coaches draw upon psychology and psychoanalysis coupled with business strategy, all in the service of increasing employee performance and organizational productivity. It is also closely related to intentional forms of professional mentoring.

But an internal coach is not the only option. Professionals can independently enlist an "external coach," and these freelance trainers have given increased attention to spirituality as part of their work, serving clients who seek meaning and vision in addition to practical business skills.[25] The transition from coaches serving professional development alone to a more holistic focus has spawned the creation of "life coaching," which expands from professional development and training to personal development of mind, body, and spirit. One author describes coaching as a potential counterbalance to the pressures of modern life: "by enlisting a coach we can often begin to focus on what really is important to us, and begin to shape what we need to do to be more in line with that."[26] When coaches help clients establish priorities, find work-life balance, articulate values, and identify life purpose, the ties to spirituality becomes evident. Life coaches become personal chaplains and gurus who help their clients make sense of life and find success in all of its areas.

Life coaching finds its conceptual roots in the emerging field of "positive psychology." In fact, it is very nearly the clinical arm of positive psychology as a discipline. Advocates of positive psychology assert that psychology as a field has become fixated on the pathological by focusing on fixing what is wrong rather than achieving what is good. In contrast,

> Positive psychology emphasizes well-being, satisfaction, happiness, interpersonal skills, perseverance, talent, wisdom, and social responsibility. It is concerned with understanding what makes life worth living, with helping people become more self-organizing and self-directed.[27]

In its highest form, life coaching takes this emerging theoretical knowledge and applies it to the lives of individuals in an environment that honors change without stigmatizing change as healing.

At the same time, this concern for change and "deeper" life issues must be packaged and sold for a fast-paced, success-oriented culture. Indicative of this speeded-up lifestyle is that much of coaching is done over the phone.[28] One coaching organization advertises its "short-term, results-oriented approach for finding meaning, purpose, and direction."[29] This same organization promises to answer important philosophical and spiritual questions like "who am I?" and "how can I integrate my spirituality into my everyday life?" in the same abbreviated time frame.[30] The focus on goal attainment, an attribute of all forms of coaching, quickly transforms aspects of spirituality to instrumental ends for a more fulfilling and meaningful life, and it may work best that way. As a result of one of the few studies on life coaching's effectiveness, Anthony Grant from the University of Sydney in Australia actually counsels coaches not to devote too much time to personal reflection because that does not support a client's goal attainment; self-reflection, says Grant, can make a person feel worse, leading to failure rather than success. Instead, "life coaching should be a result-oriented solution-focused process, rather than an introspective, overly philosophical endeavor."[31] In the end, it is about the results.

To get to those results, the descriptions and literature of life coaching repeatedly reference the methods of mind power (see chapter 4), asserting that problems can be overcome and success can be achieved through positive mental images and visualization. Life coaching actively and personally encourages visualization through various exercises. In one method called "the miracle question," a life coaching client is asked to imagine "if you woke up tomorrow, and a miracle happened and the solution was somehow present, what would be happening?" The purposefully religious imagery of a miracle is meant to inspire creative thinking and problem-solving that would normally be inhibited by the client's "self-regulation."[32] In another visualization exercise, a client is asked to follow an imaginary beam of light through time to a point twenty years in the future and to encounter the client's future self. The guided exercise allows the client to ask questions of the future self, merge with that future self, and then visualize through the future self's own eyes what is to come, creating an inspiring image than can be referenced when the exercise is complete.[33] Other exercises such as "dreaming" or focused goal setting also connect life coaching to mind power philosophies of success.

Some coaches have blurred the lines between chaplain and coach by advertising themselves as "spiritual life coaches." In 2007 the *New York Times* reported on a survey of six thousand coaches by PriceWaterhouseCoopers in which 18 percent indicated that they specialized in spirituality.[34] From assessing personal beliefs to values clarification to asking questions about one's purpose in life, almost all life coaching has some element of spirituality in it, even though it might not always be articulated as such. In this way, life coaching functions almost like a form of spiritual direction for the "spiritual but not religious." Whereas classic forms of spiritual direction within Christianity would involve sampling new types of Christian prayer or St. Ignatius's spiritual exercises, life coaching offers similar counsel and activities but without requiring confessionally specific God language. At Coaching-4-Clergy, a former Methodist pastor coaches an ecumenical mix of forty-five priests, pastors, and rabbis per month, and at Whitehawk Spiritual Consulting, Gavin Young claims to be a Quaker-influenced Roman Catholic who utilizes a deck of Tarot cards in his coaching.[35] An eclectic mix of religious practices can be present in the life coach's tool kit, all in the service of the client's preferences and goals.

Among self-styled spiritual life coaches, the confusion with spiritual direction can be even more bewildering because some life coaches specifically designate themselves as "Christian coaches." As a Christian coach, Kate Theriot of Coaching for Change prays with clients and asks them to draw pictures for each decade of life, showing how their image of God has changed and what it is today.[36] Tony Husted at The Christian Coach promotes his "expert coaching, modeling, and mentoring from a Christian Worldview . . . [that] empowers individuals and in turn communities, that honor God through excellent living." While he uses a variety of coaching techniques that could be found elsewhere, Husted touts his "Christian worldview" as the distinctive element of his coaching practice, and he offers a biblically based series of faith statements for prospective clients to consider.[37] Protestants have shown increased interest in spiritual direction, pointing to the need and desire for a form of spiritual support and growth that goes beyond traditional pastoral care, and since pastoral care is too often crisis oriented, spiritual direction can serve as a worthy complement. Despite its authoritative sounding name, spiritual direction differs from Christian coaching in that it is focused only on creating an environment for discernment and reflection. The coaching model is intensely future-directed and intent on problem-solving and achieving personal goals.[38] Faith-based coaching uses spirituality as a means to personal ends rather than as a means to engage the person in something greater than themselves.

Perhaps nothing is more indicative of life coaching's intense individualism, as well as its arrival as a cultural trend, than the addition of life coaching to the pantheon of *For Dummies* books published by John Wiley and Sons. In *Life Coaching for Dummies* (2007), author Jeni Mumford outlines the elements of life coaching from her experience as a coach who "applies whole life-coaching techniques to her work with people and with businesses."[39] *Life Coaching for Dummies* is not a how-to manual for professional coaches but a resource for "tuning into your inner coach." Advocating her do-it-yourself approach, Mumford writes:

> The good news is that you also have an inner coach, cheering you on to have a go and celebrating your progress. The inner coach speaks from your future. That version of you who knows how it all turns out and is bursting to tell you that everything is going to be just fine![40]

The book offers exercises that a reader might use to explore issues of values, work, relationships, and overall well-being. All of the characteristics of life coaching are present (except for the coach), allowing the reader to have a coaching experience in an even more individualistic way.

The author of *Jesus, CEO*, Laurie Beth Jones, offers another example of self-coaching but this time in an avowed Christian form with her book *Jesus, Life Coach* (2004). Like her other books, this one is full of short personal stories from Jones's life and quick references to scripture and the life of Jesus. From her research on life coaching and her experience as a coach herself, Jones says she was "struck by how qualified and how perfect Jesus is as a life coach."[41] The main themes describe how making Jesus into your personal life coach will increase your focus, balance, productivity, and fulfillment. While the rhetoric of "Jesus as life coach" can sound much like the rhetoric of Christian discipleship with respect to the reader's relationship with Jesus, traditional understandings of Christian discipleship call the individual to work for Jesus; coaching, on the other hand, puts Jesus to work for the individual. In one metaphorical example, Jesus holds the ladder as readers climb towards their dreams.[42] As interpreted by Jones, when Jesus is a person's life coach, goals are achieved and results improve.

Because it is so new, there has been little analysis of the coaching trend. Journalistic accounts of coaching estimate that there are 20,000 to 40,000 executive and life coaches around the world, and over 8,000 are members of the International Coach Federation.[43] The survey by PriceWaterhouseCoopers estimated that there were 30,000 coaches worldwide but as many as 50,000 were possible. The same survey indicated that coaching is an overwhelmingly feminine occupation (68.7 percent); it serves a predominate female clientele (56.5 percent); and only 39.2 percent are full-time coaches.[44] The training and background for coaches can also vary dramatically. Some life coaches may indeed have no training at all, but forms of training available include books, weekend conferences, online courses by a variety of organizations, and a new graduate-level certificate in coaching offered by Columbia University in New York. The program at Columbia includes course work in coaching as well as supervised coaching, not unlike the fieldwork requirements of professional counselors and clergy, in addition to separate tracks for internal and external coaches.[45] Anthony Grant and Michael Cavanagh of the new Coaching Psychology Department at the University of Sydney are at the forefront of professionalizing coaching, but they freely admit the discipline has not yet become standard. There are no barriers to entry into the profession, no common body of knowledge, no educational standards, no professional association to screen, admit, and discipline members, and no enforceable code of ethics.[46] Coaching in general and life coaching in particular can be almost anything the coach and client want it to be.

Life coaching thus meets a cultural need of our time, offering fast and highly individualized attention to spirituality and questions of ultimate meaning that are tied to professional work. Additionally, because coaches are supposed to be value neutral, they also may be more attractive than professional clergy who could be seen as potentially judgmental of certain values and life priorities. Whether a workplace chaplain or a personal life coach, Americans are seeking spiritual guidance outside the boundaries of traditional religious communities and independent of a tradition's own ordering of moral and spiritual practices. Instead, the needs of the individual and the employer take precedence, and spirituality becomes a means to their ends of goal attainment, self-fulfillment, morale, and productivity.

Faith Communities Respond

Previous chapters have chronicled the diverse ways faith communities and their representatives have sought to connect faith and work over time—from the Protestant Reformation to faith-based businesses and on to the industrial missions and workplace chaplaincy described here. Yet even as the establishment tradition, much of Christianity has struggled with these connections despite its resources in theologies of vocation and calling. In *Church on Sunday, Work on Monday*, Laura Nash and Scotty McLennan assert that a deep chasm exists between clergy and their parishioners in business, which prevents Christian congregations from offering interesting and engaging alternatives to the workplace spirituality movement.[47] Liberal churches have been interested in critiquing capitalism as an economic system without considering the people who work in the system, and their ministries are very engaged in the lives of individuals except for their work.[48] Conservative churches, while often more receptive to capitalism, also have limited examples of connecting faith to work except when that connection is for evangelism and church growth; Roman Catholic parishes, despite focus on the laity in Vatican II documents, have been limited actors as well. Yet congregations from a broad cross-section of Christianity combined with parachurch organizations and groups from Judaism and Islam are attempting to create new models of ministry that take seriously the work of their faithful and offer an alternative or supplement to corporate-sponsored spirituality and the many do-it-yourself approaches.

Because it conforms to established notions of social ministry as well as concern for the poor, perhaps the most prevalent form of congregational ministry related to work has been outreach to the unemployed. At St. Thomas the Apostle Catholic Church outside Chicago, a ministry to the unemployed began in 2001. Weekly meetings follow a Friday morning Mass, and monthly meetings feature a speaker. But the heart of the "Jobs Ministry" at St. Thomas is networking, skill development, and a "prayerful support group." The parish estimates that 180 employed volunteers minister to 300 job seekers from various faith traditions at any one time.[49] At Westside Baptist Church in suburban Dallas, skills in interviewing and resume writing are combined with prayer and presentations on "keeping our faith through transition."[50] Individual synagogues in New York have offered similar programs for Jews, and building on the Hebrew word for "livelihood," the Orthodox Union of Jewish congregations organized its own job search website, www.ParnossahWorks.org to allow nationwide networking for professional employment.[51] Outreach to the unemployed allows faith communities to express their concern for the economic well-being of program participants, but these programs also, explicitly and implicitly, affirm the value of work as a place of meaning-making and faith expression. Both a loss of income and a loss of meaning accompany unemployment, but too often congregational concern for work ends when employment is found.[52]

Just as programs for the unemployed connect to established ideas about social ministry, other efforts by religious communities to link faith and work usually take form under other existing ministry categories. In worship, many Christian congregations have experimented with creative ways to recognize and affirm work as a place to live out one's faith. The 1,200 worshipers at Community Presbyterian Church in Danville, California, have dedicated symbols of church members' work (uniforms, aprons, tools, and chalk, etc.), and on a designated Sunday they watch an inspiring slide show of members in their workplace.[53] Other congregations highlight faith in the workplace through sermons or homilies, offer prayers in worship on workplace issues, and sometimes even "commission" individuals for ministry in their chosen professions.[54]

But those congregations who have engaged workplace faith at all have been most active in educational programs to foster faith-work connections, including retreats, classes, special events, and regular groups. At Rivermont Presbyterian Church in Lynchburg, Virginia, the "First Monday Club" brings together congregational members for a lunch and speakers who talk about their personal efforts to connect work and faith.[55] At the Lutheran Church of the Holy Spirit in Emmaus, Pennsylvania, a "Monday Connection" breakfast group has a long history of congregational members bringing real life case studies from their work for discussion and communal guidance, and a Lutheran church in a downtown Minneapolis offers Bible study for business people on Thursday and Friday afternoons as well as a more general conversation on faith at work on Wednesdays.[56] One-time events by congregations are also common: a Roman Catholic parish in Ohio offered a workshop on "Searching for Christ in Your Workplace" and a Presbyterian congregation in Chicago invited Laura Nash to share her research from *Church on Sunday, Work on Monday*.[57]

While many Christian congregations offer occasional events, programs, and worship opportunities, only a few have made the relationship between faith and work a central component of their congregational mission and ministry. Again, at the Lutheran Church of the Holy Spirit, the congregation's Center for Faith in Life was developed to bridge the perceived gap not only between faith and work but also faith and other areas of life such as family and community. Within the center, a "ministry in occupation" group plans regular educational events on such general topics as "Christian ethics and business" and more specific topics related to individual occupations; the congregation is also easily able to notify people who work in these areas because the congregational directory lists the occupation and employment of all church members.[58] St. Mark's Episcopal Church in downtown San Antonio established a similar program with an exclusive focus on work at its Center for Faith in the Workplace. The center seeks to enact a vision "for every worklife to become a place of spiritual life, where people discover meaning in the fruitfulness of their work and find wholeness in their work relationships."[59] Through ecumenical support, the center has now become The Work + Shop with ongoing ties to the congregation but also with its own space for meetings and retreats. What distinguishes this program, however, is its distinctive method of Bible study related to faith in the workplace. Rather than studying scripture and then asking, at the end, "what does this mean in my life," The Work + Shop begins with the personal. As the group's leaders describe it,

> Our practice reverses the process. Our discussion begins with an experience in the daily life of one of the participants. Then members of the group begin to suggest passages and story from scripture that might serve to illuminate the experience.[60]

While potentially inviting proof-texts and other forms of biblical interpretation that clergy and theologians would find abhorrent, the congregation at St. Mark's joins with Holy Spirit in reorienting traditional Christian education so that the experience of work becomes an equal dialogue partner with scripture and theology.

Reflecting on the divide between faith and work in the lives of Christians, theological seminaries are often identified as places for change, and many have responded creatively to affirm faith at work and to train church leaders for congregational faith-at-work ministries. Too often, however, seminary outreach to laity in the form of summer schools and workshops offer a lighter version of clergy education rather than programs geared toward living out faith in the workplace. The Evangelical Academies of postwar Germany provided an early model for direct outreach to laity, bringing together people from occupational groups for dialogue, research on social problems from a perspective of faith, and theological education that intentionally addressed faith at work.[61] American seminaries have adopted programs like these and created others. Individual courses on workplace spirituality or Christian vocation and work can be found at several institutions, but a small number of seminaries have established centers or institutes. In his book on the Christian faith at work movement, David Miller touts the efforts of the Center for Faith and Culture he formerly led at Yale University's Divinity School; the center offers conferences for clergy and business professionals, and Miller taught a course with students from the divinity school and MBA students from Yale's School of Management.[62] At Luther Seminary in St. Paul, Minnesota, a grant from the Lilly Endowment established the Centered Life program to assist clergy and laity in making their congregations places where vocation and a Christian workplace spirituality is supported and nurtured. The program offers books and workshops, but its most significant agendas train congregational trainers to foster faith-work discussions on vocation and gifts. Their unique assessment instrument also allows congregational leaders to survey church members and identify how the congregation is succeeding and failing to equip members for vocations at work, home, community, and church, creating "Centered Life Congregations."[63]

Among more evangelical Christian seminaries there are two other notable exemplars. In Pasadena, California, Fuller Seminary has the only endowed chair in ministry of the laity, offering classes and research on faith at work, and its Max DePree Center for Leadership offers training, consulting, and executive coaching that focuses on organizational leadership within the context of Christian faith. At Gordon-Conwell Seminary near Boston, Massachusetts, the Mockler Center for Faith and Ethics in the Workplace was established in 1994 and named after a former chairman of Gillette Corporation. This center offers courses for students that are sometimes taught by business executives like Tom Phillips, retired CEO of Raytheon Corporation. It provides continuing education and supports students who are interested in workplace issues and are enrolled in the seminary's Doctor of Ministry program.[64] Unfortunately, such efforts, whether at more mainline or evangelical institutions, are rare in theological education. Surveys of seminary students indicate that they learn very little about business and economic institutions; what they do learn may be flawed; and they know these deficits will be problematic in their future ministries.[65]

Historically, when traditional religious institutions have failed or been inadequate, new organizations have been established with more specialized focus; among advocates for workplace spirituality these organizations have also been critical. Within Christianity, they are sometimes referred to as "parachurch organizations," but they have taken form outside Christianity as well. Among Christians alone, a 2003 directory counted more than 1,200 faith-at-work organizations and institutions that ranged from small, local groups meeting for study of the Bible and workplace issues to regional and national organizations with publications and professional staff.[66] Adding groups and organizations from Judaism and Islam expands this even further. As an example of a small group, Rabbi Burton L. Visotzky, a professor at Jewish Theological Seminary in New York, reported a decade ago in *Inc.* magazine about his ecumenical group study of the Hebrew Bible among business people in midtown Manhattan (see chap. 2 for descriptions of scriptural studies by various faith traditions in the workplace).[67] Muslim employees at Boeing have studied the Koran; Microsoft employees have learned about the Torah; and the former Bell Atlantic (now Verizon) had a Christian Bible study.[68] Just because sacred texts are studied in the workplace does not mean, however, that these groups address workplace issues, but certainly the opportunity is readily available. The very environment can create a flavor and orientation that would not be present if the same group met at a mosque, synagogue, or church, and workplace groups create networks of professionals on site among whom faith is not a taboo but a welcome subject of conversation.

At the regional level, small groups and more established institutions provide opportunities to connect faith and work that are both similar and different than local organizations. In St. Louis, the Aquinas Business Forum, sponsored by the Aquinas Institute of Theology, functions like many local groups with monthly meetings for prayer, Bible study, and reflection on workplace issues in light of Catholic social teachings.[69] In contrast, the Crossroads Center in Chicago is a more institutionalized nonprofit organization offering multiple events, speakers, and workshops through its Center for Faith at Work; Crossroads often collaborates with both the Career Transition Center of Chicago, a faith-based organization (including Christian and Jewish partners) for the unemployed, and the Chicago chapter of the International Coaching Federation, one of the largest professional organizations for executive and life coaches.[70] In Kerrville, Texas, Laity Lodge offers programs in a rural retreat center setting for a regional audience interested in faith at work. More evangelical in its Christian focus, the lodge is operated by a private foundation with a long commitment to the faith-at-work movement, and this includes operating a website, www.thehighcalling.org, that offers online Bible study and meditations on faith at work.[71]

Perhaps the most interesting regional group is the Forum for Faith in the Workplace located in Columbus, Ohio. Christian in origin and mission, the forum organizes small groups on faith-at-work and collaborates with congregations to offer events, classes, and programs. For several years, it collaborated with two area seminaries to offer a course, "Empowering the Ministry of the Laity in the Workplace," for students preparing to be Methodist and Lutheran pastors, and since 1988 it has presented an annual award to an individual or group who has been a leader in helping others make connections between faith and work.

The greatest diversity among faith-at-work organizations is at the national level where old and new, large and small, representatives from diverse religious traditions can all be found. Many national organizations are organized around local chapters, including the Christian Business Men's Committee (CBMC). The oldest organization in the faith-at-work movement, the CBMC was founded in the 1930s, and one of the key leaders was R. G. LeTourneau, who had started hiring workplace chaplains around the same time. With headquarters and staff in Chattanooga, Tennessee, this evangelical Christian organization has maintained its male focus, claiming more than 50,000 members around the world and 18,000 in the United States.[72]

One of the newest national groups is Legatus, a distinctively Roman Catholic organization for high-level business leaders. Started in 1987 by Tom Monaghan, the founder of Domino's Pizza, Legatus's sixty chapters are present across the United States and host regular meetings in addition to the national organization's events. After meeting Pope John Paul II, Monaghan had a vision to establish Legatus, naming it for the Latin word for "ambassador" to emphasize how the organization's members are "ambassadors in the marketplace." Membership, the groups claims, "gives you the opportunity to deepen your relationship with God and discover how Catholic truth and values can help you meet the ethical challenges you face on a daily basis."[73] Since only CEOs and other high-level business executives are eligible for membership, Legatus is a Catholic version of the older Fellowship of Companies for Christ (FCC), which offers evangelical Christian business leaders a similar forum with national events and local chapters (see chap. 2).

Without local organizations, supporting a national parachurch organization can be challenging; nonetheless, several within the faith-at-work movement have been successful. The Coalition for Ministry in Daily Life is primarily Protestant but ecumenically Christian with a focus on information sharing through a national newsletter, an annual meeting, and networking. The coalition's membership is a who's who of leaders in the faith-at-work movement, including denominational representatives, the director of Luther Seminary's Centered Life program, and the co-director of St. Mark Episcopal Center for Faith in the Workplace in San Antonio. A former leader of the coalition has also been an executive with another national organization associated with Intervarsity Christian Fellowship. Under the leadership of Pete Hammond, Intervarsity has been a strong presence through its "Marketplace Ministries and Ministry in Daily Life." Intervarsity is well known for its projects on college and university campuses. Its specialized programs in business, nursing, and other graduate schools helps build consciousness of faith-at-work issues among future professionals.[74]

Beginning in the mid-twentieth century, brand-specific organizations of Christian professionals started up with groups like the Christian Legal Society (for lawyers) and the Fellowship of Christian Peace Officers (for police). Most often with an evangelical focus, at least thirty Christian professional societies exist in the United States, bringing together Christian engineers, teachers, psychologists, pharmacists, nurses, and social workers. The Christian Pharmacists Fellowship International, for example, hosts annual meetings for both practicing pharmacists and students in pharmacy schools, and the association advocates for "the right of Christian pharmacists, based upon biblical principles and their moral convictions, to exercise their conscience within the realm of professional practice," including the refusal to dispense medications for abortion.[75]

But evangelical Christians are not alone in forming professional faith-based organizations. Adherents to Islam have organized the Islamic Medical Association, the National Association of Muslim Lawyers, the International Muslim Association of Scientists and Engineers, and the Muslim Finance Association. The Minaret Business Association (MBA), named after the spires of an Islamic mosque, closely resembles Legatus and the Fellowship of Companies for Christ but its membership consists of wealthy Muslim business owners. MBA was founded in 2000 and has a headquarters in Chicago and chapters around the world. It too holds an annual meeting and other activities in an effort to connect faith and work, responding to the "widening gap between Islamic values and actual practices among Muslim businessmen."[76] Within Judaism, similar developments are present. There is the Shomrim Society for Jewish police officers, the Mesorah Society for Jewish psychiatrists, and the Orthodox Jewish Occupational Therapy Chavrusa, which provides opportunities to discuss faith and work as well as strategies and potential conflicts in the practicing of the profession in full accord with Jewish law. On a regional level, the Jewish Business Association of Colorado, founded in 1995, offers business owners an opportunity to meet, network, and advertise (not unlike evangelical Christian's *The Shepherd's Guide*) but the Jewish Business Association, despite its name, is open to all, regardless of religion.⁷⁷

As these examples further demonstrate, not all forms of workplace spirituality are "spiritual but not religious." Among congregations and other religious communities there are notable exemplars, but the most interesting and exciting forms of tradition-specific workplace spirituality have and continue to be developed outside the church, synagogue, and mosque. Traditional religious communities certainly might consider whether they are willing to consign workplace spirituality to life coaches, books, and corporate-sponsored spirituality; perhaps they can even co-opt the coach model and offer life coaching as a form of ministry, but it is doubtful. The silence and inactivity of the vast majority of faith communities seems to indicate their disinterest, but independent faith-based organizations may prove to be a worthy alternative. Whether parachurch organization or religiously identified professional association, these groups form the foundation of what David Miller has termed the "faith at work movement." Some have long histories, some are very new, but they are the most likely alternative to "generic" spirituality and the spiritual resources offered by a worker's employer.

Signs of a Backlash?

Yet despite the widespread cheers and support for various forms of workplace spirituality—from books to life coaches and from chaplains to faith-based businesses—there have been other voices crying foul. One of the most important critics has been Tom Peters, a management guru himself and co-author of the canonical business book *In Search of Excellence* (1982). As the author of other important management tomes and as a sought-after speaker and consultant on business innovation, Peters has been a great advocate for new and creative ways of thinking about productivity and expressing gratitude to employees, but in the 1990s he drew a sharp line separating his efforts from the workplace spirituality movement. In his nationally syndicated newspaper column Peters stated in 1993 that too much attention, even then, was devoted to workplace spirituality and efforts that, he said, "blur the borders between church and corporation." Unlike the workplace spirituality advocates, he did not see the innate connection between spirituality and creativity, writing:

> By all means let's empower, then empower some more. Those who fail to tap the imagination and curiosity of workers will fail in the viciously competitive '90s. Good riddance. But in tapping the needed imagination and curiosity, let's leave the Bible, the Koran and facile talk of spiritual leaders at home.[78]

These few words in a newspaper article titled "In Praise of the Secular Corporation" unleashed something of a firestorm. Peters reported that he received more negative responses to this column than anything else he had written—with the possible exception of criticizing Ross Perot's bid for the presidency. Peters did not back down, writing later in his subscription newsletter that he regarded workplace spirituality, even as a concept, to be revolting because it threatens human liberty and free speech by imposing religious doctrine throughout the corporate workplace.[79]

Peters may very well have been prophetic. From 1992 to 2008, the Equal Employment Opportunity Commission (EEOC) reported a significant rise in religion-based complaints of employment discrimination. Complaints during this period increased more than 135 percent from 1,388 in 1992 to 3,273 in 2008—the highest number of claims ever. Although complaints for gender and racial discrimination outnumber religion complaints by a factor of ten, complaints about race and sex have remained fairly constant over the same period while religion-based complaints have almost doubled.[80]

While workplace spirituality has grown, it also appears that some employees are pushing back through the legal system. The 1964 Civil Rights Act made religion a protected activity in the workplace, requiring that places of employment not discriminate on the basis of religion and that they make "reasonable accommodations" for religious expression in the workplace. The idea behind religious accommodation is that employers should be sensitive to the religious, beliefs, values, and identities that employees bring to the workplace. A survey by the Society for Human Resources Management found that requests for time off for religious observances were the most frequent accommodation requested, and "display of religious materials" was the second.[81] But other frequent sources of challenge for employers are the desire to wear religious clothing and certain grooming practices. For example, a Muslim woman may request to wear a hijab or head covering; a Sikh man may request to wear a turban and carry a ceremonial dagger; a conservative Christian woman may insist on wearing a skirt instead of pants; and an Orthodox Jewish man may want to continue wearing a beard. While all of these may be perfectly acceptable to some employers, it can be an issue for others who insist on uniform employee appearance because of their marketing strategy or for safety reasons.

Although the Civil Rights Act, its later amendments, and Federal regulations all call for employees to accommodate the religious expression of employees, many of the Supreme Court decisions have weakened the demands on employers. The text of the Civil Rights Act, as amended, demands that employers provide "reasonable accommodations" to an employee's religion, but it also states that no employer is required to make an accommodation that would be an "undue hardship" on the employer's business. In 1977 the definition of "undue hardship" was put to the test in a *Trans World Airlines, Inc. v. Hardison*, and it became clear that the courts found almost any hardship to be undue. Hardison was a clerk at a TWA maintenance facility when he converted to the World Wide Church of God. Because his new church celebrated the Christian Sabbath on Saturday and prohibited its adherence from Sabbath work, Hardison refused to change his schedule when another employee went on vacation. After not showing up for work on the assigned Saturday, Hardison was fired. He alleged religious discrimination, but the U.S. Supreme Court disagreed. If TWA had honored Hardison's request, it would have been forced to pay premium wages to another employee, totaling $150 in extra pay. The court ruled that this amount, even for a large corporation, was still enough to be an undue hardship.[82]

After the Hardison case, the EEOC sought to counter the notion that religious accommodation was unnecessary, clarifying what was demanded of employers even with a fairly low standard for undue hardship. But in 1986, another Supreme Court case further limited the obligation of employers by stating, if choices of accommodation are available, the employer rather than the employee has the right to choose.[83] In matters of religious accommodation, states frequently provide greater levels of accommodation than federal law. As an example, while most states long ago abandoned "blue laws," a few still have some type of law prescribing or allowing workers to choose a Sabbath. Georgia, Kentucky, and Minnesota all have some form of Sabbath observance laws, and South Carolina's law requires that any employee be granted Sunday off (Saturday if requested) even though that law exempts the entire textile industry.[84]

It is impossible to explain the exact cause of rising workplace discrimination complaints, but journalists and scholars are already developing several hypotheses. First, increasing religious diversity in the workplace may be an obvious source of tension. As the United States has become more religiously diverse, especially with immigration from Asia and Africa, the workplace has become more religiously diverse as well.[85] While growing diversity does not necessarily lead to tension or discrimination, those concerns are certainly possible, especially when religious belief has public manifestations in the workplace. James Morgan theorizes that new immigrants have not been "indoctrinated with the traditional U.S. view that expressing faith at work is inappropriate" and may in fact believe that such religious expression at work, including display of symbols and practices, is essential to faithfulness.[86] The need for space and time for Muslim prayers, the addition of a scarf or kipa to a work uniform, or a small painting of Lakshmi on a desk can all be understood as forms of workplace spirituality by the individual, but they each push boundaries and force a decision on what constitutes a "reasonable accommodation."

In response to the lack of clarity in the law as well as the legal difficulty in achieving religious accommodation, congressional leaders, beginning the in the 1970s, began to call for changes in federal law. In its most recent form, the proposed Workplace Religious Freedom Act would require that the costs of any accommodation be measured by a legally established set of factors. Thus, the bill uses language similar to the Americans with Disabilities Act (1990) to define when an accommodation is justified. The Americans with Disabilities Act requires employers to accommodate someone with a disability as long as the disability does not interfere with the "essential function" of the position; the Workplace Religious Freedom Act would similarly require that an employer provide a religious accommodation as long as an essential function is not affected.[87] While the act has been endorsed by a wide spectrum of religious denominations and groups, it has attracted an odd combination of opponents, which include the American Civil Liberties Union (ACLU) and the U.S. Chambers of Commerce. The U.S. Chambers of Commerce criticism is, predictably, that the new law would place additional and unwarranted requirements on businesses, but the ACLU complains that the Workplace Religious

Freedom Act will have too many adverse effects on third parties beyond the employer-employee relationship. While advocates have rejected their arguments, the ACLU claims that by expanding the boundaries of religious accommodation, employees would be able to justify discrimination against women, minorities, and homosexuals based on their own religious convictions, and a whole series of accommodations that have been previously rejected by the courts—from a police officer's refusal to protect an abortion clinic to an employee's request to uncover a Ku Klux Klan tattoo—could now be allowed under the proposed law's new standard.[88]

Surprisingly, the American workplace most accommodating to religious beliefs and practices is likely the U.S. Government, and as the largest employer in the country, this is worth noting. In 1997 the Clinton Administration issued the "White House Guidelines on Religious Exercise and Religious Expressions in the Federal Workplace." Even though the guidelines have neither the force of law nor even the power of official federal regulations, they do indeed outline for civilian governmental agencies rules and examples that offer great religious freedom for federal employees. Often simply clarifying current law, the guidelines explain how private religious expression is allowed in work areas, including posters or Koran reading during breaks; they explain how religious expression, speech, and invitations can be directed at fellow employees until someone is asked to stop; and they provide basic examples of what constitutes religious discrimination.[89] The heart of the guidelines is that religious expression and speech should not be treated any differently than other forms of expression and speech in the workplace. If personal displays or break-time reading materials are allowed on desks, then religious displays or reading materials must also be allowed. If employees are allowed to have a fantasy football league in the cafeteria at lunch, then employees are permitted to have a Koran study group.

In addition to accommodation of religious beliefs and practices an employee may bring to the workplace, the Civil Rights Act also prohibits discrimination based on religion in the same way that it prohibits discrimination based on race, gender, age, and national origin. This raises special concerns with respect to the rise of Christian companies. Even though an owner may identify his or her business as Christian, religious discrimination in employment is still illegal. A Christian business cannot hire only Christians, employ only Christians as managers, favor Christians in any way connected to their employment, or discriminate against non-Christian employees. For example, in the case *Blalock v. Metals Trades,* the claims of a Christian company were specifically rejected by the courts as discriminatory. When Blalock, an employee at Metals Trades, changed membership to a church different than the company's owners he received a termination letter stating:

> Larry was hired with the full knowledge and understanding that Metals Trades is a Christian Company and our rule book is the word of God, or the Bible. He was in full accord and very excited. . . . I hated to lay him off as there are all too few men willing to commit themselves to Jesus— especially salesmen. Larry's problem is that he refuses to submit himself to those in authority over him and the Bible makes it clear that we are to be in submission. Larry was let go for strictly secular reasons but the root of his problem is spiritual, as the scriptures will show.[90]

Here, the courts found a perfect example of religious discrimination be- cause the employee's religious views were the basis of his dismissal rather than a "secular" reason connected to work performance.

While not prohibited by law, the EEOC has held that any inquiry about religion during the hiring process infers a discriminatory intent.[91] But in practice, such an inquiry may not be needed by a firm that has a fish and cross on its job advertisements since the advertisement would not en- courage a Buddhist or atheist to apply. One Christian business owner has reported that in speaking to job candidates at interviews he "explain[s] to them that we're doing God's work."[92] Under the law, this is not religious discrimination, but it too may allow a Christian company to hire only Christians (and especially evangelicals) because candidates self-select this type of enterprise for employment and others opt out because of the dis- tinctively Christian atmosphere. On the job, a new set of issues emerge, including the business' need to provide religious accommodations coun- ter to the business' religious identity. In Kentucky, a Jehovah's Witness was fired from her job as a clerk when she refused to greet incoming call- ers with "Merry Christmas" during the holidays. Since the employee ex- plained that the greeting was counter to her religious beliefs and was de- nied even a minimal accommodation (e.g., saying "Good Day" instead), the court ruled that her firing was discriminatory.[93]

As a faith-based business, Chick-fil-A faces all of these issues. Because of its unique franchise agreements, Chick-fil-A's franchisees are not em- ployees but independent contractors, and some have argued that this al- lows the company to be even more inquisitive about their franchisees' lives, including their religious convictions. While employees of Chick-fil-A's corporate offices and employees of a franchisee would be covered by laws against religious discrimination, the contractual arrangement between Chick-fil-A and its "owner-operator" likely is not.[94] However, in 2002 a Muslim from Houston, Texas, sued Chick-fil-A when, he claims, he was dismissed from the franchisee program the day after he refused to offer a prayer in the name of Jesus at a training event; Chick-fil-A later settled the lawsuit for an undisclosed amount. In 2007 *Forbes* magazine reported that Chick-fil-A has been sued at least twelve times for religious discrimination going back to 1988.[95] Furthermore, Chick-fil-A lobbied against a new rule by the EEOC that would have established clearer guidelines on religious harassment, fearing that it would legally prohibit religious expression in the workplace, changing the company's identity and "mak[ing] workplaces as devoid of religious expression as the public schools."[96]

Religious harassment is an important concern related to workplace spirituality and religion in the workplace. Just as the courts have found that sexual harassment is a form of discrimination prohibited by the Civil Rights Act, religious harassment is also prohibited. But religious harassment is not exactly the same as sexual harassment since it usually involves religious speech, which is also legally protected. The problem arises when the freedom to proselytize for one's religious faith comes into conflict with the legal prohibition against religious harassment. In one well-known case, a woman opposed to abortion wore a large button with the picture of an aborted fetus and the words "stop abortion." When the woman's coworkers complained, the employer, fearing a charge of religious harassment, prohibited the woman from wearing the button, promoting a lawsuit against the employer for failing to provide a religious accommodation. Commenting on how businesses and the courts have dealt with this legal conundrum, the authors of *Religion in the Workplace* (1998) wrote,

> These cases show that the tendency to merge the secular and religious worlds can have serious consequences in workplaces of increasing diversity. While employers may not discriminate against employees who proselytize in the workplace, proselytizing activities have the potential of interfering in normal business operations and may give rise to harassment claims by employees who object to the proselytizing. Although the dividing line between permissible and unacceptable proselytizing may be difficult to locate, the courts have begun to develop basic parameters of

conduct and have upheld employers that suppress proselytizing activities that become harassing.[97]

All of this makes religion and spirituality in the workplace a matter of risk management for companies, requiring policies and procedures as well as management training to protect the organization from the liability of civil lawsuit by an employee or criminal action by a state or the EEOC.

The use of corporate chaplains by businesses would appear to be one of the risks that a company might want to avoid, but that does not appear to have reduced interest in them. Interviewed for the *New York Times*, an attorney for the EEOC said that no employee can ever be required to speak with a chaplain (that would likely be harassment), but having a chaplain around at the workplace is not, in itself, illegal.[98] Ironically, rather than fearing lawsuits, one of the loudest complaints against corporate chaplains is that they are a ploy to reduce legal liability. Since chaplains, unlike licensed counselors that a company may employ, are not bound by confidentiality rules, they can provide a direct line of communication to company management about employee complaints or union activism.[99] Coupled with their general work to improve morale, a chaplain may also encourage an employee to resolve a dispute informally instead of seeking legal action against the company even when a lawsuit may be justified. *Christian Century* reached these same conclusions more than fifty years ago, worrying that companies would use religion for manipulative purposes and prostitute the Christian ministry.[100] More recently, the chaplains at Tyson Foods have come under fire for promoting the company's charitable work and care for employees at the same time the company was under investigation for child labor violations and hiring undocumented workers.[101]

One of the more challenging questions is how spiritual practices are being received when they are presented under the guise of professional development programs. Meditation, yoga, the writing of personal mission statements, and even Native American spiritual practices have been used for team building and tapping the creative processes of employees.[102] To many employees, these practices may be inoffensive and fit naturally into a "spiritual but not religious" lifestyle. But to a fundamentalist Christian or a devout Muslim, these same practices may be the very essence of idolatry. If the question is whether employees compelled to participate in these practices are engaging in religious activity, the EEOC would answer yes.

The EEOC has defined the religious protection of the Civil Rights Act to include "moral or ethical beliefs" and any other sincere belief that an individual might hold—whether it is found among a religious group or not.[103] Since the distinction between spirituality and religion has no meaning as a matter of law, "spiritual but not religious" practices in the workplace (and in education) may lead to the same calls for accommodation and complaints of harassment or discrimination that more traditional forms of religious practice and belief might cause.

In 1992 a court case in Washington State raised these very issues. A manager at a car dealership enrolled in a professional development program paid by his employer. After beginning the courses, titled "New Age Thinking to Increase Dealer Profitability," the employee concluded the course was anti-Christian and in violation of his Christian beliefs. He stopped participating in the course and was soon terminated by his employer, leading to a lawsuit charging religious discrimination. While the courts found that the employee's termination was not the direct result of his opposition to the training program, the case speaks clearly to the issue.[104] An employee who refuses to participate in corporate-sponsored spirituality—even when it is presented as religiously neutral and for professional development—if fired, demoted, or denied promotion, may have a legitimate religious discrimination complaint. More significantly, for business leaders and managers, as spiritual practices sneak into corporate America through mainstream training programs, it may be increasingly difficult to parse out what is religious or spiritual and what is legitimate and truly "secular" professional and organizational development.

While law and satire may appear disparate, they are both means of protest, and humor has become another way of responding to the workplace spirituality trend. As an example, Comedy Central's *The Daily Show* has ridiculed life coaching as the equivalent of paying to have a friend. In the show's "Trend Spotting" segment on March 20, 2006, correspondent Demetri Martin also mocked the loose training of life coaches who often receive their education online, in programs of dubious quality. Eight years earlier, Christopher Buckley, author of the dark comedy best seller *Thank You for Smoking*, teamed with John Tierney to mock the gurus who yoke spiritual and financial success in their book *God Is My Broker*. The book tells the story of a failing monastery whose wine tastes like used motor oil; the monastery becomes divided over which guru's advice to follow as they seek business and spiritual excellence.

However, the greatest bellwether of the reaction against workplace spirituality can be found in *Dilbert*, the cartoon that parodies all corporate and managerial fads. Scott Adams, *Dilbert's* creator, has made repeated references to workplace spirituality themes over the last ten years. The character Dogbert has been the frequent focus of these parodies, presenting himself to the pointy-headed manager as a consultant who "can make your employees more creative and spiritually fulfilled" not just via poetry and dance but also as a feng shui consultant who identifies evil spirits in the office. Feng shui has been a particular object of Adams's scorn with at least four strips ridiculing it. Office prayer has also been ridiculed at least twice with a character in one dressed as a witchdoctor asking for "permission to hold daily prayer services in a conference room" and promising to "do it before work" and "of course clean up any blood."[105]

Julie Davis, a communication theorist, has called *Dilbert* a "supportive comic strip" because it allows people "to vent their frustrations with the system" and "cope with their problems." When readers see issues they face described in a *Dilbert* comic strip they have a sense of solidarity with others, and they have a sense that their subjective feelings about the workplace have greater validity.[106] Six years after Adams began the *Dilbert* strip, he was downsized from his own job at Pacific Bell, and since then he has relied on letters and input from his readers for the content of the strip.[107] While it is impossible to know for certain, the presence of workplace spirituality in *Dilbert* would indicate that Adams is getting feedback on its practices in his reader mail, and readers are longing for the type of solidarity that Davis describes. While many practitioners of workplace spirituality in its different forms likely find Adams's treatment to be insulting, *Dilbert's* attention to these themes indicates workplace spirituality's "arrival" as a cultural trend. Parody may not be the highest form of flattery, but it is only warranted (and funny) when enough people understand the basic premise. Spirituality in the workplace has crossed that threshold and is now a significant theme in both American religious life and business practice.

7

The Future of Workplace
Spirituality

It could have been the plot of almost any modern-day romance novel. A couple, living in married bliss, invites two guests for an extended stay. The first is a friend and former military officer, unemployed but highly skilled, who the husband hopes can assist with a major home renovation and landscaping project. The husband looks forward to the male comradery and help with design and construction, but he also wants to aide his friend's spirit as well as his pocketbook in a time of need. The second guest is the wife's niece for whom she has great affection undoubtedly due to love for her late sister. The niece resembles the sister, and the wife is heartbroken that her niece has been sent to a boarding school where the staff is uncaring, and where the niece fails to thrive. Soon all four of the novel's characters are living together, and the couple's shared life begins to unravel. Rather than a new relationship between the two guests, the husband develops affections for his wife's niece, and the wife falls in love with her husband's friend. Tragedy ensues.

This novel by Johann Wolfgang von Goethe is set in the nineteenth century on a large estate, yet the interesting conversation among the characters is not about farming but chemistry—the chemistry of elements and the chemistry of love. Goethe's title for the novel, *Elective Affinities*, tells it too. Explaining the complexities of chemical reactions, the visiting friend also foreshadows what will happen between all of them. He says,

Imagine an A so closely connected with a B that the two cannot be separated by any means, not even by force; and imagine a C in the same relation to a D. Now bring the two pairs into contact. A will fling itself on D, and C on B, without our being able to say which left the other first, or which first combined itself with the other.[1]

In addition to his literary pursuits, Goethe also explored the sciences, and in that novel he borrowed a relatively new term from chemistry and applied it to a completely different realm of human activity. Just as elements have idiosyncratic forms of attraction, Goethe implied, so might humans.[2]

While Goethe borrowed the term from natural science, most likely Max Weber learned of it through reading Goethe. The term "elective affinity" had never before been employed in the emerging social sciences, but as early as 1904 Weber began using it regularly, appreciating its power to explain and interpret the complex relationships between ideas, institutions, and behaviors.[3] Weber was especially intrigued by the many elective affinities between theological doctrines and forms of economic organization, and this chemical-turned-literary term offered him a means in the social sciences to explore connections that could not simply be described as cause and effect. Rather, the metaphor is more magnetic.

Each of the previous chapters has described how religion and business are finding new elective affinities—magnetic attractions that allow them to come together in specific developments—but in this concluding chapter, the focus changes from the past and present to the future. Will the workplace spirituality movement continue? What will it be like? Where will new elective affinities emerge? Within these developments are also new examples and understandings of religion itself. While religion and spirituality in America are being de-centered from traditional religious institutions, they are not totally free floating and have found other institutional homes. The corporate office, the local bookstore, the family enterprise, and the university's business department have already provided the setting for the new religious movement of workplace spirituality, but it is a movement in tension with itself because it can easily emerge from opposing religious worldviews. This chapter then also places the workplace spirituality movement within the context of American religious life and assesses its future impact on businesses, higher education, and traditional religious communities.

The New Generation of Workplace Spirituality

As we learned in chapter 2, the Baby-Boom generation has been instrumental in the increased interest in workplace spirituality. Raised in a period of economic abundance, shaped by the social change of the 1960s and 1970s, and benefiting massively from higher education, the Baby Boomers shaped both the American workplace and American religion. The Boomers were also the largest generational grouping ever seen in American history, and their sheer size continues to allow them to exert great influence on American work, religion, and culture. In 2008, however, the first group of Boomers reached the age of sixty-five, and as Boomers begin to retire, trend watchers are looking at the succeeding generations to predict what changes may be in store. Generation X, which followed the Boomers (born 1961–81), attracted only limited attention because they are a much smaller group, the result of a significant decline in birth rates. It is the generation following the Xers that has garnered the real interest. They have been called Generation Y, Generation Next, and the Boomer Babies, but Millennials is a term that has stuck, and this is the group most likely to shape the future of workplace spirituality.[4]

Almost all of the indicators point to new developments over the next two decades. The Millennials surpass the Boomers in size, are more diverse than any generation in American history, and were changing American culture already in the 1990s when they were just children and teens. More than 35 percent of Millennials are nonwhite or Latino, and due to the higher fertility rates of recent immigrants, 20 percent of Millennials are second-generation Americans. They value their parents immensely, and they have spent more time with their parents than preceding generations even though it is the generation with the highest percentage of working mothers. Their lives as children included more time in organized sports and less in spontaneous neighborhood activities, less time at church and more time at school. And in their teen years Millennials were more likely to be paid for chores at home and less likely to have outside jobs. Perhaps as a result, 40 percent of Millennial teens reported that in the future they would value working at home. They also reported that they would place less emphasis on personal recognition in their work and more on helping others.[5]

Studies of Millennials have also revealed the distinct characteristics of their religious or spiritual identity, and what may be most striking overall is their reverence. Millennial teens have cited faith or spirituality as second only to their parents among the important influences on their lives.[6] And 51 percent of Millennial teens said that faith was "very important" or extremely important" in "shaping daily life" while 49 percent reported that faith was "very important" or extremely important" in "shaping major life decisions."[7] Yet despite easily professed identities, the conclusion reached by Christian Smith from his survey research on teens was that the religion of most Millennials could be named "moralistic therapeutic deism." It is a faith concerned about morality but not sin, believing that religion and morality should help people even though God does not intervene in history. "In short," Smith writes, "God is something like a combination Divine Butler and Cosmic Therapist: he is always on call, takes care of any problems that arise, professionally helps his people to feel better about themselves, and does not become too personally involved in the process."[8]

Over the past five years, authors and business leaders have also become almost obsessed about a feared "clash of generations" at work, worrying that Boomers, Xers and Millennials will not be able to labor together productively or that the Millennials will be unable to replace the highly productive Boomers. A common complaint about Millennial workers is that their sheltered and regimented childhoods lead them to seek high levels of structure and supervision at work, perhaps dampening creativity. Soon after David Brooks described Bobos (see chap. 1), he also lamented about the Millennials as the "organization kids" whose time for play was even scheduled with "dates."[9] At work, these same kids are now young adults who want their supervisors to offer clear and specific instructions, "check in" regularly, and offer frequent praise. Millennial workers are also reported to be almost completely conflict-avoidant in the workplace in contrast to their Boomer and Xer co-workers who "tend to be more edgy and abrupt, and have worked in business environments where yelling in a meeting wasn't all that strange."[10] The strong relationship with parents can even manifest itself on the job with parents becoming actively involved in the employee-employer relationship, negotiating hours or pay, and even accompanying their children to interviews.[11]

But there are also several positive developments likely to emerge from the Millennials joining the workforce, and many of these relate to themes that have become part of the workplace spirituality movement inaugurated by the Boomers. A desire for "balance" is frequently invoked when referring to the Millennials at work, and this echoes a Boomer theme as well as the workplace spirituality movement's quest for "holism." In *Millennials Rising*, the forecast of Neil Howe and William Strauss is that "young workers will demand that employers adjust to the needs of workers who wish to build careers and families at the same time and to lead lower-stress lives than their parents did."[12] But what this exactly means is still unclear, and employers may not yet need to fear that Millennials will always want to leave work early. While Millennials may describe their desire for work-life balance, their responses are not compared to previous college graduates of earlier generations; instead, they are compared to attitudes of current workers who may have a better understanding of what the concept really means.[13] Regardless, the quest for balance could take many forms, including a greater focus on the Sabbath as well as less time and interest in work as a place of meaning.

A second likely trend of Millennials in the workplace will be the increased importance of teams and collaborative work environments. From the time they were small children, Millennials have had a team orientation. Surveys show that they see individualism as a serious social problem, and their experiences with organized sports, school projects, and community service have taught them to work collaboratively.[14] As described in chapter 2, the desire to develop relationships of trust and collaboration, often around storytelling and shared spiritual practices, has been an element of workplace spirituality. Unlike the Boomers, who rebelled from community norms only to desire social bonds later, Millennials have had this orientation from the beginning, which seems to be unique with this particular group. Millennials want and expect deep personal and communal relationships in their work, and consultants are encouraging companies to institutionalize these practices through mentoring programs and casual office environments as well as management philosophies that encourage bosses to be "pleasant and easy to get along with."[15]

Millennials have also grown up in an environment in which religion and spirituality were readily discussed and expressed—from politics to Oprah—and so they are very open to both religious diversity and opportunities for conversation about beliefs. Several surveys have reported that Millennials informally "talk about religion" regularly with their friends, and while Millennials may understand faith or spirituality to be "personal," they do not seem to equate that with "private."[16] Even more significant is that most inter-religious contact for young people is now occurring at work and not through friendships or religious settings. To some degree, the work setting makes inter-religious interaction more unavoidable since people are not as free to select their workplace colleagues. The evidence also reveals that inter-religious contact at work reduces religious orthodoxy.[17] In other words, the workplace, while not entirely a religious melting pot, can make religious adherents less likely to believe that their convictions are absolute and universal. As a result, this combination of religious diversity at work and the Millennials' greater openness to conversation about faith will likely create greater opportunities for inter-religious dialogue and understanding.

If it was not already clear that there is no returning to Taylor's scientific management, the last trend of Millennial workers confirms it: Millennials want to have fun at work, and they want their work to have meaning. Having fun at work may seem obvious enough, but one consultant encourages employers to conduct surveys to learn whether workers find their work environment to be fun and enjoyable.[18] Another consultant recommends a regular "fun budget" for offices as well as "creativity parties" for group brainstorming.[19] The search for meaning, however, may be more complicated. It can include fun, but it also can include opportunities to volunteer through work and a focus on a company's social responsibility. Researchers note that Millennials more than any other generation have experience with community service, and "more than half of workers in their twenties prefer employment at companies that provide volunteer opportunities."[20] As consumers, Millennials also indicate by large margins that they are more likely to buy products from a company and more likely to trust the company itself when it exhibits strong social and environmental commitments.[21] Claiming a major transition in values, Tim Sanders, a former Yahoo! Executive, claims in his book *Saving the World at Work* that multiple surveys are indicating how young people are making social issues prominent in their job searches. They are seeking out responsible companies, avoiding those with poor social and environmental records, and even taking lower salaries when given a choice between employers practicing social responsibility and those who are not.[22]

Yet most significantly, Millennials view themselves as special with a generational sense of calling and purpose. Howe and Strauss contend that,

> Boomers gained fame as the generation that asked "why"? Gen Xers earned theirs as the generation that made ironic fun of such big questions ("why ask why?"). Millennials are showing themselves to be the generation to ask the question "why not?" They assume that the big questions will require big answers—answers that work, answers that they themselves (more than other generations) will have to implement.[23]

Millennials want to understand how their work fits into the big picture of the company, and how the company serves the social goals they value. At the same time, one forecaster concludes that the inability for Millennials to find jobs that support their social goals will further increase the demand for life coaches and other career guides.[24] Overall, combining their high regard for spirituality generally and a practical or applied spirituality more specifically, it is likely that Millennials will at least bring attitudes receptive to workplace spirituality if not an aggressive seeking of religious and spiritual meaning.

In addition to their preexisting theism and team spirit, what the Millennials also bring to the table is the potential to transform workplace spirituality through technology. When Martin Luther began his engagement with the theological concept of vocation and the possibility of faith and everyday work being connected, he had a powerful new tool at his disposal: the printing press. Scholars of the Reformation have repeatedly pointed to the emergence of the movable type press and the widespread availability of books and other print resources as a critical factor in the spread of Protestant ideas, and disseminating throughout these ideas was the theology of vocation.[25] In our day and time it is no secret that the new media is the Internet, and since it is already making an impact on religion generally, it will likely be an important force in the future of workplace spirituality as well. As Brenda Brasher has written, "Using a computer for online religious activity—an intriguing, albeit marginal pastime to which interactive computing was put in the late twentieth century—could become the dominant form of religion and religious experience in the next century. If so, religious expression and experience will change dramatically."[26] And the degree to which workplace spirituality is one aspect of religious expression, that will change too.

In thinking about the development of the Internet and its relationship to religion, Christopher Helland has sought to distinguish "religion online" and "online religion." Whereas the former describes a process of information dispersal, not unlike the printing press of five centuries earlier, the latter attempts to capture the way the Internet allows its users to participate in religious activity and not just read or learn about it.[27] Of course, many websites do both, and they likely want to do both. This is certainly the case with Belief.net, perhaps the most well known, ecumenical religious website. Belief.net offers a combination of articles, discussion "threads," prayer circles, and memorials.[28] There is even an online quiz— the "belief-o-matic"—that allows people to learn how their personal convictions fit within a wide religious pantheon.

As it has done with almost all other types of information, the Internet will undoubtedly become, if it has not already, a major source for information about religion.[29] But this is not what has most interested and troubled commentators. Instead, it is the significance of online interaction and whether this interaction will replace traditional forms of religious community. The idea that religious community should be a form of face-to-face interaction is not anything new, but it has had to be articulated in a way never necessary before. The tendency to characterize Internet interactions as "virtual" carries with it the assumption that it is not real in the same way face-to-face interactions are. But those who are a part of online interactive communities do not consider them any less real, and they frequently complement existing face-to-face relationships rather than replacing them. Studies have also shown that despite fears of superficiality and deception, online relationships have also been effective in providing emotional support.[30] The founder of Belief.net, Steve Waldman, notes that the "web offers a paradox: its intimacy often leads to intimacy. People open up, reveal things about themselves, and pose questions they'd otherwise be embarrassed to ask."[31] This may be especially true for youth and young adults, the so-called digital natives who, when they were growing up, spent twice as much time playing video games as they did reading and for whom "computer games, email, the Internet, cell phones and instant messaging are integral parts of their lives."[32]

Survey research among young adults indicates that the vast majority who seek religious or spiritual information on the Internet are already religiously committed and part of traditional forms of religious communities. Among those who seek religious information online, 24 percent reported that they did so several times a week, and another 38 percent were online several times per month. But more striking was that 85 percent were members of a religious community, 85 percent reported they prayed or mediated daily, and 75 percent attended worship services at least once a week. Based on this evidence, the sociologist Robert Wuthnow concluded that religious "seeking" online was a supplement to traditional religious community and traditional sources of religious information.[33] But as we saw in chapter 4, the religious bookstore often serves very similar purposes. Both the Internet and the bookstore allow religious seekers to find information not available in traditional religious communities, perhaps because the information is unorthodox or because it is too specialized. Online communities also have the potential to unite believers who share spiritual or religious interests but have not found others with similar interests in their geographic area.[34] Either way, the Internet provides a new and potentially unlimited spiritual marketplace as well as a venue for expressions of workplace spirituality.

Workplace spirituality already has a substantial presence online. The clearest examples are in the "religion online" category of information and resources, and this is to be expected as Boomers have utilized the Internet as an alternative communication medium. The various parachurch groups offer the clearest examples of these informational uses of the Internet. For example, the Fellowship of Companies for Christ has an extensive website with resources, organization information, and details about groups and events. However, the website serves only to lead its readers to face-to-face programs like the Business Leadership Groups or the organization's regional and national conferences. The same could be said for the relatively simple website by the Coalition for Ministry in Daily life as well as congregational websites that describe and promote various types of groups and educational activities. New forms of technology are also allowing for new forms of media like podcasts and e-books, and a few books in the *Jesus, CEO* series can already be downloaded as podcasts. Amazon.com allows readers to not only submit their personal reviews of books, like *Jesus, CEO*, which has more than fifty customer reviews, but also to create book lists on certain themes, including workplace spirituality. But now Amazon.com is attempting to move beyond this one-way communication to something more interactive.

The more interactive uses of the Internet, most recently termed Web 2.0, are beginning to offer opportunities for workplace spirituality, but certainly this is the greatest area for potential growth. Posts on blogs about workplace spirituality are plentiful, and the next generation of FCC's Business Leadership Groups could easily be a social networking site or a group on MySpace.com. An example on this cutting edge has been Scrupples.net founded by Mike McLoughlin in 2002. With over 2,500 users, the self-described mission of Scrupples (an acronym for Serve Christ Radically in an Uncompromising People Loving Entrepreneurial Spirit) is to serve "all Christians in the marketplace who walk out their faith in difficult and challenging circumstances . . . they put their faith on the line as they serve God and others in the marketplace."[35] While not all discussion groups and threads have remained current, it provides an interesting venue and model for evangelical Christians especially to engage one another on issues such as business ethics, entrepreneurship, and workplace prayer.[36] An even larger presence on the web is MyChurch.org, a social networking site that offers the potential to connect individuals, congregations, and parachurch ministries. As more of these digital natives become curious about workplace spirituality, it is likely that online communities will offer a new, virtual dimension to the workplace spirituality movement. Perhaps the new Koran study at an office will be online rather than around a lunch table, or online communities for faith discussions could be supported by a corporate website and serve employees stationed all over the world. Millennials will likely seek and create these new opportunities as they increasingly enter the workforce over the next decade.

Social and Environmental Responsibility

When Patricia Aburdene predicted the rise of spirituality in business in *Megatrends 2010*, the context she described was a new "conscious capitalism" where workplace spirituality and socially and environmentally responsible management would thrive together.[37] Philosophers and theologians have argued for centuries, against each other and between themselves, about the relationship between ethics and theism or spirituality, and certainly there can be social responsibility in businesses and other organizations without any explicit mention of God and the divine. The continued interest in and growth of socially and environmentally responsible workplaces will offer additional opportunities for Americans to live out their spiritual values and convictions in explicit and implicit ways. The type of corporate mission and culture that supports this kind of social responsibility is the same model that is hospitable and perhaps even encouraging of authentic expressions of faith and spirituality at work.

Tim Sanders describes the changes taking place in American business as nothing less than a revolution. It is, he argues, a "responsibility revolution" that makes a dramatic change with past practices and moves American business in a completely new direction toward a full-scale adoption of policies, practices, cultures, and attitudes that support social and environmental responsibility. Other periods of business transformation, from the Industrial Revolution of the nineteenth century to the "quality revolution" of the 1980s and 1990s, provide the models for Sanders, and he makes the case that the responsibility revolution is following a similar set of five steps that have guided other periods of significant change.[38] In the first two steps, new developments like the Internet and, more importantly, new values begin to make an impact on how commerce is conducted. Corporate scandals, a growing recognition of environmental crisis, a renewed desire for community in the midst of a "war on terror" set the stage for people wanting to make a difference and live their values as consumers, investors, and workers. As noted with the Millennials especially, increasing numbers of Americans appear to exercise greater care in their shopping, buying products that are environmentally sensitive and from socially responsible companies, and the amount of money invested in designated socially responsible mutual funds as well as other mutual funds with "screens" to weed out irresponsible companies has exploded. In 2003, $150 billion in assets were held by socially responsible mutual funds like Pax World Fund, Calvert Group, an increase from just $150 million in 1971 and a 50 percent increase from just two years earlier. Sanders's conclusion from these developments is that the combination of socially conscious consumers and investors can thus exert great force in two directions on business practice.

The third force Sanders foresees is employees, and he joins the concerns of consumers and investors with what he says is the desire by workers to be socially and environmentally responsible. He writes,

A final note about the New Order—for many of you it will bring welcome news. Here's why: You may already be practicing socially responsible behavior at home. You recycle trash, think about fuel emissions, volunteer to help gather toys for tots at Christmas, or shop at the local farmers' market and buy from local merchants. Maybe you've been frustrated that you've had to leave those sensibilities at home; by the time you arrive at your job, you're no longer someone who thinks about good, but someone who thinks only about work. Maybe you've reluctantly swallowed your conscience from nine to five. One of the greatest blessings of the Responsibility Revolution is that you'll be able to take your values to work with you instead of leaving them at home. In fact, your company desperately needs you to do so. The Responsibility Revolution's unique offer is this: the chance to lead a purpose-driven life, 24/7/365.[39]

Oddly borrowing from evangelical Rick Warren in support of his argument, Sanders concludes that change is clearly in the making.

Recognizing the changing circumstances and embracing the new values, a group of pioneering innovators emerges in a business revolution, argues Sanders, and this has been no exception in the area of social and environmental responsibility. In chapter 2 we saw how Tom Chappell of Tom's of Maine, Ben Cohen and Jerry Greenfield of Ben & Jerry's Homemade Ice

Cream, Max DePree of Herman Miller Furniture, and Howard Schulz of Starbucks Coffee were described as being on this cutting edge, and several other companies and their founders could be added to the list. Sanders names Aveda hair and personal care products and its founder Horst Rechelbacher as well as Patagonia and its founder Yvon Chouinard.[40] Julius Walls Jr., CEO of Greyston Bakery in New York has been recognized for his efforts to hire the homeless and unemployed—people who may previously have been unemployable because of a history of crime, prison, or drug abuse.[41] Ray Anderson of Interface Carpets is a frequent speaker and author on community and environmental responsibility in business because of his efforts to eliminate waste and make his carpet factories carbon neutral.[42] Timberland, the maker of boots and clothes, and its CEO Nathan Swartz are known for their many charitable works but also for the strict code of conduct they impose on their suppliers to prevent worker exploitation and child labor.[43] And even more could be named.

Either by the descriptions offered about them or, quite commonly, by their own business autobiographies, these pioneers become management gurus in the "hero managers" vein. There is clearly an interest in and market for stories about those who create and successfully operate socially and environmentally responsible businesses. Chouinard (*Let My People Go Surfing*), Ray Anderson (*Mid-Course Correction*), and Tom Chappell (*The Soul of a Business*), and Ben Cohen and Jerry Greenfield (*Ben & Jerry's: The Inside Scoop*) are all examples of this kind of hero manager. Perhaps it is because, in Sanders's terms, people are curious about the front-line business revolutionaries and how commerce will be transformed, or perhaps it is hope for an alternative approach to business, even though the reader may never be able to have the same experience at work. The motivation for buying a pioneer's business biography or autobiography may not be entirely known, but the market for such books seem insatiable.

The terms and language used by leaders, advocates, and books related to corporate social responsibility are foreign to traditional business language. No longer is there the single "bottom line" of financial results, but there is also a "double bottom line," calculating financial returns and community impacts, and a "triple bottom line" that measures outcomes related to "people, planet, and profits." Instead of businesses being "profit-driven," they are (or should be) "values-driven."[44] There are entrepreneurs, and then there are "social entrepreneurs" who seek to harness the power of capitalism and profit-making for solving social and environmental problems. They also vary on whether they engage spirituality and religion in describing their work and motivation, with some naming explicitly religious themes (Timberland's Swartz and his practice of Orthodox Judaism), others expressing themselves as "spiritual but not religious" (Interface's Anderson), and still others seeking to avoid any mention of spirituality or religion and only affirming their commitment to the social good and environmental sustainability. The Social Ventures Network, an organization of "pioneers" in the area of social and environmental responsibility in business founded in 1987, posed a question on its blog about the role of spirituality, and the subject proved divisive despite their shared, overarching social goals.[45]

Although Sanders and others are clearly playing the role of futurists, predicting the new direction of American business by reading the signs of the times, their cheerleading for social and environmental responsibility as well as the proselytizing tone of the pioneers-turned-hero-managers needs to be tempered by more sober observations. The realities of community and environmental responsibility may not be equal to all of the hype. In what may be the only comprehensive and data-driven look at the "responsibility revolution," David Vogel of the University of California's Hass School of Business argues in *The Market for Virtue* that the social responsibility movement is making only limited impact on American commerce overall. Even more, Vogel concludes, it is impossible to claim, universally, that "doing well" environmentally and socially always leads to "doing good" economically in either the short- or long-term. Despite saying that they prefer socially conscious companies, the vast majority of consumers do not make socially conscious choices when they actually buy; despite saying that they prefer socially conscious firms for employment, there is no evidence that social responsibility helps companies in recruiting or retaining employees. There is also little to be gained by socially responsible investing because, again overall, the financial markets do not reward social responsibility nor do they penalize irresponsibility.[46] In fact, some of the best-known socially responsible companies of the 1990s, including Ben & Jerry's Homemade and The Body Shop, were bought when profits and shareholder values—more traditional measures of success—lagged, and Anderson's Interface Carpet has been unprofitable for some time. This has led some to conclude that socially responsible firms may do better if they are privately held and not subject to the logic of the stock markets (and studies of success like Vogel's) that excludes all but financial considerations.[47]

Vogel does not conclude that corporate social responsibility is a bad idea, but he wants to ensure that the enthusiasm does not overshadow the facts. Perhaps more importantly, Vogel emphasizes that for some companies, social responsibility is a direct benefit because it "is part of their corporate strategy and business identity: it is a way for them to differentiate themselves from their competitors and is often linked to their strategies for attracting and retaining customers or employees." A second category of firms, corporations like McDonalds, Nike, or Wal-Mart, can also benefit from corporate social responsibility because they want to avoid being targeted by shareholder and consumer activists. In other words, while organizations like Patagonia want to be distinguished by their corporate virtue, other organizations choose to practice greater social and environmental responsibility precisely to avoid being distinguished and having their brands tarnished.[48] In a strange hybrid of the two, a third option now developing is large corporations with no clear reputation for social responsibility (or irresponsibility, for that matter) buying smaller, more environmentally and socially aware businesses. As examples, Colgate-Palmolive purchased Tom's of Maine, and Green and Black, a firm that buys and sells Fair Trade chocolate, was bought by the British conglomerate Cadbury Schweppes.[49] As a result, social responsibility can become one among many strategies for market share and corporate success, but that does not make it a revolution poised to take over American business culture. In fact, Vogel fears that all the hype and enthusiasm over corporate environmental and social responsibility will distract from the forms of governmental regulation that really change business behavior and even provide the best climate for voluntary regulation through corporate environmental and social responsibility movements.[50]

Yet Vogel's analysis may tell us the most about the relationship between spirituality and the many advocates, supporters, and pioneering practitioners of corporate and environmental responsibility. While in some individual cases there may be elective affinities between certain beliefs and specific socially responsible practices, more appropriately the practices and convictions related to environmental and social responsibility are best understood as a system of beliefs in and of themselves. As *Fortune* magazine writer Mark Gunther states, they have *faith*. "Faith provides the fuel that energizes these people as they strive to do business better. Some have faith in God. Others do not. But all of them have faith in the goodness of people, faith in the possibility of change and, perhaps most surprising, faith that corporations can become a powerful force for good in the world."[51] And if their convictions are truly faith-driven, then neither Vogel's analysis nor any other collection of facts and figures will persuade them otherwise.

Notably, the first part of Sanders's book draws on a term from politics—revolution—, but he concludes the book with themes from theology. He describes the need to "evangelize" (his term) about the difference social and environmental practices in business are already making, and he hopes to "convert" (again his term) other business leaders to the cause.[52] The biographical and autobiographical books on environmental and social responsibility are nothing less than conversion narratives or testimonies that explain how the business leader came to see the light and join the faithful, and like all other testimonies, whether that of Paul on the road to Damascus or a sinner at a revival, their purpose is to edify and call others to repentance and conversion. The kingdom, they believe, is coming, but it is a new way of doing business that will save the world.

Workplace Spirituality and the Changing Character of American Religion

Salvation can be a tricky idea. A century ago Max Weber observed that affluent groups tended to be not very interested in religious notions of salvation, leading prophets and redeemers over the centuries and across the world's religions to distrust wealth, its acquisition, and its use. The two highest states for salvation religions have always been rebirth and redemption, but one's views about what redemption might be have close ties to one's current (or perceived) status.[53] Those in economic want foresee salvation as milk and honey. Those who are economically stable or prosperous might only fear environmental calamity, and so they can understand salvation very differently, perhaps using terms like "sustainability" in the same way the poor might speak of heavenly mansions and streets paved with gold.

From his study of both comparative religion and economic activity, Weber concluded that the inherent problems religious traditions have with economic life provide only two paths to salvation.[54] The first is a form of asceticism, but it is an "inner-worldly asceticism" in which the believer simultaneously rejects the allure and benefits of worldly possessions while plunging into the world as an instrument of god. It is from this approach that religious understandings of vocation and calling emerged. The believer "feels himself to be a warrior on behalf of god" who seeks to engage the world and even transform it according to god's will.[55] This was precisely what Martin Luther and the other Protestant reformers imagined, but Weber also saw it in the caste system of India; there, too, the people understood their place and related work as divinely appointed.[56] In contrast, the other approach Weber described was defined by inactivity and, as much as possible, a withdrawal from the world. He likened this approach to that of the contemplative mystic who rejects the world and seeks to live apart, if no other way than psychologically. The mystic is "other-worldly," finding spiritual or religious meaning outside this world and longing for the realm of the divine. But despite their shared suspicion of worldly activity as a threat to devotion and faith, practitioners of one approach categorically reject the other. The conflict is inevitable, says Weber,

> From the standpoint of a contemplative mystic, the ascetic appears, by virtue of his transcendental self-maceration and struggles, and especially by virtue of his ascetically rationalized conduct within the world, to be forever involved in all the burdens of created things, confronting insoluble tensions between violence and generosity, between empirical reality and love. The ascetic is therefore regarded as permanently alienated from unity with god, and as forced into contradictions and compromises that are alien to salvation. But from the converse standpoint of the ascetic, the contemplative mystic appears not to be thinking of god, the enhancement of his kingdom and glory, or the fulfillment of his will, but rather to be thinking exclusively about himself. Therefore the mystic lives in everlasting inconsistency, since by reason of the very fact that he is alive he must inevitably provide for the maintenance of his own life. This is particularly true when the contemplative mystic lives within the world and its institutions.[57]

The ascetic can thus find some religious or spiritual meaning in work, and elective affinities are possible because faith and economic life intersect. But for the mystic, work is something that must be endured, if it is necessary at all, until contemplation can be resumed. Weber saw no middle ground.

Nonetheless, times change and so do economic systems as well as religious and spiritual practices. In 1998, the sociologist Robert Wuthnow claimed that the search for salvation and religious meaning in the United States had twice been reoriented since Weber's analysis in the early twentieth century. In order to make his point, Wuthnow fashioned a narrative of American religious history that made the 1950s the high point for a "spirituality of dwelling" in *After Heaven: Spirituality in America Since the 1950s*. The nineteenth-century religious landscape of the United States was quite diverse with an odd collection of religious communities, spiritualists, and mind power adherents, but in 1956 church membership totaled 80 percent of all Americans—the highest level in history. From this, Wuthnow concluded that religious leaders of the mid-twentieth century convinced the American public that congregational membership and congregational participation, "dwelling" Wuthnow called it, was the highest form of spiritual expression. Congregations thus held something close to a monopoly on spirituality and religious life.[58]

In many respects, the dwelling that Wuthnow described was a form of culturally enforced mysticism where the religious congregation was a place apart from the world and from the rest of life. It was sacred space while everything else was profane, and for that reason a congregation could be understood and called a "sanctuary," a place for the contemplation of God in worship and for clearly identifiable religious or spiritual activities. In the postwar period, church construction boomed, distinctions in religious practices based on economic class were made uniform, and to be outside "organized religion" was tantamount to being without faith altogether—a serious problem in an age of conformity and fears of godless communism.[59] While Weber described the mystic not as "dwelling in" but as "possessing" the holy, the metaphors are related because they place or locate the divine in a fixed way, in contrast to the inner-worldly ascetic, whose relationship to the holy is always defined by action.[60]

This was undoubtedly disappointing to the leaders of the World Council of Churches who, after World War II, envisioned the Christian life as a full engagement in the world, recovering and renewing vocation as a theological ideal. Yet this did not happen, and so the 1950s and 1960s saw a small group of marginalized voices attempting to be prophetic, all to no avail, about the need for greater engagement between faith and work. In the same sort of conflict that Weber said was always present, one duo of this-worldly ascetic authors equated the mystical age of "dwelling" with paralysis and being "God's frozen people."[61] The critics called for a Christianity of action, and Wuthnow concluded that this same period also bred a spiritual shallowness, in part, because it compartmentalized faith from other aspects of life, including no relationship between faith and work.[62]

The second change after Weber was a significant transformation "from dwelling to seeking" in which American religion was reoriented away from traditional religious communities and toward a wider, more diverse collection of places, practices, and experiences (ibid., 40). Here Wuthnow's narrative was not unlike Wade Clark Roof's *A Generation of Seekers*, published only a few years earlier, but while Roof was primarily interested in the changing pattern of religion and spirituality among the Baby Boomers, Wuthnow claimed to see a larger transformation in American life and culture beginning in the 1960s. Whereas before Americans sought to find God in identified sacred places, Wuthnow asserted "that people have been losing faith in a metaphysics that can make them feel at home in the universe and that they increasingly negotiate among competing glimpses of the sacred, seeking partial knowledge and practical wisdom" (ibid., 3). To explain the complexity of what was happening, Wuthnow resorted to a mixed set of metaphors, referring to contemporary faith and spirituality as "a patchwork quilt" and describing people of faith with the exilic image of "God's people having been dispersed" (ibid., 2, 4). Gone were the days—as short in number as they may have been—when religion and spirituality could be easily received and exclusively found at churches, synagogues, and mosques. Something more like the religious eclecticism of the nineteenth century was re-emerging.

In this new period, techniques for self-improvement became popular, and notions of spiritual "discipline" became less focused on behaviors and more on attitudes, reassurance, and a faith in goodness (ibid., 89, 95, 100, 103). As a result, many religious leaders and academic observers worried that the new religious seeking would too easily become consumeristic, and Wuthnow described the rise of a "religion industry" consisting of "publishers, therapists, independent authors, and spiritual guides of all types." The commodification of spirituality might even be inevitable because freedom implies choice, and choice leads to habits of consumption, looking for the right religious or spiritual fit (ibid., 11–12, 66–67). Wuthnow thought that the greatest temptation would be for Americans to view spirituality primarily as a quick fix that could be bought and sold. As he stated, "spirituality has become big business, and big business finds many of its best markets by putting things into small, easy-to-consume packages" (ibid., 132). Many Americans in the 1970s and 1980s, already understood spirituality and religion in highly individualistic terms that were criticized forcefully at that time by social theorists, including the now infamous denouncement of "Sheilaism" and other forms of expressive individualism in Robert Bellah's *Habits of the Heart* (ibid., 150). As previous chapters have already indicated, these fears were not unwarranted, and the growing use of marketplace language to describe faith was not limited to the workplace.

Wuthnow's work was important in that he not only critiqued the changing character of American religious and spiritual life, but he also sought to advance an alternative position focusing on religious and spiritual practices that would move beyond techniques and quick fixes to sustained and hopefully more communal methods of "seeking connection with the divine." Wuthnow saw a focus on practices as the best hope for the American worldview of seeking. He also took heart in the fact that to engage a practice is to participate in a tradition and find a "center" outside oneself and the particular needs or desires of the moment (ibid., 181–88). He referenced interviews with practitioners of spiritual direction as well as deep and rich forms of prayer and meditation. In one case, these practices were maintained in conjunction with conventional membership in a congregation, and in another case they were not, but even for the congregational member, it was the spiritual practice that defined his spiritual identity and not the membership and its focus on dwelling (ibid., 171–78).

Wuthnow noted that a focus on spiritual practices frequently, if not always, had some social or institutional grounding. These practices involved institutions such as congregations, religious orders, retreat centers, Internet sites, and publishers, making them at least social if not communal. The challenge was that even devoted practitioners could still hold their communal ties loosely and profess limited interest in the institutions themselves. Wuthnow's informants had great commitment to their practices, but they held much more utilitarian views of the institutions by which the practices were supported (ibid., 181–83). But practices also have rules dictated by a tradition, and they are not easy in their time requirements and commitment, allowing the practices to shape and form the practitioner as he or she conforms to the practice and its parameters (ibid., 178–79). Overall, Wuthnow wanted to recognize and lift up the institutional, social, and communal dimensions of practices, but he could not escape coming back to the individual and the centrality of his or her relationship with the divine.

In Weberian terms, Wuthnow was still hoping to reclaim some sort of mysticism even though the mystic's relationship to sacred spaces, communities, or institutions might be in flux or absent. But contemporary mysticism is no longer uniformly other-worldly. The contemporary mystic is not the medieval Christian or Buddhist monk that Weber envisioned. Instead, the new mystic finds joy at work or in the marketplace; labor is a path to meaning, and shopping is a form of therapy. Weber discussed the possibility of "inner-worldly mysticism," but his primary references excluded economics, focusing on eroticism and even religiously inspired orgies.[63] Inner-worldly mysticism is a way of being in the world that is completely opposite of the religious ascetic, and at the same time, but differently, it is a way of being mystical that is in complete opposition to the contemplative. However, the changes in spiritual and economic life as well as the rise of certain forms of workplace spirituality reveal that the options for relating God and mammon are no longer twofold but threefold—inner-worldly asceticism, inner-worldly mysticism, and other-worldly mysticism. Elective affinities are only possible with the two approaches that have an inner-worldly orientation. Even more, the chances of ordinary Americans finding a real, other-worldly mystic are almost impossible, and there is virtually no way to be ordinary in America if you are not fully immersed in the American economic system, leaving inner-worldly asceticism and inner-worldly mysticism as the only options available.

Some of the confusion over contemporary workplace spirituality is caused by the larger tension between traditional ways of describing vocation and calling, which are drawn from practices of inner-worldly asceticism and the new, inner-worldly mysticism connected to changes in American spirituality since the 1960s. Since there is not a long tradition for this second form of mysticism in relationship to economic life, terms connected to vocation and calling have frequently been adopted and redefined for use within inner-worldly mysticism. A person may identify a sense of calling as a means to describe deeply personal meaning, happiness, and joy in work, but this is not how an inner-worldly ascetic would use the term nor is it how Luther or Calvin would have described a Christian's vocation. For the ascetic, a calling is about duty and an assignment from God, which is to be completed whether it is joyful or not; more specifically, in Christian theology, it is a cross to bear. While there may be two ways of being spiritual "in" the workplace, they share only one vocabulary.

Because Weber presents the mystic and the ascetic plus inner-worldly and other-worldly as ideal types, it should not be too much of a surprise when blurring occurs between them. What continues to interest critics, however, is how workplace spirituality's expressions can more closely resemble Weber's original two ways for the faithful to engage the economic. Being "spiritual not religious" is such a malleable idea that it is easily exploited in workplace spirituality with the individual tempted by what is easy and institutions tempted by what sells. As repeatedly identified, workplace spirituality is especially vulnerable to quick-fix techniques when supplied by employers who have mixed motives for their religion and spiritual engagement. Wuthnow's advocacy of practices attempts to pull mysticism back to the other-worldly, recognizing that this can be only a corrective more than a return to the ideal.

Of course, critics of inner-worldly mysticism can also take heart by being realists and recognizing that workplace ecstasy cannot be sustained forever. What the Christian tradition named as a curse, most workers recognize as the simple drudgery of work that cannot be fully escaped and can often result in a crisis. An office meditation room, reading *Jesus, CEO*, or knowing that you work for a Christian company may simply not be enough when layoffs occur. Wuthnow's hope is that all seekers will recognize the fleeting character of so many spiritual techniques and resources, seeking instead those with depth and staying power as well as a community and tradition to guide them. Workplace spirituality practitioners already have some resources for this as they often see work as a community, and they have several parachurch groups that offer networks connected to traditions yet are unencumbered by traditional religious institutions.

On the other side, advocates of renewed emphasis on vocation are willing to grant that some happiness and joy might be found in work itself, but they want workers who are sufficiently ascetic so as to make *service* their primary goal rather than simply personal joy or enrichment. A related tension is that the inner-worldly ascetic needs to be sent into the world and fully immersed in it, but religious leaders responding against spiritual seekers and inner-worldly mysticism may discourage practices of vocation because they challenge the authority of religious institutions and their monopoly on religious and spiritual meaning. The places for workplace spirituality in this approach include work but also other locations where workplace meaning is sought, whether it is a congregation, bookstore, parachurch group, university business classroom, or online forum. A continued focus on place is also significant for the inner-worldly ascetic because it de-centers the church or other religious hierarchies without needing to re-center religious meaning exclusively in the individual.

While Wuthnow concludes that mysticism is all that's left, de-centering religious institutions can also allow other places to be invested with meaning. Rather than a dualistic secular-sacred divide, the entire world is deemed sacred so that work in any area can assume religious and spiritual meaning; continued attention to place allows workplace spirituality adherents to reframe the religious meaning of work not as in individualistic spirituality but as "local theologies" tying person and place together under a sense of divine will.

Local theology is a term from Christian missions that describes the abandonment of projects to create universal theologies or universal theories of religious meaning. A frequent criticism of missionary activity has been its indifference or even hostility to local cultures, but more important has been the criticism that theological systems claim to be universal and eternal, even in the face of profound cultural differences and changing circumstances.[64] Local or "little" theologies take seriously those issues of culture and context as well as issues of place. Among the practitioners of workplace spirituality, religious or spiritual seeking is always grounded in a desire for personal relevance, and the hope is for personal "contextualization," literally the weaving of a spiritual meaning into everyday life and work.[65] At their best, this is what forms of workplace spirituality and the concept of vocation do when they find religious and spiritual purpose in human labor, in the places where labor occurs, and with the people who share in the same or similar work. Weber's elective affinities are possible between the sacred and seemingly profane, and these affinities have the power to change both attitudes and behaviors. While techniques and quick fixes for workplace meaning will continue to be bought and sold, what the workplace spirituality movement indicates is that people yearn for systems of meaning that are little and local yet deep and communal, created for a particular occasion.[66] They can then become practices that, rather than being consumed by adherents, can shape and form the practitioner, allowing for personal meaning-making to grow alongside service. This is the most promising future for workplace spirituality.

Uncertainty Ahead

What remains to be seen is whether the aftermath of recent economic turmoil and recession will significantly change the American workplace and workplace spirituality. As we saw in chapters 1 and 2, economic uncertainty was a powerful motive in the development of the workplace spirituality movement in the 1980s and 1990s, and it was the vast economic and social changes from industrialization that produced company towns and welfare capitalism with religion as an employee benefit. Yet a fundamental tension is now likely. While news media are reporting a surging interest in faith generally in response to the economic crisis, simultaneously, corporate sponsored spirituality, like all employee benefits, may be cut back or eliminated unless clear links to productivity and profits can be demonstrated.[67] Traditional religious communities and parachurch organizations could step in to fill the gap, but nonprofit organizations will also feel the financial squeeze if donations shrink and attendance wanes.

Economic shifts will certainly influence other aspects of workplace spirituality as well. Interest in life coaching may soar amid layoffs and economic uncertainty, but the newly unemployed will have a hard time paying for it. Huge debts may make economic and spiritual asceticism popular as an antidote to previous excesses, and calls for spirituality in business tied to high moral standards may also be heard as Americans lament the corporate greed and outright dishonesty that was at least partially to blame for the mess. A new "green" political agenda by the administration of President Barack Obama may also solidify the place of business leaders like Ben Cohen and Jerry Greenfield, Tom Chappell, and Ray Anderson in a pantheon of spiritually motivated, green business prophets if the U.S. government leads a substantial effort in this direction.

Amid all the economic volatility, the ultimate future of workplace spirituality is impossible to predict, but whatever occurs will be shaped by Millennials entering the workforce, new technologies, and faith in more socially and environmentally responsible business models. Inner-worldly ascetics with their focus on dutiful service will labor alongside inner-worldly mystics who seek spiritual joy, and both will claim ownership of that classic Christian idea of "calling" despite significantly different ideas of what the concept actually means. Evangelical Christians will read the next sequel to *Jesus, CEO* (or listen to it as a podcast) and those who are spiritual but not religious will find new management gurus among the world's religious traditions (perhaps *The Wisdom of Gandhi for Effective Marketing?*). Religious diversity at work will undoubtedly grow, creating great opportunities for both inter-religious dialogue and inter-religious conflict with lawsuits and friendships produced as results. It is even possible that the growing diversity of practices will make "workplace spirituality" obsolete as an overarching term, requiring religious and academic observers to create new categories and subcategories. And, also worthwhile, scholars of religion may seek greater collaborations in the engagement and study of these practices with their business department colleagues. Much remains to be seen.

It was one hundred years ago that Max Weber recognized the complex yet fertile relationship between religion and economic life. In this new century both religion and the economy have changed and are changing, but their relationships remain. Predicting the exact shapes and forms of those relationships may be impossible, but knowing that new elective affinities will emerge requires no oracle.

Notes

NOTES TO CHAPTER 1

1. Patricia Aburdene, *Megatrends 2010* (Charlottesville, VA: Hampton Roads Publishing, 2005), xviii–xix.

2. Michelle Conlin, "Religion in the Workplace," *BusinessWeek*, November 1, 1999, 150–58.

3. Barbara Ettorre, "Religion in the Workplace: Implications for Mangers," *Management Review* 85 (December 1996): 16.

4. John Naisbitt and Patricia Aburdene, *Megatrends 2000* (New York: William Morrow, 1990), 294.

5. Robert S. Michaelson, "Changes in the Puritan Concept of Calling or Vocation," *New England Quarterly* 26 (September 1953): 326–28; Richard Steele, *The Religious Tradesman* (Harrisonburg, VA: Sprinkle Publications, 1989), 19.

6. Isaac Watts, introduction to *Religious Tradesman*, by Richard Steele, iii–iv.

7. Steele, *Religious Tradesman,* 10–11.

8. Max Weber, *The Protestant Ethic and the Spirit of Capitalism*, trans. Talcott Parsons (London: Routledge Classics, 2001), xxxi.

9. Sean McCloud, "Putting Some Class Into Religious Studies: Resurrecting an Important Concept," *Journal of the American Academy of Religion* 75 (December 2007): 851–52.

10. Gen. 1:26 and 2:15 (New Revised Standard Version).

11. Gen. 3:17–19 (NRSV).

12. Klaus Bockmuehl, "Recovering Vocation Today," *Crux* 24 (1988): 26.

13. Paul S. Minear, "Work and Vocation in Scripture" in *Work and Vocation: A Christian Discussion*, ed. John O. Nelson (New York: Harper and Brothers Publishers, 1954), 61–63.

14. John Calvin, *Institutes of the Christian Religion*, ed. John T. McNeil (Louisville, KY: Westminster/John Knox Press, 1960), 1270–71; Donald R. Heiges, *The Christian's Calling* (Philadelphia: Muhlenberg Press, 1958), 58.

15. Calvin, *Institutes,* 1256–57.

16. Ibid., 724–25.

17. Louis T. Almen, "The Doctrine of Vocation in Luther and Calvin" (ThM

thesis, Princeton Theological Seminary, 1955), 210–11 ("Let each of you remain in the condition in which you were called" [NRSV]).

18. William Perkins, "A Treatise of the Vocations or Callings of Men," in *Working*, ed. Gilbert Meilaender (Notre Dame, IN: University of Notre Dame Press, 2000), 112–13.

19. Michaelson, "Changes in the Puritan Concept of Calling or Vocation," 328.

20. Ibid., 327–28.

21. Ibid.

22. Barbara Holkert Andolsen, *The New Job Contract* (Cleveland, OH: Pilgrim Press, 1998), 8–24; Judith A. Neal, "Spirituality in Management Education: A Guide to Resources," *Journal of Management Education* 21 (1997): 122.

23. Martin Rutte, "Spirituality in the Workplace," in *Heart at Work*, ed. Jack Canfield and Jacqueline Miller (New York: McGraw Hill, 1998), 221.

24. Patricia Aburdene, "The Spiritual Path of Leadership," (presentation, "Spirituality at Work: The New Values-Based Productivity Conference, Washington, DC, June 27, 1998).

25. Robert Reich, *The Work of Nations* (New York: Alfred Knopf, 1991), 178.

26. Ibid., 182–83.

27. Jerry Adler, "The Rise of the Overclass," *Newsweek*, July 31, 1995, 34–44.

28. David Brooks, *Bobos in Paradise: The New Upper Class and How They Got There* (New York: Simon and Schuster, 2000), 40.

29. Ibid., 110, 133–35.

30. Richard Florida, *The Rise of the Creative Class* (New York: Basic Books, 2002), 8.

31. Ibid., 80–82.

32. Ibid., 167–69.

33. Ibid., 192–93.

34. Thomas H. Davenport, *Thinking for a Living* (Boston: Harvard University Press, 2005), 3–7, 11, 15, 20.

35. Ibid., 13–14.

36. Jerry Useem, "Welcome to the New Company Town," *Fortune* 141 (January 10, 2000): 68.

37. James Autry, "Corporate Education Day Convocation" (lecture, Wartburg College, Waverly, IA, November 17, 1998).

38. See Arlie R. Hoschild, *The Time Bind: When Work Becomes Home and Home Becomes Work* (New York: Henry Holt and Company, 1997).

39. W. A. Visser't Hooft, ed., *The Evanston Report: The Second Assembly of the World Council of Churches* (New York: Harper and Brothers, 1955), 168.

40. Pope John Paul II, "Laborem Exercens," in *Catholic Social Thought: The Documentary Heritage*, eds. David O'Brien and Thomas Shannon (Maryknoll, NY: Orbis Press, 1992), 384–89.

41. See William Diehl's *Christianity and Real Life* (Philadelphia: Fortress

Press, 1976), *Thank God It's Monday* (Philadelphia: Fortress Press, 1982), and *The Monday Connection* (San Francisco: Harper San Francisco, 1991).

42. Robert Wuthnow, *The Crisis in the Churches: Spiritual Malaise, Fiscal Woe* (New York: Oxford University Press, 1997), 56–57.

43. Ibid., 63.

44. Dirk Johnson, "In Georgia, a Matter of Faith," *Newsweek*, March 28, 2005, 29.

45. Rick Warren, *The Purpose Driven Life: What on Earth Am I Here For?* (Grand Rapids, MI: Zondervan Publishing, 2002), 227–31.

46. Daisy Maryles, "Rick Warren Matters," *Publishers Weekly*, January 23, 2005, http://www.publishersweekly.com/article/CA490723.html?q=%22daisy+mar yles%22+%22purpose+driven+life%22 (accessed February 21, 2008).

47. Catherine L. Albanese, *A Republic of Mind and Spirit* (New Haven, CT: Yale University Press, 2007), 13–15, 69–72.

48. Ian I. Mitroff and Elizabeth A. Denton, *A Spiritual Audit of Corporate America* (San Francisco: Jossey-Bass, 1999), xvi; Richard Camino and Don Lattin, *Shopping for Faith* (San Francisco: Jossey-Bass, 1998), 36.

49. Robert C. Fuller, *Spiritual, But Not Religious* (New York: Oxford University Press, 2001), 5.

50. Wade Clark Roof, *A Generation of Seekers* (San Francisco: HarperCollins, 1993), 56–57.

51. Fuller, *Spiritual, But Not Religious,* 17.

52. Leigh Schmidt, *Restless Souls: The Making of American Spirituality* (New York: Harper Collins, 2005), 13–14.

53. Roof, *Generation of Seekers,* 2.

54. Ibid., 34, 56–57.

55. Ibid., 122–23.

56. Rutte, "Spirituality in the Workplace," 222; Neal, "Spirituality in Management Education," 122.

NOTES TO CHAPTER 2

1. Stanley Buder, *Pullman: An Experiment in Industrial Order and Community Planning* (New York: Oxford University Press, 1967), 29.

2. Melvin Kranzberg and Joseph Gies, *By the Sweat of Thy Brow* (New York: G. P. Putnam's Sons, 1975), 41, 66–68.

3. Ibid., 69–70.

4. Adam Smith, *An Inquiry into the Nature and Cause of the Wealth of Nations* (New York: E. P. Dutton and Co., 1911), 4–5.

5. Thomas K. McCraw, "The Evolution of the Corporation in the United States," in *The U.S. Business Corporation: An Institution in Transition*, eds. J. Meyer and J. Gustafson (Cambridge: Ballinger Publishing Co., 1988), 2–3.

6. Ronald E. Seavoy, *The Origins of the American Business Corporation, 1784–1855* (Westport, CT: Greenwood Press, 1982), 4–6.

7. McCraw, "The Evolution of the Corporation in the United States," 5.

8. Ibid., 4.

9. Alfred Chandler, Jr., *The Visible Hand* (Cambridge, MA: Belknap Press, 1977), 415, 451.

10. Anthony Sampson, *Company Man: The Rise and Fall of Corporate Life* (New York: Random House, 1995), 22, 26.

11. Lee Hardy, *The Fabric of This World* (Grand Rapids, MI: W. B. Eerdmans Publishing Co., 1990), 130–32.

12. Frederick W. Taylor, *The Principles of Scientific Management*, facsimile of original 1911 edition (Norcross, GA: Industrial Engineering and Management Press, 1998), 28.

13. Hardy, *Fabric of This World,* 134.

14. David Harvey, *The Condition of Postmodernity* (Cambridge, MA: Blackwell Publishers, 1989), 125–26.

15. Alan Briskin, *The Stirring of the Soul in the Workplace* (San Francisco: Jossey-Bass, 1996), 106, 109.

16. Buder, *Pullman,* 38, 49–50, 89.

17. Ibid., 34–35.

18. Ibid., 42.

19. Ibid., 3–4.

20. Ibid., 66.

21. Stuart Brandes, *American Welfare Capitalism* (Chicago: University of Chicago Press, 1976), 76–82, 98–102.

22. Liston Pope, *Millhands and Preachers* (New Haven, CT: Yale University Press, 1942), 38–40.

23. Ibid., 96–98.

24. Ibid., 39, 104–6.

25. Brandes, *American Welfare Capitalism,* 38.

26. Harvey, *Condition of Postmodernity,* 126.

27. Brandes, *American Welfare Capitalism,* 1–2; Sanford M. Jacoby, *Modern Manors: Welfare Capitalism Since the New Deal* (Princeton, NJ: Princeton University Press, 1997), 12–14.

28. Jacoby, *Modern Manors,* 14; Charles Howard Hopkins, *The Rise of the Social Gospel* (New Haven: Yale University Press, 1940), 245–51.

29. Brandes, *American Welfare Capitalism,* 1–5.

30. Jacoby, *Modern Manors,* 11–13, 17.

31. Brandes, *American Welfare Capitalism,* 67.

32. Jacoby, *Modern Manors,* 18–19.

33. Bruce E. Kaufman, *The Origin and Evolution of the Field of Industrial Relations in the United States* (Ithaca, NY: Industrial and Labor Relations Press, 1993), 22.

34. Jacoby, *Modern Manors*, 44.

35. Ibid., 19–20, 84.

36. Kaufman, *Origin and Evolution*, 26.

37. Ibid., 77.

38. Ibid., 78.

39. Hardy, *Fabric of This World*, 144.

40. Emile Durkheim, *On Morality and Society*, ed. Robert Bellah (Chicago: University of Chicago Press, 1973), 139, 169.

41. James C. Dingley, "Durkheim, Mayo, Morality and Management," *Journal of Business Ethics* 16 (1997): 1121.

42. Neal Chalofsky et al., "The Meaning of Work: A Literature Review" (working paper, George Washington University, 1997), 2.

43. Frederick Herzberg et al., *The Motivation to Work* (New York: John Wiley and Sons, Inc., 1959), 60, 113; Hardy, *Fabric of This World*, 151–53.

44. Mary B. Young, "Hard Bodies, Soft Issues, and the Whole Person," in *A Fatal Embrace?*, eds. Frank W. Heuberger and Laura Nash (New Brunswick, NJ: Transaction Publishers, 1994), 21–22.

45. Edgar H. Schein, *Organizational Culture and Leadership* (San Francisco: Jossey-Bass Publishers, 1986), 6.

46. D. Stephen Cloniger, "Corporate Social Responsibility and the Business Manager: An Ethical Inquiry" (PhD diss., Emory University, 1985), 38.

47. Charles Conrad, "The Ethical Nexis: Conceptual Grounding," in *The Ethical Nexus*, ed. Charles Conrad (Norwood, NJ: Ablex Publishing, 1996), 22.

48. Connie Bullis, "Organizational Values and Control," in *The Ethical Nexus*, 82; Robert Jackall, *Moral Mazes* (New York: Oxford University Press, 1988), 38.

49. Harrison M. Trice and Janice M. Beyer, *The Cultures of Work Organizations* (Englewood Cliffs, NJ: Prentice-Hall, 1993), 150–54.

50. Paul DiMaggio, "The Relevance of Organizational Theory to the Study of Religion," in *Sacred Companies*, eds. N. J. Demerath III et al. (New York: Oxford University Press, 1998), 8–9.

51. Jerry Useem, "Welcome to the New Company Town," *Fortune* 141 (January 10, 2000), 62.

52. Young, "Hard Bodies, Soft Issues, and the Whole Person," 18–19.

53. "100 Best Companies Have an Edge," *Compensation and Benefits Review* 31 (May 1999): 9.

54. Young, "Hard Bodies, Soft Issues, and the Whole Person," 18–19.

55. Stewart D. Friedman et al., "Work and Life: The End of the Zero-Sum Game," *Harvard Business Review* 76 (November/December 1998): 119–29.

56. Steven Greenhouse, "Ford to Offer Social Services to Workers and Retirees," *New York Times*, November 22, 2000, C8.

57. Jill Elswick, "A Symphony of Nontraditional Benefits," *Employee Benefits News* 14 (March 200): 39, 52.

58. Frank W. Heuberger and Laura Nash, introduction to *Fatal Embrace?*, 2–3.

59. Judith A. Neal, "Spirituality in Management Education: A Guide to Resources," *Journal of Management Education* 21 (1997): 123.

60. Bob Ronser, "Is There Room for the Soul at Work,?" *Workforce* 80 (February 2001): 82–83.

61. Ian I. Mitroff and Elizabeth A. Denton, *A Spiritual Audit of Corporate America* (San Francisco: Jossey-Bass Publishers, 1999), 125–30.

62. Martin Rutte, "Create a Chicken Soup Group in Your Workplace" (Santa Fe, NM: unpublished paper, n.d.).

63. Peter Senge, *The Fifth Discipline* (New York: Doubleday, 1990), 239–45.

64. David Whyte, *The Heart Aroused: Poetry and the Preservation of the Soul in Corporate America* (New York: Doubleday, 1994), 79–80.

65. Ibid., 13.

66. Michelle Conlin, "Religion in the Workplace," *Business Week*, November 1, 1999, 151–52.

67. Stephen E. Plum, "Ford Teams Take Vows in Detroit Monastery," *Ward's Auto World* 29 (June 1993): 40–41.

68. Unsigned review of *Working with Spirit: To Replace Control with Trust*, by Richard L. Gutherie, http://www.workingwithspirit.com/generic.html (accessed July 25, 2001).

69. G. Pascal Zachary, "The New Search for Meaning in 'Meaningless' Work," *Wall Street Journal*, January 9, 1997, B1.

70. Richard Barrett, "Spiritual Unfolding at the World Bank," Corporate Transformation Tools, http://www.corptools.com/text/spiritun.html (accessed September 1, 1998).

71. Barrett, "Liberating the Corporate Soul," Corporate Transformation Tools, http://www.corptools.com/text/amaart.html (accessed September 1, 1998).

72. Tom Chappell, "Workplace Spirituality" (lecture, "Spirituality at Work: The New Values-Based Productivity Conference, Washington, DC, June 28, 1998).

73. Ben Cohen and Jerry Greenfield, *Ben & Jerry's Double Dip* (New York: Simon and Schuster, 1997), 51.

74. Self promotion of enlightened business practices is not without risks. Charges of hypocrisy come when firms fail to measure-up to self-described values. The Body Shop, founded by Anita Brock, was for many years seen as an example of values-centered business, but it has also been faulted for failing to live up to its mission and even outright deception on the natural quality of its ingredients. See John Entine, "Shattered Image," *Business Ethics* (September/October 1994), reprinted in *Business Ethics Annotated Edition*, ed. John Richardson (Guilford, CT: Dushkin Publishing, 1996), 2001–206.

75. Katja Hahn D'Errico, *The Impact of Spirituality on the Work of Organization Development Consulting Practice* (PhD diss., University of Massachusetts at Amherst, 1998), 320–22.

76. Patricia Hardin, "What's Your Sign? Companies Use Otherworldly Assessment Methods to Choose the Right Employees," *Personnel Journal* 74 (September 1995), 66.

77. Krista Kurth, "An Exploration of the Expression and Perceived Impact of Selfless Service in For-Profit Organizations" (PhD diss., George Washington University, 1994), 319.

78. Jacoby, *Modern Manors*, 44.

79. Philip H. Mirvis, "Human Development or Depersonalization? The Company as Total Community," in *A Fatal Embrace?*, ed. Heuberger and Nash, 136–38.

80. Michael Walzer, *Spheres of Justice* (New York: Basic Books, 1983), 6.

81. Pope, *Millhands and Preachers*, 264.

82. Ibid., 276–77, 282–83.

83. Ibid., 278, 331–32.

84. Michelle Conlin, "Religion in the Workplace," *Business Week*, November 1, 1999, 152.

85. Catherine L. Albanese, "The Subtle Energies of the Spirit: Explorations in Metaphysical and New Age Spirituality," *Journal of the American Academy of Religion* 67(1999): 317–18.

86. Joe Holland, "A Postmodern Vision of Spirituality in Society," in *Spirituality and Society*, ed. David Ray Griffin (Albany: State University of New York Press 1988), 50–55.

87. Richard Kyle, *The New Age Movement in American Culture* (Lanham, MD: University Press of America, 1995), 132–33.

88. Max L. Stackhouse, "Reflections: Secular Ministrations in Personal Development Programs—A Theological Perspective," in Heuberger and Nash, *Fatal Embrace?*, 248–49.

89. Ibid., 249.

90. Matthew Fox, "Spirituality for a New Era," *New Age Spirituality: An Assessment* (Louisville: Westminster/John Knox, 1993), 209.

91. Barbara Ettorre, "Religion in the Workplace: Implication for Managers," *Management Review* (December 1996): 15–18.

92. Douglas A. Hicks, *Religion and the Workplace: Pluralism, Spirituality and Leadership* (Cambridge: Cambridge University Press, 2003), 113–14.

93. Neal, "Spirituality in Management Education," 123.

NOTES TO CHAPTER 3

1. Gary J. Johnson, "A Christian Business and Christian Self-identity in Third/Fourth Century Phrygia," *Vigiliae Christianae* 48 (1994): 341, 350.

2. Ibid., 341.

3. Ibid., 360–61.

4. George M. Marsden, *Religion and American Culture* (San Diego: Harcourt Brace Jovanovich, 1990), 265–68.

5. Ibid., 270.

6. Ibid., 270–71.

7. William G. McLoughlin, Jr., *Modern Revivalism* (New York: The Ronald Press, 1959), 82–85.

8. Marsden, *Religion and American Culture*, 179–80.

9. McLoughlin, *Modern Revivalism*, 420.

10. "Billy Sunday Holds a Council of War," *New York Times*, April 10, 1917, 22.

11. Marsden, *Religion and American Culture*, 180.

12. Christian Smith, *Christian America? What Evangelicals Really Want* (Berkeley, CA: University of California Press, 2000), 55.

13. A. James Reichley, "The Evangelical and Fundamentalist Revolt," in *Piety and Politics*, ed. Richard John Neuhaus and Michael Cromartie (Washington, DC: Ethics and Public Policy Center, 1987), 86.

14. Jeffery L. Sheler, "The Christian Capitalists," *U.S. News and World Report*, March 13, 1995, 54.

15. Ibid.

16. Fellowship of Companies for Christ International, "About Us," http://www.christianity.com/CC_Content_Page/0,,PTID38930|CHID144625|CIID,00.html (accessed August 7, 2003).

17. Robert J. Tamasy, "What Is CBMC?" in *Jesus Works Here*, ed. Robert J. Tamasy (Nashville: Broadman and Holman Publishers, 1995), 252–53.

18. Nabil A. Ibrahim et al., "Characteristics and Practices of 'Christian-Based' Companies," *Journal of Business Ethics* 10 (1991): 124–25.

19. Ibid., 127.

20. Ibid., 128.

21. Ibid., 128–29.

22. Ibid., 130.

23. Ian I. Mitroff and Elizabeth A. Denton, *A Spiritual Audit of Corporate America* (San Francisco: Jossey-Bass, 1999), 62–65.

24. Ibid., 63–69.

25. Ibid., 58, 74.

26. Ibid., 72.

27. Daniel Machalaba, "More Employees Are Seeking to Worship God on the Job," *Wall Street Journal*, June 25, 2002, B1, B2.

28. Chick-fil-A, "A Brief History," http://www.chick-fil-A.com/content/about/history.htm (accessed July 25, 2001).

29. Jack Hayes, "Chick-fil-A Sours as Collins Hands Reins to Cathy," *Nation's Restaurant News*, June 11, 2001, 1, 6.

30. S. Truett Cathy, *Chick-fil-A, Inc.: A History Maker in Foodservice* (New York: The Newcomen Society of the United States, 1998), 10.

31. Ibid.

32. Chick-fil-A, "Company Fact Sheet," www.chick-fil-A.com/content/about/comfact.htm (accessed July 25, 2001).

33. Donald J. McNerney, "Creating a Motivated Workforce," *HR Focus* 73 (August 1996): 1.

34. Chick-fil-A, "Company Fact Sheet."

35. McNerney, "Creating a Motivated Workforce," 1.

36. Edward C. Baig, "Profiting with Help from Above," *Fortune* 115 (April 27, 1997), 36.

37. Ibid.

38. S. Truett Cathy, *It's Easier to Succeed Than to Fail* (Nashville: Oliver Nelson, 1989), 156–57.

39. S. Truett Cathy, *Eat Mor Chikin: Inspire More People: Doing Business the Chick-fil-A Way* (Decatur, GA: Looking Glass Books, 2002), 102–6.

40. Ibid., 142.

41. Cathy, *Chick-fil-A, Inc.*, 22.

42. Cathy, *Eat Mor Chikin*, 92.

43. Ibid., 145–47.

44. Ibid., 193.

45. C. William Pollard, *The Soul of the Firm* (Grand Rapids, MI: Harper Business and Zondervan Publishing Co., 1996), 32.

46. Joseph A. Maciariello, "Credo and Credibility," in *Faith in Leadership*, eds. Robert Banks and Kimberly Powell (San Francisco: Jossey-Bass Publishers, 2000), 213.

47. Pollard, *Soul of the Firm*, 18.

48. Elizabeth Rouke and April D. Gasbarre, "ServiceMaster Inc.," *International Directory of Company Histories*, vol. 23, ed. Tina Grant (Detroit: James Press, 1998), 428.

49. Marion E. Wade with Glenn D. Kittler, *The Lord is My Counsel: A Businessman's Personal Experiences with the Bible* (New York: Prentice Hall, 1987), 82–83.

50. Rod Willis, "ServiceMaster: The Details Make the Whole Thing Work," *Management Review* 76 (October 1987): 28–29.

51. Wade, *The Lord is My Counsel*, 139.

52. "Healthcare Hall of Fame," *Modern Healthcare*, September 14, 1992, 34.

53. Pollard, *Soul of the Firm*, 79.

54. "Healthcare Hall of Fame," 34.

55. Ibid., 20–21.

56. Pollard, *Soul of the Firm*, 25.

57. Ibid., 17.

58. Maciariello, "Credo and Credibility," 205, 208; Calmetta Y. Coleman, "Religious Roots Sprout Divine Results at ServiceMaster," *Wall Street Journal*, September 13, 1995, B4.

59. See Dennis P. McCann and M. L. Brownsberger, "Management as a Social Practice: Rethinking Business Ethics after MacIntyre," in *On Moral Business*, eds. Max L. Stackhouse et al. (Grand Rapids, MI: W. B. Eerdmans Publishing, 1995), 508–13.

60. Pollard, *Soul of the Firm*, 127–30.

61. Ibid., 14–15.

62. Robert K. Greenleaf, *Servant Leadership* (New York: Paulist Press, 1977), 13.

63. Willis, "ServiceMaster: The Details Make the Whole Thing Work," 29.

64. Hobby Lobby, "Message Ads," http://www.hobbylobby.com/site3/minstry/message.cfm (accessed July 1, 2003).

65. "David Green," *Chain Store Age* 73 (December 1997): 126.

66. Debbie Howell, "Hobby Lobby's Heavenly Ascension," *Discount Store News* 39 (January 2000): 26.

67. Hobby Lobby, "Company Information," http://www.hobbylobby.com/site3/company/company.cfm (accessed June 26, 2003).

68. Howell, "Hobby Lobby's Heavenly Ascension," 26.

69. David Green with Dean Merrill, *More Than a Hobby* (Nashville: Thomas Nelson, 2005), 166.

70. Hobby Lobby, "Statement of Purpose," http://www.hobbylobby.com/site3/company/statement.htm (accessed June 26, 2003).

71. Howell, "Hobby Lobby's Heavenly Ascension," 26.

72. Hobby Lobby, "Statement of Purpose."

73. Mardel Christian and Educational Supply, "Our Mission," http://www.mardel.com/company.mission.cfm (accessed July 3, 2003).

74. Max Weber, "The Protestant Sects and the Spirit of Capitalism," in *From Max Weber: Essays in Sociology*, ed. H. H. Gerth and C. Wright Mills (London: Routledge and Kegan Paul Ltd., 1952), 304–5.

75. Ibid., 305.

76. Ibid, 306.

77. Ibid., 302–03.

78. Ibid., 312–13.

79. Thrivent Financial for Lutherans, "Facts and Figures," http://www.thrivent.com/aboutus/facts/index.html (accessed August 7, 2003).

80. Hakala Associates Inc., *A Common Bond: The Story of Lutheran Brotherhood* (Minneapolis: Lutheran Brotherhood, 1989), 16. Quote is from the King James (Authorized) Version.

81. The Shepherds Guide, "About TSG," http://www.shepherdsguide.com/about_home.html (accessed February 12, 2002).

82. *The Shepherd's Guide: Greater Louisville*, 9th annual ed. (Louisville, KY: The Shepherd's Guide, 2001).

83. Christian Yellow Page, "Accountability." http://www.christianyellowpage.com/index.cfm?nav=Accountability (accessed August 7, 2003).

84. Tammerlin Drummond, "In God We Advertise," *Los Angeles Times*, July 29, 1991, 2.

85. Ibid.

86. Steven Erlanger, "For Ultra-Orthodox of Israel, A Modern Marketplace Grows," *New York Times*, November 2, 2007, A1.

87. Renee Rose Shield, *Diamond Stories: Enduring Change on 47th Street* (Ithaca, NY: Cornell University Press, 2002), 15, 62, 82.

88. Barak D. Richman, "Community Enforcement of Informal Contracts: Jewish Diamond Merchants in New York," The Harvard John M. Olin Discussion Paper Series, No. 384, September 2002, 13, 25.

89. Shield, *Diamond Stories*, 58.

90. Ibid., 92.

91. Ibid., 46; Richman, "Community Enforcement of Informal Contracts," 7.

92. Shield, *Diamond Stories*, 185–86.

93. Ibid., 35.

94. Richman, "Community Enforcement of Informal Contracts," 39–40.

95. Max L. Stackhouse, *Public Theology and Political Economy* (Grand Rapids, MI: W. B. Eerdmans, 1987), 43–44.

96. Ibid., 91–92.

97. Jean Miller Schmidt, *Souls or the Social Order* (Brooklyn, NY: Carlson Publishing, 1991), 136–39.

98. Randall Balmer, *Mine Eyes Have Seen the Glory: A Journey into the Evangelical Subculture of America* (New York: Oxford University Press, 1989), 18; George Marsden, *Fundamentalism and American Culture* (New York: Oxford University Pres, 1980), 80–85.

99. Marsden, *Fundamentalism and American Culture*, 89–90.

100. Frank E. Gaebelein, "Evangelicals and Social Concern," *Journal of the Evangelical Theological Society* 25 (March 1982): 19.

101. Eric Schlosser, *Fast Food Nation: The Dark Side of the All-American Meal* (New York: Perennial Books, 2002), 140–42.

102. National Interfaith Committee for Worker Justice, "Poultry Justice Campaign." http://www.nicwj.org/pages/issues.Poultry.html (accessed September 12, 2003).

103. Catholic Bishops of the South, "Voices and Choices," http://www.americancatholic.org/News/PoultryPastoral/english.asp (accessed September 12, 2003).

104. Melonee McKinney Hurt, "Offering More than Chicken Sandwiches," *American Profile Magazine*, February 25, 2007, 7.

105. Balmer, *Mine Eyes Have Seen the Glory*, 316.

NOTES TO CHAPTER 4

1. Laurie Beth Jones, *The Path* (New York: Hyperion, 1996), 215–21. In this book, Jones includes references to her professional career and the writing of her earlier book *Jesus, CEO.*

2. Jones, *Jesus, CEO* (New York: Hyperion, 1995), xviii.

3. Ibid., xi.

4. Ibid., 87.

5. Ibid., 22–23.

6. Ibid., xiv.

7. Ibid., 304–5.

8. Jones, *Jesus, Inc.* (New York: Hyperion 2001), xiii.

9. Gary Lawrence, *The State of Faith: God in the Workplace* (Minneapolis: Kirk House Publishing, 2002), 6.

10. Robert Wuthnow, *The Crisis in the Churches* (New York: Oxford University Press, 1997), 63, 259, n10.

11. Ibid., 68–69.

12. Ibid., 80–81.

13. Laura Nash and Scotty McLennan, *Church on Sunday, Work on Monday* (San Francisco: Jossey-Bass Publishers, 2001), 126.

14. Julia Duin, "Faith Fuels Spiritual Capitalism," *Insight On the News*, September 8, 1997, 37.

15. Jeremy Lott, "Jesus Sells," *Reason* 34 (February 2003), *http://www.reason.com/0302/fe.jl.jesus.shtml* (accessed March 26, 2004).

16. Phyllis A. Tickle, *Re-Discovering the Sacred* (New York: Crossroads, 1995), 18.

17. Peg Tyre, "The Almighty Dollar," *Newsweek*, January 24, 2005, 68.

18. Tickle, *Re-Discovering the Sacred*, 120, 179n4.

19. Robert C. Fuller, *Spiritual But Not Religious* (New York: Oxford University Press, 2001), 155.

20. Wade Clark Roof, *Spiritual Marketplace* (Princeton, NJ: Princeton University Press, 1999), 141.

21. Jeremy Carrette and Richard King, *Selling Spirituality* (London: Routledge, 2005), 15.

22. Roof, *Spiritual Marketplace*, 75.

23. Phyllis A. Tickle, *God-Talk in America* (New York: Crossroads, 1997), 33.

24. Tickle, *Re-Discovering the Sacred*, 36–52.

25. Ibid., 46–47.

26. Ibid., 39–43.

27. Lead Like Jesus, "About," http://www.leadlikejesus.com/about/ (accessed August 18, 2008).

28. Nash and McLennan, *Church on Sunday, Work on Monday*, 145.

29. Ibid., 166–67.

30. Ibid., 145.

31. Ibid., 92–93.

32. Ibid., 167.

33. Richard M. Fried, introduction to *The Man Nobody Knows,* by Bruce Barton, (Chicago: Ivan R. Dee Publisher, 2000), vii–viii; Leo P. Ribuffo, "Jesus Christ as Business Statesman: Bruce Barton and the Selling of Corporate Capitalism," *American Quarterly* 33 (Summer 1981): 221.

34. Bruce Barton, *The Man Nobody Knows* (Indianapolis: Bobbs-Merrill Co., 1925; repr., Chicago: Ivan R. Dee Publisher, 2000), 4.

35. Ribuffo, "Jesus Christ as Business Statesman," 222; Fried, introduction to *The Man Nobody Knows,* xxi.

36. Ribuffo, "Jesus Christ as Business Statesman," 215.

37. Ibid., 213, 220.

38. Rolf Lunden, *Business and Religion in the American 1920s* (New York: Greenwood Press, 1988), 102.

39. Ibid., 105.

40. "Jesus As Efficiency Expert," *Christian Century* 42 (July 2, 1925), 352.

41. "No Comment Department," *Christian Century* 112 (October 11, 1995), 917.

42. Barton, *Man Nobody Knows,* 88–89.

43. Ibid., 38.

44. Ibid., 15–18.

45. James Rorty, *Our Master's Voice* (New York: John Day, Co., 1934; repr. by Arno Press, 1976), 318–20.

46. Bruce Barton, *The Man Nobody Knows and The Book Nobody Knows* (Indianapolis: Bobbs-Merrill, 1956), 101–2, quoted in Ribuffo, "Jesus Christ as Business Statesman," 229.

47. Max L. Stackhouse, "Jesus and Economics: A Century of Reflection," in *The Bible in American Law, Politics and Rhetoric,* ed. James Turner Johnson (Philadelphia: Fortress Press and Chico, CA: Scholars Press, 1985), 109.

48. Ribuffo, "Jesus Christ as Business Statesman," 211.

49. Shailer Matthews, *The Social Teachings of Jesus* (New York: The Macmillan Co., 1909), 132–57.

50. Janet C. Olson, "*In His Steps*: A Social Gospel Novel," in *Religions of the United States in Practice,* vol. 1, ed. Colleen McDannell (Princeton: Princeton University Press, 2001), 254–45.

51. William C. Graham, *Half Finished Heaven: The Social Gospel in American Literature* (Lanham, MD: University Press of America, 1995), 79–80.

52. Gary Scott Smith, "Charles M. Sheldon's *In His Steps* in the Context of Religion and Culture in Late Nineteenth Century America," *Fides et historia* 22 (1990): 47n1.

53. Graham, *Half Finished Heaven,* 60.

54. James H. Smylie, "Sheldon's *In His Steps*: Conscience and Discipleship," *Theology Today* 32 (April 1975): 35.

55. Brad Jackson, *Management Gurus and Management Fashions* (London: Routledge, 2001), 9.

56. Thomas H. Davenport and Laurence Prusak, with H. James Wilson, *What's the Big Idea* (Boston: Harvard Business School Press, 2003), 76–77.

57. Andrzej Hucznski, *Management Gurus* (London: Routledge, 1993), 40–42.

58. Ibid., 50.

59. Ibid., 11; David Bough, "Business Auto/biography," *Encyclopedia of Life Writing*, vol. 1, ed. Margaretta Jolly (London: Fitzroy Dearborn Publishers, 2001), 161–62.

60. Ken Blanchard, foreword to *What Would Buddha Do at Work*, by Franz Metcalf and B. J. Gallagher Hateley (Berkeley, CA: Seastone Press/Berrett-Koehler Publishers, 2001), xii.

61. Lloyd Field, *Business and the Buddha: Doing Well by Doing Good* (Boston: Wisdom Publications, 2007), 23, 42–44, 163–68, 181–83.

62. Laurie Beth Jones, *Jesus, Entrepreneur* (New York: Three Rivers Press, 2001), 24.

63. Stephen R. Covey, *The 7 Habits of Highly Effective People* (New York: Fireside Books, 1989), 18–21.

64. Jackson, *Management Gurus and Management Fashions*, 96, 102–3.

65. Ibid., 106.

66. Covey, *7 Habits*, 106–9.

67. Ibid., 18.

68. Richard M. Huber, *The American Idea of Success* (New York: McGraw-Hill Book Company, 1971), 227.

69. Ibid., 295.

70. Ibid., 135.

71. Ibid., 295–98.

72. Dennis Voskuil, *Mountains into Goldmines: Robert Schuller and the Gospel of Success* (Grand Rapids, MI: W. B. Eerdmans, 1983), 125.

73. Norman Vincent Peale, *The Power of Positive Thinking* (Engelwood Cliffs, NJ: Prentice Hall, 1952), 16–17.

74. Ibid., 53

75. Voskuil, *Mountains into Goldmines*, 128–30.

76. Lakewood Community Church, "Sermon Listing," http://www.lakewood.cc/sermon_listing.htm (accessed March 8, 2005).

77. Joel Osteen, *Your Best Life Now* (New York: Warner Faith, 2004), 3.

78. Bruce Wilkinson, *The Prayer of Jabez: Breaking Through to the Blessed Life* (Sisters, OR: Multnomah, 2000), 17.

79. Ibid., 32.

80. Ibid., 86–87.

81. Rodney Clapp and John Wright, "God as Santa," *Christian Century* 119 (October 23, 2002), 29–31.

82. Philip Zaleski, "In Defense of Jabez," *First Things* 116 (October 1, 2001), 10–11.

83. Huber, *American Idea of Success*, 256.

84. Ibid., 226, 282–83.

85. Covey, *7 Habits*, 51.

86. Huber, *American Idea of Success*, 11–12.

87. Covey, *7 Habits*, 113–16.

NOTES TO CHAPTER 5

1. Anita Wadhwani, "Lipscomb Course Draws on Christian Values in Business," *Tennessean*, August 19, 2006, 5B.

2. George Marsden, *The Soul of the American University: From Protestant Establishment to Established Nonbelief* (New York: Oxford University Press, 1994), 36–38.

3. Martin Luther, "To the Councilmen of All Cities in Germany That They Establish and Maintain Christian Schools," in *Luther's Works*, vol. 45, eds. Walther I. Brandt and Helmut T. Lehmann (Philadelphia: Fortress Press, 1962), 353.

4. Martin Luther, "A Sermon on Keeping Children in School," in *Luther's Works*, vol. 46, eds. Robert C. Schultz and Helmut T. Lehmann (Philadelphia: Fortress Press, 1967), 217–18.

5. Marsden, *Soul of the American University*, 37.

6. Ibid., 29.

7. Ibid., 14.

8. Ibid., 170.

9. Alfred Chandler, Jr., *The Visible Hand* (Cambridge, MA: Belknap Press, 1977), 7, 491.

10. Ibid.

11. Samuel J. Wanous et al., *A Chronology of Business Education in the United States, 1635–2000* (Reston, VA: National Business Education Association, 2000), 3–5.

12. Ibid., 7.

13. Steven Schlossman et al., introduction, *The Beginnings of Graduate Management Education in the United States* (Santa Monica, CA: Graduate Management Admissions Council, 1994), 3–4; Paul S. Hugstad, *The Business School in the 1980s* (New York: Praeger Special Studies, 1983), 2.

14. Marsden, *Soul of the American University*, 115.

15. Ibid., 153–54.

16. Mark R. Schwehn, *Exiles from Eden* (New York: Oxford University Press, 1993), 11–13.

17. Marsden, *Soul of the American University*, 150.

18. Ibid., 333, 415.

19. Ibid., 282–83.

20. Ibid., 317–29.

21. Philip Gleason, *Contending with Modernity: Catholic Higher Education in the Twentieth Century* (New York: Oxford University Press, 1995), 288–90.

22. Ibid., 295.

23. Ibid., 314–16.

24. Frank Pierson et al., *The Education of American Businessmen: A Study of University-College Programs in Business Administration* (New York: McGraw-Hill, 1959), 41.

25. Michael Sedlak and Steven Schlossman, "The Case Method and Business Education at Northwestern University," in *Beginnings of Graduate Management Education*, 22–33.

26. Warren G. Bennis and James O'Toole, "How Business Schools Lost Their Way," *Harvard Business Review* 83 (May 2005): 98.

27. Mie Augier and James G. March, "The Pursuit of Relevance in Management Education," *California Management Review* 49 (Spring 2007): 133, 131.

28. "Survey of Project Directors of the Lilly Program for the Theological Exploration of Vocation." In 2007, the author surveyed eighty-five project directors using a survey with six open response questions. The response rate was 34 percent, and some project directors attached additional information to their surveys. The complete survey is available from the author.

29. Calvin College, "Economics and Management: Bringing Christian Values into the Marketplace," http://www.calvin.edu/academics/economics-business.htm (accessed October 3, 2007).

30. Shirley J. Roels, "Infusing Non-Theological Disciplines with Vocational Reflection: Business Management as a Case Application" (lecture, Program for the Theological Exploration of Vocation Conference, Indianapolis, Indiana, February 9, 2007).

31. "Survey of Project Directors of the Lilly Program."

32. Jeff Van Duzer, "It's Not Your Business: A Christian Reflection on Stewardship and Business," *Journal of Management, Spirituality & Religion* 4 (2007): 107–16.

33. Lipscomb University, "Innovative Lipscomb Class Combines Business and Christianity," http://www.lipscomb.edu/filter.asp?SID=14&fi_key=724&co_key=10163 (accessed October 4, 2007).

34. Lipscomb University, "Basic Training Student Comments," http://www.lipscomb.edu/gsearch.asp?cx=008213778838108855072%3Axts7pgcdnws&cof=FORID%3A11&q=%22Basic+training+student+comments%22#172 (accessed October 4, 2007).

35. Foundation Center, "Top 100 U.S. Foundations by Asset Size," Foundation

Center, http://foundationcenter.org/findfunders/topfunders/top100assets.html (accessed October 2, 2007).

36. Resources for American Christianity, "In Higher Education—Church-Related," http://www.resourcingchristianity.org/WhatsBeenLearned. aspx?ID=87&t=4&i=324 (accessed October 2, 2007).

37. Craig Dykstra, "The Theological Exploration of Vocation: Plenary Conference Address (2003)," Program for the Theological Exploration of Vocation, http://www.ptev.org/hints.aspx?iid=22 (accessed February 22, 2007).

38. "Survey of Project Directors of the Lilly Program."

39. Ibid.

40. Michael Naughton and Ameeta Jaiswal-Dale, "Christian Faith and the Management Profession Syllabus," Program for the Theological Exploration of Vocation, http://www.ptev.org/Syllabus.aspx?iid=84 (accessed October 3, 2007).

41. Karen P. Manz et al., "The Language of Virtues: Toward an Inclusive Approach for Integrating Spirituality in Management Education," *Journal of Management, Spirituality & Religion* 3 (2006): 114.

42. Carol K. Barnett, Terence C. Krell, and Jeanette Sendry, "Learning to Learn about Spirituality: A Categorical Approach to Introducing the Topic into Management Courses," *Journal of Management Education* 24 (2000): 576.

43. Robert A. Giacalone, "A Transcendent Business Education for the 21st Century," *Academy of Management Learning & Education* 3 (2004): 417.

44. Manz et al., "The Language of Virtues," 106.

45. Parker Palmer, *The Courage to Teach* (San Francisco: Jossey-Bass, 1998), 1–7; Karen P. Harlos, "Toward a Practical Pedagogy: Meaning, Practice, and Applications in Management Education," *Journal of Management Education* 24 (2000): 617–19; Richard A. Kernochan, Donald W. McCormick, Judith A. White, "Spirituality and the Management Teacher," *Journal of Management Inquiry* 16 (2007): 63–71; Judith Neal, "Teaching with Soul: Support for the Management Educator," *Journal of Management Systems* 10 (1998): 86–87.

46. Kristen Fiani, "As Seen on YouTube: Virginia Tech Favorite," *BusinessWeek*, September 4, 2007, http://www.businessweek.com/bschools/content/jul2007/bs20070731_101079.htm?chan=bschools_undergrad+--+favorite+professors+2007_favorite+professors (accessed September 10, 2007).

47. Charles C. Manz and Christopher P. Neck, *Mastering Self-Leadership: Empowering Yourself for Personal Excellence,* 3rd ed. (Upper Saddle River, NJ: Pearson Prentice Hall, 2004), 25, 62, 69, 121.

48. University of Notre Dame, "The Notre Dame MBA: Electives," http://www.nd.edu/~mba/academics/twoYear/electives.shtml#ethics (accessed October 8, 2007).

49. Stanford University, "MBA and Sloan Elective Courses: Organizational Behavior," http://www.gsb.stanford.edu/research/courses/ob.html#OB372 (accessed October 8, 2007).

50. Manz et al., "The Language of Virtues," 121.

51. Stanford University, "MBA and Sloan Elective Courses: Political Economy," http://www.gsb.stanford.edu/research/courses/polecon.html#PE349 (accessed October 8, 2007).

52. David M. Boje, "MGT 90 Seminar in Storytelling and Consulting," New Mexico State University, http://business.nmsu.edu/~dboje/690/index.htm (accessed October 8, 2007).

53. Srikumar S. Rao, "Creativity and Personal Mastery Syllabus," Are You Ready to Succeed, http://www.areyoureadytosucceed.com/docs/Syllabus%20-%20Creativity%20and%20Pesonal%20Mastery.pdf (accessed September 15, 2007).

54. Rao, *Are You Ready to Succeed?* (New York: Hyperion, 2006), 6.

55. Scranton University, "Jerry Biberman Faculty Home Page," http://academic.scranton.edu/faculty/biberman1/ (accessed October 11, 2007).

56. Working Wizdom, "Working Wizdom Homepage," http://www.workingwizdom.com/default.htm (accessed October 11, 2007).

57. Andre L. Delbecq, "Spirituality for Business Leadership: Reporting on a Pilot Course for MBAs and CEOs," *Journal of Management Inquiry* 9 (2000): 118–26.

58. Gilbert Klaperman, *The Story of Yeshiva University* (London: The Macmillan Company, 1969), 83–84.

59. Ibid., 161.

60. "Yeshiva U. to Open School of Business in the Fall," *New York Times,* December 7, 1986, 73.

61. Moses L. Pava, "Spirituality In (and Out) of the Classroom: A Pragmatic Approach," *Journal of Business Ethics* 73 (2007): 288.

62. Ibid., 297.

63. Ibid., 295.

64. Cynthia Ann Humes, "Maharishi Mahesh Yogi: Beyond the TM Technique," in *Gurus in America,* eds. Thomas A. Forstoefel and Cynthia Ann Humes (Albany, NY: State University of New York Press, 2005), 60–61, 65.

65. Ibid., 57.

66. Ibid., 72.

67. Ibid., 67.

68. Maharishi Mahesh Yogi, *Maharishi University of Management: Wholeness on the Move* (n.p., India: Age of Enlightenment Publications, n.d.), 3.

69. Ibid., 15 and 22–23.

70. Maharishi University of Management, "Course Descriptions for the Master of Business Administration Degree," http://www.mum.edu/mba/descriptions.html (accessed September 28, 2007).

71. Ibid., "Course Descriptions for the B.A. in Business," http://www.mum.edu/business/descriptions.html (accessed September 28, 2007).

72. Ibid., "Consciousness-Based Education," http://www.mum.edu/cbe/html (accessed September 28, 2007).

73. Jane Schmidt-Wilk, "Applications of Maharishi Vedic Science to Business Management," *Journal of Social Behavior and Personality* 17 (2005): 230–31.

74. Jerry Biberman, "How Workplace Spirituality Becomes Mainstreamed in a Scholarly Organization," in *Handbook of Workplace Spirituality and Organizational Performance*, eds. Robert A. Giacalone and Carole L. Jurkiewicz (Armonk, NY: M. E. Sharpe, 2003), 421.

75. Ibid., 424–25.

76. Ibid., 422–23.

77. David Trott, "From the Chair's Corner," *Academy of Management MSR Newsletter* 6 (Summer 2006): 1.

78. Jerry Biberman and Yochanan Altman, "Welcome to the New Journal of Management, Spirituality and Religion," *Journal of Management, Spirituality and Religion* 1 (2004): 2.

79. William M. Sullivan, *Work and Integrity*, 2nd ed. (San Francisco: Jossey-Bass, 2005), 208.

NOTES TO CHAPTER 6

1. Lillemor Erlander, *Faith in the World of Work: On the Theology of Work as Lived by the French Worker-Priests and British Industrial Mission* (Uppsala, Sweden: Almquist and Wiksell International, 1991), 16–18.

2. Ibid., 81.

3. Ibid., 35–41.

4. Ibid., 152.

5. Lynn Ashley, "Tending to Business by Tending Spirits: A New Generation of Chaplains for the Workplace" (DMin thesis., Andover Newton Theological Seminary, 2003), 144–45.

6. Diana C. Dale, "Historical Outline of Industrial Mission in the United States" (National Institute of Business and Industrial Chaplains, 1998, mimeographed), 1.

7. "Praying for Gain," *Economist* 384 (August 25, 2007): 60.

8. Eve Tahmincioglu, "Face of Employee Assistance Is Often a Company Chaplain," *New York Times*, January 4, 2004, section 10, 1.

9. Lin Grensing-Pophal, "Workplace Chaplains," *HR Magazine*, August 2000, 54.

10. Ashley, "Tending to Business by Tending Spirits," 155–56.

11. Ibid., 60; David Miller, *God at Work: The History and Promise of the Faith at Work Movement* (New York: Oxford University Press, 2007), 114.

12. David B. Plummer, "Chaplaincy: The Greatest Story Never Told," *Journal of Pastoral Care* 50 (Spring 1996): 5.

13. Melba Newsome, "Hey Reverend, Let's Do Lunch," *U.S. News and World Report,* January 31, 2005, EE12.

14. Marketplace Chaplains USA, "Frequently Asked Questions," http://mchapusa.com/03faq.asp (accessed October 22, 2007).

15. Grensing-Pophal, "Workplace Chaplains," 56.

16. Bruce Shutan, "Freedom of Religion," *Plansponsor* 13 (2006): 57.

17. CBS News, "Keeping the Faith While at Work," http://www.cbsnews.com/stories/2007/04/19/earlyshow/main2707047.shtml (accessed October 22, 2007).

18. Tahmincioglu, "Face of Employee Assistance," 1.

19. Corporate Chaplains of America, "Our Mission," www.inneractiveministries.org/whomission_statement.htm (accessed June 3, 2003).

20. Mark A. Keliner, "God on the Gridiron," *Christianity Today* 43 (November 15, 1999), 77.

21. William J. Baker, *Playing with God: Religion and Modern Sport* (Cambridge, MA: Harvard University Press, 2007), 206–9.

22. Keliner, "God on the Gridiron," 80.

23. Brian W.W. Aitken, "The Emergence of Born-Again Sport," in *Religion and Sport: The Meeting of Sacred and Profane,* ed. Charles S. Prebish (Westport, CT: Greenwood Press, 1993), 208.

24. Douglas T. Hall, Karen L. Otazo, and George P. Hollenbeck, "Behind Closed Doors: What Really Happens in Executive Coaching," *Organizational Dynamics* 27(Winter 1999): 39, 43.

25. Ibid., 25.

26. Julie Starr, *The Coaching Manual* (London: Pearson Education Ltd., 2003), 10.

27. James E. Maddux, "Stopping the 'Madness': Positive Psychology and the Deconstruction of the Illness Ideology and the DSM," in *Handbook of Positive Psychology,* eds. C. R. Snyder and Shane J. Lopez (New York: Oxford University Press, 2002), 21.

28. Jennifer Wolcott, "Get a Life!" *Christian Science Monitor,* April 4, 2001, 11.

29. Life Purpose Institute, "Coaching and Consulting," http://www.lifepurposeinstitute.com/lifepurpose.html (accessed September 13, 2005).

30. Ibid.

31. Anthony M. Grant, "The Impact of Life Coaching on Goal Attainment, Metacognition and Mental Health," *Social Behavior and Personality* 31 (2003): 262.

32. Ibid., 257.

33. Laura Whitworth et al., *Co-Active Coaching: New Skills for Coaching People Towards Success in Work and Life,* 2nd ed. (Mountain View, CA: Davies-Black Publishing, 2007), 238–39.

34. Francine Parnes, "Seekers Try On Life Coaching for the Soul," *New York Times,* March 24, 2007, B5.

35. Ibid.

36. Ibid.

37. Tony Husted, "The Christian Coach," *The Christian Coach*, http://www.thechristiancoach.com/index.htm (accessed October 26, 2007).

38. Barbara B. Troxell, "Soul Friends: The Role of Spiritual Directors," *Christian Century* 115 (March 4, 1992): 247.

39. Jeni Mumford, *Life Coaching for Dummies* (Chichester, UK: John Wiley and Sons, 2007), v.

40. Ibid., 17.

41. Laurie Beth Jones, *Jesus, Life Coach* (Nashville: Thomas Nelson, 2004), xiii.

42. Ibid., 93.

43. Jennifer Wolcott and Jordon Robertson, "Motivational Speaking," *Waterloo Courier*, September 4, 2005, D10.

44. PriceWaterhouseCoopers, *Executive Summary of the Global Coaching Study* (Lexington, KY: International Coach Federation, 2007), 2–5.

45. Columbia University, "The Columbia University Coaching Certificate Program," http://continuingeducation.tc.columbia.edu/default.aspx?pageid=631 (accessed October 26, 2007).

46. Anthony M. Grant and Michael J. Cavanagh, "Towards a Profession of Coaching: Sixty-five Years of Progress and Challenges for the Future," *International Journal of Evidenced Based Coaching and Mentoring* 2 (2004): 3.

47. Laura Nash and Scotty McLennan, *Church on Sunday, Work on Monday* (San Francisco: Jossey-Bass, 2001), 9–10.

48. Ibid., 77–78.

49. St. Thomas the Apostle Catholic Church, "Historical Record of Jobs Ministry," http://www.stapostle.org/index2.php?area=ministries&data=jobminhistory (accessed November 7, 2007).

50. Westside Baptist Church, "Job Ministry," http://www.westsidebaptistchurch.com/jobministry.htm (accessed November 7, 2007).

51. Orthodox Union, "OU and FEGS Join Forces to Create Synagogue-Based Project ParnossahWorks," http://www.ou.org/oupr/2004/parnossah64.htm (accessed November 7, 2007); Warren Strugatch, "For the Jobless, Help from an Unexpected Source," *New York Times*, February 22, 2004, sec. 14, 6.

52. Nash and McLennan, *Church on Sunday, Work on Monday*, 114.

53. Pete Hammond, "Marketplace Reflections: Congregations and Workplace Faith" (Madison, WI: Intervarsity Christian Fellowship, 1995, mimeographed), 1.

54. William E. Diehl, *Ministry in Daily Life* (Washington, DC: Alban Institute, 1997), 22–25.

55. Hammond, "Marketplace Reflections," 2.

56. Diehl, *Ministry in Daily Life*, 43–45; "In the Parish," *Initiatives* 94 (November 1998), 2.

57. "In the Parish," *Initiatives* 101 (Summer 1999): 2.

58. Diehl, *Ministry in Daily Life*, 36–37.

59. St. Mark's Episcopal Church, "The Workshop: Center for Faith in the Workplace," http://www.stmarks-sa.org/cgi-bin/kingdomtools/ktpublic.rb?page_title=index (accessed November 8, 2007).

60. The Work + Shop, "Jesus Said, 'Follow me,'" http://www.theworkshop-sa.org/cgi-bin/kingdomtools/ktpublic.rb?ministry_id=1&utility=Page (accessed November 8, 2007).

61. Robert Banks, *Redeeming the Routines: Bringing Theology to Life* (Wheaton, IL: Victor Books, 1993), 157–58.

62. Miller, *God at Work*, 96.

63. Luther Seminary, "About Centered Life," http://www.centeredlife.org/about/default.asp?m=-2878#1 (accessed November 8, 2007).

64. Miller, *God at Work*, 102–3.

65. Ibid., 98.

66. Ibid., 106.

67. Burton L. Visotzky, "Bible in the Boardroom?" *Inc.* 20 (July 1998): 29.

68. David Chen, "Fitting the Lord's Work into Work's Tight Schedules," *New York Times*, November 29, 1997, A1, B4.

69. "Among Business Leaders," *Initiatives* 136 (January 2004), 1.

70. Crossroads Center, "Faith at Work," http://www.crossroads-center.org/document.php?Id=48 (accessed November 9, 2007).

71. Laity Lodge, "Welcome to Laity Lodge," http://www.laitylodge.org/index.asp (accessed November 9, 2007).

72. Miller, *God at Work*, 33–34.

73. Legatus, "The Heritage of Legatus," http://www.legatus.org/public/About_Legatus/ourHeritage.asp (accessed November 13, 2007).

74. Intervarsity Christian Fellowship, "Whole Life Stewardship," http://www.ivmdl.org/about.cfm (accessed November 9, 2007).

75. Christian Pharmacists Fellowship International, "Beliefs," http://www.cpfi.org/?BISKIT=32099426&CONTEXT=cat&cat=3 (accessed November 9, 2007).

76. Minaret Business Association, "History," http://www.mbosv.org/pView.asp?action=viewPDetails&pageID=10905&pT=History (accessed November 9, 2007).

77. Allied Jewish Federation of Colorado, "Jewish Business Association of Colorado," http://www.jewishcolorado.org/page.html?ArticleID=38368 (accessed November 9, 2007).

78. Tom Peters, "In Praise of the Secular Corporation," http://www.tompeters.com/col_entries.php?note=005397&year=1993 (accessed December 5, 2007).

79. John Renesch, "Spirit & Work: Can Business and Consciousness Co-Exist?" in *The New Bottom Line*, eds. John Renesch and Bill DeFoore (San Francisco: New Leaders Press, 1996), 19.

80. U.S. Equal Employment Opportunity Commission, "Charge Statistics," http://www.eeoc.gov/stats/charges.html (accessed March 29, 2009).

81. Karen C. Cash and George R. Gray, "A Framework for Accommodating Religion and Spirituality in the Workplace," *Academy of Management Executive* 14 (2000): 125.

82. Michael Wolf, Bruce Friedman, and Daniel Sutherland, *Religion in the Workplace: A Comprehensive Guide to Legal Rights and Responsibilities* (Chicago: American Bar Association, 1998), 104–7.

83. Robert A. Caplen, "A Struggle of Biblical Proportions: The Campaign to Enact the Workplace Religious Freedom Act of 2003," *University of Florida Journal of Law and Public Policy* 16 (December 2005), http://www.lexisnexis. com/us/lnacademic/search/journalssubmitForm.do (accessed November 9, 2007).

84. Peter M. Panken, *A State-by-State Survey of the Law on Religion in the Workplace* (Philadelphia: American Law Institute-American Bar Association, 2001), 288–89.

85. Ibid., 13; Russell Shorto, "Faith at Work," *New York Times Magazine*, October 31, 2004, 43.

86. James F. Morgan, "How Should Business Respond to a More Religious Workplace?" *SAM Advanced Management Journal* 69 (2004): 12–13.

87. Caplen, "A Struggle of Biblical Proportions."

88. Laura W. Murphy and Christopher E. Anders, "ACLU Letter on the Harmful Effects of S. 893, the Workplace Religious Freedom Act, on Critical Personal and Civil Rights (6/2/2004)," http://www.aclu.org/religion/frb/16224leg20040602. html (accessed December 4, 2007).

89. Wolf, Friedman, and Sutherland, *Religion in the Workplace*, 251–67.

90. *Blalock v. Metals Trades*, 775 F.2d 703 (6th Cir. 1985), quoted in Wolf, Friedman and Sutherland, *Religion in the Workplace*, 40.

91. Wolf, Friedman, and Sutherland, *Religion in the Workplace*, 54.

92. Shorto, "Faith at Work," 46.

93. Panken, *State-by-State Survey of the Law*, 113–14.

94. Emily Schmall, "The Cult of Chick-fil-A," *Forbes*, July 23, 2007, http:// www.forbes.com/leadership/forbes/2007/0723/080.html (accessed December 3, 2007).

95. Ibid.

96. Julia Spoor, "Go Tell It on the Mountain, But Keep It Out of the Office: Religious Harassment in the Workplace," *Valparaiso University Law Review* 31 (Summer 1997): http://www.lexisnexis.com/us/lnacademic/search/journalssubmitForm.do (accessed November 9, 2007).

97. Wolfe, Friedman, and Sutherland, *Religion in the Workplace*, 61–62.

98. Tahmincioglu, "Face of Employee Assistance," 1.

99. Michael Eidam and Ira Sager, "Got Worries? Tell Them to the Chaplain," *Business Week*, February 9, 2004, 16.

100. "A New Help to Labor Relations," *Time*, October 31, 1955, 84.

101. Kerry Hall, "Some Companies Hire Chaplains to Counsel Workers," *Waterloo Courier Church Directory 2006*, January 29, 2006, 2.

102. Cash and Gray, "A Framework for Accommodating Religion," 127.

103. Morgan, "How Should Business Respond," 14.

104. Panken, State-by-State Survey of the Law, 327–28.

105. "Dilbert Archives," http://members.comics.com/members/extra/addtofavoritestrips.do? (accessed September 22, 2005).

106. Julie Davis, "An Ideological Reading of Dilbert," in *Comics and Ideology*, eds. Matthew P. McAllister, Edward H. Sewell, Jr., and Ian Gordon (New York: Peter Lang, 2001), 293–94.

107. Ibid., 282.

NOTES TO CHAPTER 7

1. Johann Wolfgang von Goethe, *Elective Affinities*, trans. Elizabeth Mayer and Louise Bogan (Chicago: Henry Regnery Co., 1963), 43.

2. Richard Herbert Howe, "Max Weber's Elective Affinities: Sociology within the Bounds of Pure Reason," *American Journal of Sociology* 84 (1978): 372–73.

3. Ibid., 367–68, 371–72.

4. Neil Howe and William Strauss, *Millennials Rising: The Next Great Generation* (New York: Vintage Books, 2000), 12–14.

5. Ibid., 15–16, 123, 128, 134–35, 172–73, 276–79.

6. Ibid., 234.

7. Christian Smith with Melinda Lundquist Denton, *Soul Searching: The Religious and Spiritual Lives of American Teenagers* (New York: Oxford University Press, 2005), 40.

8. Ibid., 162–65.

9. David Brooks, "The Organization Kid," *Atlantic Monthly* (April 2001): 40–54.

10. Lisa Orrell, *Millennials Incorporated* (n.p.: Intelligent Women Publishing, 2007), 74–76.

11. Merrill Associates, "Call Them Gen Y or Millennials: They Deserve Our Attention," http://www.merrillassociates.com/topic/2005/05/call-them-gen-y-or-millennials-they-deserve-our-attention/ (accessed September 9, 2007).

12. Howe and Strauss, *Millennials Rising*, 314.

13. Edwin W. Koc, "The Myth of the Millennials," *NACE Journal* (March 2008): 15–16.

14. Howe and Strauss, *Millennials Rising*, 180–81; Neil Howe and William Strauss, *Millennials Go to College* (Washington, DC: American Association of Collegiate Registrars and Admissions Officers, 2003), 93.

15. Orrell, *Millennials Incorporated*, 80–81, 105.

16. Howe and Strauss, *Millennials Rising*, 234–35; Erin Potts, Roger Bennett, and Rachel Levin, "OMG! How Generation Y Is Redefining Faith in the iPod Era," www.rebooters.net/admfiles/upload/116.pdf (accessed October 22, 2008); Robert Wuthnow, *After the Baby Boomers: How Twenty- and Thirty-Somethings Are Shaping the Future of American Religion* (Princeton, NJ: Princeton University Press, 2007), 119–20.

17. Wuthnow, *After the Baby Boomers*, 102.

18. Orrell, *Millennials Incorporated*,89.

19. Bruce Tulgan and Carolyn A. Martin, *Managing Generation Y* (Amherst, MA: HRD Press, 2001), 67, 88.

20. Penelope Trunk, "What Gen Y Really Wants," *Time*, July 16, 2007, G8.

21. Sharon Jayson, "Generation Y Gets Involved," *USA Today*, October 24, 2006, 1D.

22. Tim Sanders, *Saving the World at Work: What Companies and Individuals Can Do to Go Beyond Making a Profit to Making a Difference* (New York: Doubleday, 2008), 37–38.

23. Neil Howe and William Strauss, with Pete Markiewitz, *Millennials and the Pop Culture: Strategies for a New Generation of Consumers* (Elburn, IL: Lifecourse Associates, 2006), 123.

24. Jean M. Twenge, *Generation Me* (New York: Free Press, 2006), 221.

25. Brenda E. Brasher, *Give Me That Online Religion* (San Francisco: Jossey-Bass Publishers, 2001), 14.

26. Ibid., 19.

27. Christopher Helland, "Popular Religion and the World Wide Web: A Match Made in (Cyber) Heaven," in *Religion Online*, eds. Lorne L. Dawson and Douglas E. Crown (New York: Routledge, 2004), 30–31.

28. Mark U. Edwards, Jr., "Belief.net," *Christian Century* (May 16, 2001), 4.

29. Aaron M. Cohen, "Young, Single and Spiritual," *Futurist* (July-August 2008), 17.

30. Heidi Campbell, "Challenges Created by Online Religious Networks," *Journal of Media and Religion* 3 (2004): 90–91.

31. Edwards, "Belief.net," 4.

32. Marc Prensky, "Digital Natives, Digital Immigrants," *http://www.marcprensky.com/writing/* (accessed October 22, 2008).

33. Wuthnow, *After the Baby Boomers*, 209–10.

34. Heidi Campbell, *Exploring Religious Community Online* (New York: Peter Lang, 2005), 67.

35. Scruples, "Scruples Dedication, Disclaimer & Copyright Information," Welcome to Scruples, http://www.scruples.net/ (accessed October 22, 2008).

36. Scruples, "Tree View," Welcome to Scrupples, http://www.scruples.net/ (accessed October 22, 2008).

37. Patricia Aburdene, *Megatrends 2010* (Charlottesville, VA: Hampton Roads Publishing Company, 2005), xx–xxii.

38. Sanders, *Saving the World at Work*, 16–24.

39. Ibid., 32–41.

40. Ibid., 46–47, 52–53.

41. Marc Gunther, *Faith and Fortune* (New York: Crown Business Publishing Group, 2004), 45–49.

42. Ray C. Anderson, *Mid-Course Correction* (White River Junction, VT: Chelsea Green Publishing Company, 1998), 1–3.

43. Gunther, *Faith and Fortune*, 157.

44. Ben Cohen and Mal Warwick, *Values-Driven Business* (San Francisco: Barrett-Koehler Publishers, 2006), xvi–xvii.

45. Charles Cameron, moderator of "Spirituality and Social Entrepreneurship," http://www.socialedge.org/discussions/responsibility/spirituality-and-social-entrepreneurship/ (accessed October 24, 2008).

46. David Vogel, *The Market for Virtue: The Potential and Limits for Corporate Social Responsibility*, paperback edition (Washington, DC: Brooking Institution, 2006), 33–34, 48, 58, 71–72.

47. Ibid., 71; Cohen and Warwick, *Values-Driven Business*, xxi.

48. Vogel, *Market for Virtue*, 73.

49. Ibid., viii.

50. Ibid., 168–69.

51. Gunther, *Faith and Fortune*, 1.

52. Sanders, *Saving the World at Work*, 205–7.

53. Max Weber, "The Social Psychology of the World Religions," in *From Max Weber: Essays in Sociology*, eds. H. H. Gerth and C. Wright Mills (London: Routledge and Kegan Paul Ltd., 1948), 276–80.

54. Ibid., 332–33.

55. Max Weber, *Sociology of Religion* (Boston: Beacon Press, 1963), 166–69.

56. Ibid., 42.

57. Ibid., 171.

58. Robert Wuthnow, *After Heaven: Spirituality in America Since the 1950s* (Berkeley, CA: University of California Press, 1998), 30.

59. Ibid., 31.

60. Weber, "The Social Psychology of the World Religions," 325.

61. For example, see Hendrik Kraemer, *A Theology of the Laity* (Philadelphia: Westminster Press, 1958) and Mark Gibbs and T. R. Morton, *God's Frozen People* (Philadelphia: Westminster Press, 1965).

62. Wuthnow, *After Heaven*, 40, hereafter cited in text.

63. Weber, *Sociology of Religion*, 157–58; Weber, "The Social Psychology of the World Religions," 326.

64. Robert J. Schreiter, *Constructing Local Theologies* (Maryknoll, NY: Orbis Books, 1985), 5

65. Clemens Sedmak, *Doing Local Theology* (Maryknoll, NY: Orbis Books, 2002), 95.

66. Ibid., 119.

67. Paul Vitello, "An Evangelical Article of Faith: Bad Times Draw Bigger Crowds," *New York Times*, December 14, 2008, A1.

Select Bibliography

Aburdene, Patricia. *Megatrends 2010*. Charlottesville, VA: Hampton Roads Publishing, 2005.

Albanese, Catherine L. *A Republic of Mind and Spirit: A Cultural History of American Metaphysical Religion*. New Haven, CT: Yale University Press, 2007.

Baker, William J. *Playing with God: Religion and Modern Sport*. Cambridge, MA: Harvard University Press, 2007.

Barton, Bruce. *The Man Nobody Knows*. Indianapolis: Bobbs-Merrill Co., 1925. Reprinted with an introduction by Richard M. Fried. Chicago: Ivan R. Dee Publisher, 2000.

Brandes, Stuart. *American Welfare Capitalism, 1880–1940*. Chicago: University of Chicago Press, 1976.

Briskin, Alan. *The Stirring of the Soul in the Workplace*. San Francisco: Jossey-Bass, 1996.

Brooks, David. *Bobos in Paradise: The New Upper Class and How They Got There*. New York: Simon and Schuster, 2000.

Buder, Stanley. *Pullman: An Experiment in Industrial Order and Community Planning*. New York: Oxford University Press, 1967.

Carrette, Jeremy, and Richard King, *Selling Spirituality: The Silent Takeover of Religion*. London: Routledge, 2005.

Chandler, Alfred Jr. *The Visible Hand: The Managerial Revolution in American Business*. Cambridge, MA: Belknap Press, 1977.

Cohen, Ben, and Jerry Greenfield. *Ben & Jerry's Double Dip: How to Run a Values-Led Business and Make Money, Too*. New York: Simon and Schuster, 1997.

Covey, Stephen R. *The 7 Habits of Highly Effective People*. New York: Fireside Books, 1989.

Diehl, William E. *Ministry in Daily Life: A Practical Guide for Congregations*. Washington, DC: Alban Institute, 1997.

Field, Lloyd. *Business and the Buddha: Doing Well by Doing Good*. Boston: Wisdom Publications, 2007.

Florida, Richard. *The Rise of the Creative Class: And How It's Transforming Work, Leisure, Community and Everyday Life*. New York: Basic Books, 2002.

Fuller, Robert C. *Spiritual, But Not Religious: Understanding Unchurched America*. New York: Oxford University Press, 2001.

Green, David, and Dean Merrill. *More Than a Hobby: How a $600 Startup Became America's Home and Craft Superstore*. Nashville, TN: Thomas Nelson, 2002.

Hardy, Lee. *The Fabric of this World: Inquiries into Calling, Career Choice, and the Design of Human Work*. Grand Rapids, MI: W. B. Eerdmans Publishing Co, 1990.

Heuberger, Frank W., and Laura Nash, eds. *A Fatal Embrace?: Assessing Trends in Human Resources Programs*. New Brunswick, NJ: Transaction Publishers, 1994.

Hicks, Douglas A. *Religion in the Workplace: Pluralism, Spirituality, Leadership*. Cambridge: Cambridge University Press, 2003.

Howe, Neil, and William Strauss. *Millennials Rising: The Next Great Generation*. New York: Vintage Books, 2000.

Huber, Richard M. *The American Idea of Success*. New York: McGraw-Hill Book Company, 1971.

Hucznski, Andrzej. *Management Gurus*. London: Routledge, 1993.

Jackson, Brad. *Management Gurus and Management Fashions: A Dramatistic Inquiry*. London: Routledge, 2001.

Jacoby, Sanford M. *Modern Manors: Welfare Capitalism Since the New Deal*. Princeton, NJ: Princeton University Press, 1997.

Jones, Laurie Beth. *Jesus, CEO*. New York: Hyperion, 1995.

———. *Jesus, Entrepreneur*. New York: Three Rivers Press, 2001.

——— *Jesus, Life Coach*. Nashville, TN: Thomas Nelson, 2004.

———. *The Path*. New York: Hyperion, 1996.

Kyle, Richard. *The New Age Movement in American Culture*. Lanham, MD: University Press of America, 1995.

Lunden, Rolf. *Business and Religion in the American 1920s*. New York: Greenwood Press, 1988.

Marsden, George M. *The Soul of the American University From Protestant Establishment to Established Nonbelief*. New York: Oxford University Press, 1994.

Miller, David. *God at Work: The History and Promise of the Faith at Work Movement*. New York: Oxford University Press, 2007.

Miller Schmidt, Jean. *Souls or the Social Order: The Two-Party System in American Protestantism*. Brooklyn, NY: Carlson Publishing, 1991.

Mitroff, Ian I., and Elizabeth A. Denton. *A Spiritual Audit of Corporate America: A Hard Look at Spirituality, Religion, and Values in the Workplace*. San Francisco: Jossey-Bass Publishers, 1999.

Naisbitt, John, and Patricia Aburdene, *Megatrends 2000*. New York: William Morrow, 1990.

Nash, Laura, and Scotty McLennan, *Church on Sunday, Work on Monday: The Challenge of Fusing Christian Values with Business Life.* San Francisco: Jossey-Bass Publishers, 2001.

Osteen, Joel. *Your Best Life Now: Seven Steps to Living at Your Full Potential.* New York: Warner Faith, 2004.

Panken, Peter M. *A State-by-State Survey of the Law on Religion in the Workplace.* Philadelphia: American Law Institute-American Bar Association, 2001.

Peale, Norman Vincent. *The Power of Positive Thinking.* Englewood Cliffs, NJ: Prentice Hall, 1952.

Pollard, William C. *The Soul of the Firm.* Grand Rapids, MI: Harper Business and Zondervan Publishing Co., 1996.

Pope, Liston. *Millhands and Preachers.* New Haven, CT: Yale University Press, 1942.

Roof, Wade Clark. *A Generation of Seekers: The Spiritual Journeys of the Baby Boom Generation.* San Francisco: Harper Collins, 1993.

———. *Spiritual Marketplace: Baby Boomers and the Remaking of American Religion.* Princeton, NJ: Princeton University Press, 1999.

Sanders, Tim. *Saving the World at Work: What Companies and Individuals Can Do to Go Beyond Making a Profit to Making a Difference.* New York: Doubleday, 2008.

Schmidt, Leigh. *Restless Souls: The Making of American Spirituality.* New York: HarperCollins, 2005.

Schwehn, Mark R. *Exiles from Eden: Religion and the Academic Vocation in America.* New York: Oxford University Press, 1993.

Smith, Christian, with Melinda Lundquist Denton. *Soul Searching: The Religious and Spiritual Lives of American Teenagers.* New York: Oxford University Press, 2005.

Steele, Richard. *The Religious Tradesman.* With an introduction by Isaac Watts. 1747. Reprint, Harrisonburg, VA: Sprinkle Publications, 1989.

Taylor, Frederick W. *The Principles of Scientific Management.* New York: Harper and Brothers, 1911. A facsimile of the original edition. Norcross, GA: Industrial Engineering and Management Press, 1998.

Tickle, Phyllis A. *God-Talk in America.* New York: Crossroads, 1997.

———. *Re-Discovering the Sacred.* New York: Crossroads, 1995.

Trice, Harrison M., and Janice M. Beyer. *The Cultures of Work Organizations.* Englewood Cliffs, NJ: Prentice-Hall, 1993.

Vogel, David. *The Market for Virtue: The Potential and Limits for Corporate Social Responsibility.* Washington, DC: Brooking Institution, 2006.

Voskuil, Dennis. *Mountains into Goldmines: Robert Schuller and the Gospel of Success.* Grand Rapids, MI: W. B. Eerdmans Publishing Co., 1983.

Wade, Marion E., with Glenn D. Kittler. *The Lord is My Counsel: A Businessman's Personal Experiences with the Bible.* New York: Prentice Hall, 1987.

Warren, Rick. *The Purpose Driven Life: What on Earth Am I Here For?* Grand Rapids, MI: Zondervan Publishing, 2002.

Weber, Max. *Economy and Society.* Edited by Guenther Roth and Claus Wittich. 3 vols. New York: Bedminster Press, 1968.

———. *Max Weber: Essays in Sociology.* Edited by. H. H. Gerth and C. Wright Mills. London: Routledge and Kegan Paul Ltd., 1952.

———. *The Protestant Ethic and the Spirit of Capitalism.* Translated by Talcott Parsons. London and New York: Routledge Classics, 2001.

———. *The Sociology of Religion: 1864–1920.* Boston: Beacon Press, 1963.

Wilkinson, Bruce. *The Prayer of Jabez: Breaking Through to the Blessed Life.* Sisters, OR: Multnomah Publishers, 2000.

Williams, Oliver F., C.S.C., ed. *Business, Religion, Spirituality: A New Synthesis.* Notre Dame, IN: University of Notre Dame Press, 2003.

Whyte, David. *The Heart Aroused: Poetry and the Preservation of the Soul in Corporate America.* New York: Doubleday, 1994.

Wolf, Michael, Bruce Friedman, and Daniel Sutherland, *Religion in the Workplace: A Comprehensive Guide to Legal Rights and Responsibilities.* Chicago: American Bar Association, 1998.

Wuthnow, Robert. *After the Baby Boomers: How Twenty- and Thirty-Somethings Are Shaping the Future of American Religion.* Princeton, NJ: Princeton University Press, 2007.

———. *After Heaven: Spirituality in America Since the 1950s.* Berkeley, CA: University of California Press, 1998.

———. *The Crisis in the Churches: Spiritual Malaise, Fiscal Woe.* New York: Oxford University Press, 1997.

Index

About the Author

LAKE LAMBERT III is Professor of Religion and Board of Regents Chair in Ethics at Wartburg College, Waverly, Iowa.